The Family Guide to

Disability and Personal Finances

ED ARBUCKLE

The Family Guide to Disability and Personal Finances
Copyright © 2018 by John Edwin Arbuckle

It is important that the book receives as wide a distribution as possible to support disability. Generous price discounts will be considered for volume purchases and purchases by organizations who provide financial services or products to individuals with a disability. Please see *Let's Keep the Conversation Going* at the end of the book.

The strategies outlined in this book may not be suitable for every individual, and are not guaranteed or warrantied to produce any particular results. Further, any examples or sample forms presented are intended only as illustrations. The author and publisher assume no responsibility for errors or omissions and disclaim any responsibility for any liability, loss or risk, personal or otherwise, which is incurred as a consequence, directly or indirectly, of the use and application of any of the contents of this book.

Tellwell Talent
www.tellwell.ca

ISBN
978-1-77302-732-6 (Hardcover)
978-1-77302-733-3 (Paperback)
978-1-77302-734-0 (eBook)

Ed Arle

This book is dedicated to…

Damon

Bruce, Shirley, Madeleine and Bridget

Family and friends

An army of health care and social service providers

Many supporting community-based organizations

McMaster Children's Hospital

Holland Bloorview Kids Rehabilitation Hospital

The Honourable James Flaherty

Table of Contents

Foreword 15

Acknowledgements 19

Introduction 21

About the Author. 25

Chapter 1: Disability – An Overview. 27

    PART 1 – DISABILITY. 27
        Who is a Person with a Disability? 27
        Disability and Management of Personal Finances 29
        Vulnerability 30
        Disability and the Family 31
        Disability as a Continuum 31
        Developmental Assessment. 32
        The Challenges of Disability 33

    PART 2 – FINANCES. 35
        Financial Betterment is Your Right. 35
        Family Life Cycle and Personal Finance. 35
        Financial Assistance Changes with Age. 36
        Personal Finances Aren't Just About Growth of Capital 37
        Factor in Inflation and Life Expectancy. 37
        The Four Pillars of Financial Support 38
        Transfer of Financial Assistance 39
        Trusts for More Than a Single Reason 39

PART 3 – PLANNING 40
   Setting Priorities 40
   Agreement, Confirmation and Understanding 40
   Written Records 40
   Planned Savings are Vital to Long-term Cash Flow 41
   Pooling Family Resources 41
   Customize Your Planning 41

PART 4 – ESSENTIAL FINANCIAL ISSUES AND CONCERNS 42
   Life Plan 42
   Housing and Attendant Care 43
   Long-term Money Plan 43
   The Constraints of Our Laws 43
   Competency, Guardianship and Legal Issues 44
   Financial Caregiver Continuity 44
   Trusts – Property Ownership, Taxation and Income Distribution 44
   Social Assistance 45
   Community Resources 45
   Tax Planning and Incentives 45
   Estate Planning and Wealth Continuity 46
   Key Areas of Disability and Financial Planning 46
   Summing Up 47

Chapter 2: Communities – The Glue That Binds **49**

PART 1 – THE ORGANIZATIONS 50
   Community Services 50
   The Work of Governments Behind the Scenes 51
   Not-For-Profit Organizations 52
   Funding of Community Services 52

PART 2 – HOUSING 53
   Traditional Housing Options 53
   Housing Options for Individuals with Disabilities 53
   Housing Choices and Their Effects on the Cost of Living 54
   A Private Home is Possible 54
   Social Assistance and Housing 55
   Home Care 55
   Home Ownership or Renting 56

PART 3 – COMMUNITY SERVICES 56
   Social, Recreational and Community Activities 56
   Education and Life Skills Training 56
   Local Health Initiatives Network (LHIN) 57
   Hospitals 57
   Specialized Programs – Therapies and Counselling 58

In Town Public Transportation 58

Services in the Next Town 59

Passport Program. 59

Summing Up 60

Chapter 3: Provincial Income Assistance **61**

PART 1 – INCOME ASSISTANCE. 61

Income Assistance Across Canada. 61

Asset Limits 62

Income Limits. 64

PART 2 – ONTARIO DISABILITY SUPPORT PROGRAM (ODSP) 65

Qualifying For ODSP 65

The Disability Mandate Under the ODSP. 65

ODSP Legal Structure 66

ODSP Information Sources 66

ODSP Monthly Benefits. 66

Other ODSP Benefits. 67

ODSP Income. 68

Chargeable Income and Budgetary Requirements 69

Maximizing Social Assistance. 70

Exempt Income 71

Reduction in Income Assistance – Assets and Income. 71

Canada Pension Disability Benefits 72

Disability Related Expenses 73

Retirement Income for Persons with Disabilities. 73

Inheritance Trusts. 73

Segregated Funds and Annuities 74

Avoiding Income Disqualification. 74

ODSP Case Worker. 75

Giving Up on Social Assistance 75

PART 3 – ADDING A HENSON TRUST 76

What is a Henson Trust? 76

Trust Distributions Affect Social Assistance 78

Henson Trusts – Now or Later. 78

Trusts – Complying With Ontario Law 78

Choosing a Trustee. 79

Talk to Your Family 79

Summing Up. 79

Chapter 4: Family - Support and Communication **83**

PART 1 – FINANCIAL SUPPORT 84

Ways for the Family to Offer Financial Help 84

Financial Support 85

Accommodation Support.. 85

Care Support 86

Employment of Individuals With Disabilities................. 86

Inheritances - Equal Treatment by Family 86

Reach Out for Help and Advice................................ 87

Money Management 87

Balancing Things Out With a Life Plan 87

PART 2 – LEGAL STRUCTURES 88

Property Ownership and Control.............................. 88

Personal Guardianship and Taxation........................ 89

Personal Guardianship and Legal Authority 90

Financial Caregivers 90

Summing Up.. 90

Chapter 5: Trusts – Fundamental to Planning for Disability 91

PART 1 – THE LEGALITIES OF TRUSTS......................... 92

Use of Trusts in Disability 92

What Is A Trust?.. 93

Testamentary and Inter Vivos Trusts........................ 93

Trustees... 94

Trust Distributions 94

Letter of Wishes 95

Trusts and Taxation 95

Control of a Trust for Tax Purposes.......................... 96

Tax Features of a Trust 96

New Trust Tax Rules in 2016................................... 97

Trusts and Property Ownership............................... 98

Trusts and Disability.. 98

Corporate Trustees 99

Rules Against Accumulations and Perpetuities............. 99

PART 2 – HENSON TRUSTS 100

PART 3 – PRINCIPAL RESIDENCE TRUSTS 101

PART 4 – INHERITANCE TRUSTS PROTECT INCOME ASSISTANCE 102

PART 5 – LIFETIME BENEFIT TRUSTS 102

PART 6 – LIFE INSURANCE TRUSTS........................... 105

PART 7 – QUALIFIED DISABILITY TRUSTS (QDT) 105

QDT Defined... 105

Existing Testamentary Trusts 106

PART 8 – TAX PLANNING AND COMPLIANCE FOR TRUSTS...................... 106

Trusts as Tax Free Conduits 106

Preferred Beneficiary Election (PBE) 106
21-Year Disposition.. 107
Winding up of a Trust 107
Summing Up.. 108

Chapter 6: Tax Planning – Navigating the Tax System 109

PART 1 – YOU AND YOUR TAXES – THE BASIC RULES.......................... 110
    Taxation – The Big Picture 110
    Income Tax Rates 111
    Non-Refundable Tax Credits 112
    Vulnerable or Markedly Restricted... 113
    The Value of Tax Credits... 113
    Claiming Non-refundable Tax Credits.. 113
    Tax Benefits for Individuals with Disabilities 114

PART 2 – THE DISABILITY TAX CREDIT... 116
    Disability Tax Credit 116
    Markedly Restricted 118
    Cognitive Functions Definition and Eligibility for the DTC......................... 118
    DTC Application... 119
    Child Disability Supplement.. 119
    Transferability of the DTC 120
    Tax Savings from the DTC.. 120
    Prolonged Impairment 120
    Level of Restriction... 121
    Retroactivity.. 122
    Other Tax Benefits from the DTC... 122
    The Complexity of the DTC Provision 123

PART 3 – OTHER SUPPORT FOR DEPENDENTS................................. 123
    Eligible Dependent 123
    Canada Caregiver Credit... 124
    RESPs for Persons with Disabilities – Expanded Benefit 124

PART 4 – MEDICAL EXPENSE CREDITS... 125
    Medical Expense Claim 125
    Medical Expenses by Category 125
    Medical Practitioner Payments... 125
    Attendant Care 126
    Medications and Other Prescriptions 128
    Medical Devices and Equipment.. 129
    Home Modification Tax Benefits 129
    Transportation and Travel Expenses... 129

PART 5 – REFUNDABLE AND DEDUCTIBLE AMOUNTS........................ 130
    Refundable Medical Expense Supplement.. 130

Disability Supports Deduction 130

Enhanced Child Care Expenses.. 131

Working Income Tax Benefit and Disability Supplement............................. 131

PART 6 – PLANS AND GRANTS 131

Study Grants.. 131

Life-long Learning Credit 131

Home Buyer's Plan 131

PART 7 – OTHER BENEFITS FOR PERSONS WITH DISABILITIES..................... 132

Canada Child Benefit (CCB)... 132

Child Disability Benefit (CDB) (supplement to CCB)................................ 132

Preferred Beneficiary Election (PBE) 132

PART 8 – TAX PLANNING 133

Tax Planning – Show Me the Ways.. 133

Taxes Delayed are Taxes Saved 133

Obtaining Tax Credits for Past Years.. 134

Credits for Family Members Age 18 and Over 134

Advocate for Tax Fairness.. 134

Tax Credit Transfers... 135

Summing Up.. 136

Chapter 7: RDSPs – A Generous Pension Plan for Disability 141

PART 1 – RDSP OVERVIEW 141

RDSP – The Basic Concept and Purpose 141

Qualifying as an RDSP 142

Loss of RDSP Eligibility... 142

RDSPs and Social Assistance 143

The Savings Potential of RDSPs 143

RDSP Timelines 143

RDSP Beneficiary... 144

RDSP Account Holder 145

Allowable Investments... 145

RDSP Budget Amendments 145

PART 2 – CONTRIBUTIONS AND OTHER RDSP FUNDING SOURCES 146

Rules and Limits.. 146

Government Assistance – Bonds and Grants 146

Calculation of Bonds and Grants 147

Repayments of Bonds and Grants 148

Ten Year Carryover Rule 148

Transfers from RRIFs and RRSPs... 149

RESP Transfers for Disability 150

Early RDSP Funding 150

PART 3 – RDSP WITHDRAWALS 151

The Pension (LDAP) Withdrawal Formula 151

Shortened Life Expectancy 152

Taxation of Payments to Beneficiary. 152

Early Withdrawals. 152

Events Requiring Grant and Bond Repayments 153

Death of a Beneficiary 153

PART 4 – PLANNING FOR RDSPS 153

Financial Advisors. 153

Planning for Early Withdrawals. 154

Contribution Planning 154

RDSPs are for the Long-term. 155

Comparing an RDSP to a Henson Trust 155

Estate Planning 155

RDSP and Guardianship. 156

Summing Up. 156

Chapter 8: Estate Planning – A Different Path. 159

PART 1 – ESTATE PLANNING FOR DISABILITY – AN OVERVIEW. 160

Why Estate Planning for Disability is Different. 160

Estate Planning Overview. 160

Two Kinds of Beneficiaries 161

Life Plan. 162

Trusts or Outright Bequests 162

Choosing Trustees, Executors and Others 162

Caregiver Succession. 162

Capacity and Its Implications. 163

Guardianship and Estate Planning 163

Treating Beneficiaries Differently. 165

Provincial Social Assistance Constraints 165

PART 2 – WILLS, PROBATE AND RELATED ISSUES 165

Practical Estate Planning. 165

Estate Distributions 167

Capacity to Make a Will. 167

Survivor Financial Rights. 168

Dependent Relief Provisions 169

Survivor Pension Benefits. 169

Corporate Executors 169

A Will Checklist 169

PART 3 – TRUSTS IN ESTATE PLANNING 170

Trusts – Issues, Tax Benefits and Other Considerations 170

Six Trusts For Estate Planning 171

    Qualified Disability Trusts...172

    The Henson Trust...172

    Who are the Final Trust Beneficiaries?................................173

PART 4 – PLAN TRANSFERS...174

    Death of a RRSP or RRIF Plan Holder................................174

    RRSP/RRIF and RESP Rollover to RDSP.............................174

    Lifetime Benefit Trust..175

    Inheritance Trust..175

    Summing Up...175

Chapter 9: Charitable Giving - A Winning Proposition 177

PART 1 – THE CASE FOR GIVING BACK.....................................177

    A Winning Proposition 177

    How Will Your Gift be Used?...178

    Tax Credits for Donations..178

    Community Foundations 178

    What's the Value to You of a Donation?..............................179

    Current and Testamentary Gifts......................................180

    Charitable Bequests...180

PART 2 – CURRENT GIFT GIVING 180

    Donating Cash 180

    Donating Capital Property...181

    Donating Publicly Listed Securities and Other Assets 181

    Donating Life Insurance - Cash Value 181

PART 3 - DONATING WHAT'S LEFT OVER 182

    Life Insurance Proceeds 182

    What's Left in a Henson Trust?.......................................182

    Residual Interest in Property...183

    RRSPs and RRIFs 183

    Summing Up...183

Chapter 10: Seniors – Plan Ahead to Stay Ahead 185

PART 1 – AGING CAN INFLUENCE FINANCIAL OUTCOMES......................185

    Financial Planning For Seniors.......................................185

    The Wisdom that Comes with Age 186

    Risk Changes in Retirement 186

    The Scarcity of Funds 187

    Time to Recover Is Short 187

    Family Financial Advice 188

    Borrowing Money from the Bank of Mom and Dad 188

    The Family Cottage..189

PART 2 – CAPACITY AND UNDUE INFLUENCE 189
   It's a Complex World For Seniors 189
   Seniors – Age Reduces Capacity 190
   Capacity Tests Can Be Different 190
   Vulnerability 193
   Signs of Undue Influence 193
   Financial Literacy and Risk 194

PART 3 – DOCUMENTATION AND THE BLURRING OF PROPERTY OWNERSHIP 194
   Did You Mean to Give Up Ownership? 194
   Financial Power Of Attorney 195
   Trusts Can Replace Wills 196

PART 4 – PROFESSIONAL ADVISORS 196
   Advisors Should Be Holistic 196
   Independent Advice 196
   Choosing a Suitable Money Manager 196
   Fiduciary Obligations of Advisors 197
   Summing Up 197

Chapter 11: Financial Planning and Investing – Some Guiding Principles 199

PART 1 – FINANCIAL PLANNING 200
   What's in a Financial Plan? 200
   A Personal Financial Check-up 200
   Budgeting for the Future 200
   Reaching Out for Financial Advice 202
   Lifetime Financial Needs 202
   Financial Concerns Unique to People with Disabilities 203
   Phasing in Family Support 203
   Capital Needs – A Snapshot 204
   Structuring Financial Support and Asset Ownership 205
   Consider Inflation 206
   The Time Value of Money 207
   Maximizing Financial Resources 207
   Capital Resources 208
   The Income Gap 209
   Maximizing RDSP Income 209
   Tax and Legal Constraints of Trusts 210

PART 2 – MONEY MANAGEMENT 211
   Bedrock Rules for Investing 211
   Accumulation Years and Preservation Years 211
   Long-Term Investing 212
   Family Support - The Savings Pots 213
   Self-Investing - Can You Do It on Your Own? 213

Why Do Investors Fail?. 214
Advisors and Personal Finances 214
Financial Institutions Provide Expertise and Special Financial Products. 215
PART 3 – INVESTMENTS AND DISABILITY. 216
Investments and Financial Products 216
Tax-Free Savings Accounts. 217
Life Insurance. 218
Term, Whole Life or Universal Life?. 219
Insurance and Disability 219
Annuities 220
Segregated Funds - A Good Product for Disability. 220
Life Funding Road Map 221
Letter of Wishes 223
Engage and Move Forward. 223

Bibliography 225

Appendix A – Summary of Figures 229
Figures 229

Appendix B – Helpful References 233
Relevant Legislation/Regulations (Ontario). 233
Helpful Studies And Submissions. 234
Provincial Laws Impacting Individuals With Disabilities. 234
Websites 234

Appendix C - Publications. 237
Income Tax Folios. 237
Alerts 238

Glossary 239
Abbreviations. 239

Let's Keep the Conversation Going 247
Social Media. 247
Newsletters. 247
Book Discount Privileges 248
Speaking 248

Foreword

Damon is our son and Ed's grandson. His disabilities and the life-long challenges that stemmed from birth were Ed's inspiration to write this much needed book.

Since the day Damon was born, he has moved mountains. We want to share Damon's story so others can benefit from his journey and have a better road map in coping with the challenges that lie ahead for the parents of a special needs child.

Damon is very happy by nature. Armed with a warm smile and a charming personality, he is absolutely lovable – an exceptional kid really! When this journey began for us, Damon's parents, there were many moments of uncertainty and heartbreak. We experienced a roller coaster of emotions, which is daunting for any parent. There is no manual to consult for coping with a newborn in distress, which is what we faced with Damon a few days after he came into the world.

I had a typical pregnancy for the first eight months with the usual bouts of discomfort that go along with being pregnant. One morning I woke up with pain in my stomach which quickly became unbearable, so we rushed to the hospital to get medical attention. The doctors did some tests and made sure the baby was okay. They believed that appendicitis was the cause of the pain, but confirming this in the late stages of pregnancy is not easy. It was agreed that they would perform an appendectomy. Even though there was a good chance things were normal, the doctors didn't want to take this risk – two lives were at stake. As it turned out, appendicitis was not the cause.

The pain continued and my breathing was becoming shorter and more laboured. At this point the doctors suspected pneumonia or a pulmonary embolism. After a couple of days of monitoring, the symptoms worsened and the decision was made to transfer me to McMaster Children's Hospital. I was admitted to the Intensive Care Unit and quickly assessed. A pulmonary embolism was ruled out and a change was made to the antibiotic prescribed to treat me for pneumonia.

Damon was born two days later. He was delivered seemingly fine and he showed no signs of distress, which was a relief! A few days later we noticed that Damon was having difficulty nursing and that he was listless. His breathing was shallow, so we asked for another examination. After waiting for two hours while he was being examined, we were met by a doctor who told us that Damon had stopped breathing and had to be resuscitated. He was now in the Neonatal Intensive Care Unit at McMaster on a ventilator and in critical condition. The next seventy-two hours were the longest three days of our lives as we waited to see if Damon would pull through.

To our relief, he did start to get better and continued to get stronger. He was put on antibiotics to treat bacterial meningitis. Once a week for the next three weeks an ultrasound of his head was done to ensure there was no infection or brain damage. The first ultrasound showed that he was fine, the second showed a small mark on his brain and the third showed significant brain damage. A team of doctors showed up in my hospital room to deliver the incredibly bad news while I held Damon in my arms. I looked at Damon, wondering what life held in store for him and how we would cope. His prognosis was grim. We were told that he would probably have substantial physical and intellectual special needs that might prevent him from walking or even talking and that he would most likely be confined to a wheelchair for the rest of his life. Our world was turned upside down.

We took him home on Remembrance Day – a day we would never forget. It was the beginning of the next phase of Damon's journey. Shortly thereafter we met with a transition team at McMaster that helped us find community organizations we would come to rely on for Damon's therapies over the next several months and years. Each week brought many appointments and exercises to help Damon with his development. We were very fortunate to receive so much help from family, friends and all the community services we were put in touch with.

By the age of eight months Damon had been through many medical challenges, but he was making progress. Over the next few years we watched him grow into a toddler. He took longer than the average child to start walking, but eventually he did. He also began talking. While progress was little by little, he was headed in the right direction.

Once in school, Damon really thrived. His vision steadily improved, going from legally blind as an infant, to 20/200 as a toddler and then to roughly 20/80 today. It's quite amazing how the parts of his brain that were not damaged took over and allowed him to develop in ways we did not think were possible. His walking became steadier and his vocabulary made remarkable strides and continues to do so. He loves school and his greatest strength is his positive attitude. His sisters, Madeleine and Bridget, watch out for Damon and include him in family activities. Indeed, the whole family was and continues to be amazingly supportive.

Damon is a teenager now and lives with us in Cambridge, Ontario, attending high school in a life skills class with about eight other children. He is a proud member of the Cambridge Ice Hounds hockey team, enjoys movies, likes going to the library and attends camp in the summertime.

The journey so far has been a long one for Damon, and it's not over! He receives lots of help from community resources and agencies. He continues to travel to McMaster a few times a year for assessments of his growth and development.

Today, Damon is a very happy, sociable young man who is capable of taking on all challenges; he continues to defy the odds. His life is truly a miracle and he continues to have a positive impact on our family and all those around us. Damon has had many ups and downs in his life, but through it all he remains an example that anything is possible. We hope this book will make your own journey a little easier so that you too can find financial, government and community resources to help you through the challenges you might come up against in the future.

Bruce and Shirley
Proud parents of Damon

DAMON

Acknowledgements

Four very special people guided me through the creation of this book. All four are my mentors, my colleagues and my friends.

Alison Canavan

Alison lives in the nation's capital and is very involved in her community. She provides strategic planning advice and hands-on leadership in marketing and event planning for Blackberry in Canada and around the world. Alison's years of experience have helped me get this book out to the wide reading audience for which it is intended.

Ron Malis

Ron Malis, a Toronto-based financial advisor, has dedicated his entire practice to advising individuals with disabilities and their supporting family members. Ron advises parents of children with disabilities on how to supplement government disability benefits, including the Ontario Disability Support Program and the Registered Disability Savings Plan. He is a sought-after speaker and has appeared on television, print media and the radio.

Donna McCaw

Donna and I have had many lunches together to talk about my book. Her thoughts and experience have been a great help to me. Donna has authored several books herself—the latest one and recently revised, *It's Your Time,* is about getting ready for retirement. Besides being an author, Donna is an engaging speaker, a workshop presenter and a world traveller. You can find her on the web at www.donnamccaw.com.

Terry Wichman

Terry has been a good friend and colleague for many years—we were both tax partners at the same national accounting firm many years ago. He has retired as a tax partner at PricewaterhouseCoopers and currently works at BDO providing specialized tax advice to clients of their Waterloo office. Terry reviewed several sections of this book and I thank him for his thoughtful suggestions.

I also wish to thank so many people who took the time to give me their thoughts from personal experiences, knowledge and backgrounds in disability.

Alex Nayyar	Gary Whetung	Martina Rozsa
Alison Rogers	Jamie Martin	Maxine Hyndman
Angela Hovey	Janet Huber	Patricia Henry
Ann Bilodeau	Jesse Spence	Paula Saunders
Ann Caine	Jim Kibble	Rino Racanelli
Barry Monaghan	John and Betty Lyn Enns	Ritesh and Rini Bhargava
Becky Verdun	John Lennox	Rosemary Smith
Brian Cowan	Karen Veloriote	Rudy Dorner
Caroline Arbuckle	Katherine Loveys	Scott Wildfong
Courtney Horowitz	Kathy Smith	Shaune Lawton
David Chilton	Kevin Buko	Shelley Hyndman
Dayna Degiorgio	Lana Sanichar	Sheryl Khanna
Don Shouldice	Laurie Mawlam	Spence and Janet Clark
Douglas Griffeon	Linda Hazlett	Sue Lantz
Dr. Peter Fitzgerald	Lindsey Hutchison	Tracy Franks
Eileen Reppenhagen	Lyman MacInnis	
Garreth Fallis	Mark Seymour	

A special tribute and a big thanks to my administrative assistants, Gerrie Laurin, Valerie McClung, Krista Spurrell, Amanda Power and Amber LeBlanc, for their dedicated hard work. They never complained about typing the manuscript many times over. They made the book a better one with their thoughtful suggestions. Pat Henry also made an amazing contribution by adding her thoughtful comments in the final revisions of the book. Tellwell Publishing helped me navigate the labyrinth of self-publishing and I am particularly grateful to Roxanne van Germert, Lenore Kennedy and Rebecca Steinmann.

And finally, thanks to Bob Blaney of Manitoulin Island for his photograph of the monarch butterfly. His butterfly was a perfect choice for me and is used throughout this book and in all of my writings about disability.

Introduction

Strange as it may seem, there has not been a book written thus far to guide individuals, their families, caregivers and their advisors through the financial complexities of disability in Canada. When I decided to write this book, I realized that the biggest challenge would be to help readers understand the total picture of such financial planning in a clear and relevant way. I believe that I have done that. With ever increasing government regulations, albeit with the best of intentions, it's difficult and expensive for families to obtain adequate advice, plan for the future and set priorities.

The primary focus of this book is on individuals in the prime of their lives with significant disabilities. Specifically, this book addresses individuals who have significant, continuing or recurring cognitive or physical disabilities. Consequently, these individuals are usually restricted in their activities of daily living: tending to their personal care, functioning in the community, participating in the workplace, and living their lives in a conventional way. These individuals include young children and adults who are unable to cope on their own.

However, there are others who may not have an identifiable disability, but are not capable of making good decisions, holding a job, relating well to others or living independently. They are vulnerable and have difficulty qualifying for government programs. Sometimes even family connections have disappeared for them, so they must struggle for access common support systems on their own. Reducing the complexity of qualification for government assisted programs would be a breakthrough for these individuals.

Disability does not respect the boundaries of age. A person may live with a disability from birth or may experience one in a later stage of life. Seniors have a significantly different set of financial issues than children or mid-life adults because the finances of mature adults are usually better organized. Much of what is in this book can apply to seniors, but the information is not a perfect fit since the contents relate to people with disabilities in the prime of their lives. The challenges specific to seniors with disabilities are discussed in chapter 10.

Individuals with disabilities and their families can face a host of difficulties in obtaining their rightful financial support (for instance, social assistance, tax benefits and strategies resulting from good financial planning and tax planning). The financial world relating to disability is a complex system to navigate so a coordinated approach with professional assistance is invaluable.

It can be a challenge for families to find information that makes sense to them. Laws are complicated, and professionals can be guarded or give unclear advice. Some families face the choice between maximizing government support versus setting aside more income and wealth in order to provide loved ones with a better quality of life. For families with modest means, government support is essential. Others with more financial resources have more options, but often face challenges of fairness and complicated planning structures.

Families with a child, spouse or parent with a disability come from all walks of life. Some will have good communication skills and can make the system work—others will not. My goal is that this book will be a roadmap for navigating disability and related financial planning. I hope it will give you more confidence, less heartache and result in better financial outcomes as you address your family's unique situation.

This book provides an overview of provincial and Canadian disability laws and references on where to find them. Laws are filtered through regulations and interpretations which tend to be unclear. Is there a solution? Yes! I urge you to dig deeply, to refuse to accept an answer until you are satisfied with it, and to challenge any advice you believe to be wrong.

I have relied on information that is current at the time of writing but may have changed since publication. From a provincial perspective, most of this book is based on Ontario law, but I have included information from other provinces to the extent possible. The book contains numerous charts and tables to help readers grasp the concepts no matter how complex the situation.

This book is intended to be a guide for planning, but is not meant to be used in lieu of professional advice on financial issues related to disability. In the end, everyone should seek help from professional advisors such as lawyers, accountants, tax specialists or others. Professionals themselves may find this book useful in understanding areas where they lack familiarity. Educators can use this book as a resource. Lawyers, financial planners and other advisors may use this book as a reference guide in delivering their services with a greater understanding of disability.

This book goes hand-in-hand with our website on disability, www.thefamilyguide.ca, and our more general financial planning website, www.personalwealthstrategies.net. Between these two websites you will find a rich source of information on financial and tax planning for disability. Also, I intend to follow this book with smaller Family Guide publications covering specific areas of disability planning: Disability and the RDSP, Disability and Estate Planning, and Disability and Income Tax.

The complexity of rules and regulations in this area is a serious burden on families and needs to be addressed. I hope this book will be a catalyst for advocates to challenge this complexity and demand better communication and support from all levels of government. Laws are admittedly complex, but that should not stand in the way of more resources dedicated to disability issues being available.

My primary reason for writing this book is to help readers work through their own situation and develop a better financial plan. In addition to a financial plan, a life plan which sets out long-term goals is also important. Writing this book has been personally rewarding. It has caused me to become even more reflective on policy issues surrounding disability in Canada and will help me advocate for better policies in this area. I hope you will enjoy reading this book and that it will assist you and your family in finding resolutions to the financial complexities of disability.

Ed Arbuckle

About the Author

Ed is a member of the Society of Trust and Estate Practitioners. He is also an alumnus of both KPMG and PwC. He qualified as a chartered accountant in Kingston, Ontario. After moving to Kitchener, Ontario he became a tax partner and office managing partner with Coopers and Lybrand. In 1985, Ed was awarded the designation of Fellow of the Institute of Chartered Accountants (FCA) because of his significant contribution to the profession and his extensive community involvement. That same year he attended an advanced management program in Oxford, England.

Ed's practice concentrates primarily on personal tax planning, retirement planning, estate planning, and planning for individuals with disabilities. He currently contributes articles on financial and tax planning to the MoneySaver magazine.

Community involvement has been a lifetime priority for Ed. He has served on boards and volunteered for organizations such as Red Cross, Big Brothers, the Kitchener-Waterloo Chamber of Commerce, the Kitchener-Waterloo Art Gallery, and as a minor hockey coach. Most recently, he served as treasurer on the Board of Directors of the Waterloo-Wellington Community Care Access Centre.

CHAPTER 1

Disability – An Overview

When a family is confronted with the reality of a disability, it's a scary time. They ask themselves many questions. What will we do? How will we adjust? Can we afford the new costs we are going to incur? And, what's going to happen to our lives in the long term? These questions can be overwhelming, but it is quite remarkable how most people take charge. The process will be never-ending, so families need as much determination as they can muster.

At the onset of a disability, the family is in unfamiliar territory—be it with a newborn child, a traumatic health issue or a devastating injury caused by an unfortunate accident. The seriousness may not be completely in focus at first, but in time reality sets in and the family begins to understand that major adjustments to the norms of daily living will be required. Often there is little time to make adjustments.

PART 1 – DISABILITY

Who is a Person with a Disability?

I was part way into my writing when I was asked how I define individuals with disabilities. It's fair to say that we all have challenges. However, the scope of a disability and its challenges can be as wide or as narrow as you can imagine.

I am writing a book for people with significant disabilities who will need a different approach to personal finances and a helping hand, most likely for the long term. Smart financial planning will be important because, without it, life will be difficult or even unbearable at times. All people with disabilities are entitled to the benefits and services available to them to reduce the costs created by their disability; they, or their families, should go looking for these benefits.

In its final report, A Framework for the Law as It Affects Persons with Disabilities (September 2012), the Law Commission of Ontario defines disability as follows.

No single definition of "disability" can fully capture experiences of persons with disabilities. Definitions of disability must recognize the complexity that results from the interaction of an individual with his or her environment. For example, the particular context in which the term is raised—such as employment or housing—will matter, as well as the way in which stereotyping affects the perception of an impairment. Definitions must relate to particular contexts and purposes, and a definition that is of assistance in considering one aspect of the experience of disability may not be illuminating in another.

Definitions found in the Ontario Disability Support Act (ODSP) and the Canadian Income Tax Act are also helpful.

Figure 1.1   ODSP Definition of Disability

- The individual has a substantial physical or intellectual impairment that is continuous or recurrent and expected to last one year or more
- The effect of the impairment on the person's ability to attend to his or her personal care, function in the community and function in a workplace which results in a substantial restriction in one or more of these activities of daily living
- The impairment and its likely durations and the restriction in the person's activities of daily living have been verified

The definition of disability in the Income Tax Act for the disability tax credit, unlike under ODSP, contains no reference to the ability for a person to function in the community or workplace.

Figure 1.2   ITA Definition of Disability

- The individual has one or more severe and prolonged impairments
- The effects of the impairment or impairments are such that the individual is significantly restricted in performing one or more than one of the basic activities of daily living

The ODSP definition of disability is based on the premise that the disability affects personal care, functioning in the community or functioning in the workplace. This is quite different from the definition in the Income Tax Act which is based on a person's ability to perform basic activities of daily living. Consequently, it is possible for a person with a disability to qualify for social assistance and not qualify for income tax benefits or vice versa. The definition of a person with a disability used in this book is an individual with a significant cognitive or physical challenge that is long-lasting.

Disability and Management of Personal Finances

Broadly speaking, a disability may be either physical or cognitive. Individuals with only physical disabilities can make legally binding agreements, own property, sign a will or make elections under the Income Tax Act. They have few impediments to good decision-making.

Individuals with cognitive disabilities, generally speaking, fall into one of two categories. Some individuals with an intellectual disability do not have the capacity to plan, comprehend or reason. Other individuals with an adaptive disability have challenges in responding to social interactions, setting and keeping goals, making appropriate judgements or interacting well with others. However, they may still have the intellectual capacity to own property, sign contracts, live on their own or have a will. It is important to know the distinction between intellectual and adaptive functioning in financial planning when it comes to legal capacity, the requirements for guardianship, or the use of trusts in financial management and planning, as shown in Figure 1.3.

Figure 1.3 Physical or Cognitive Disability

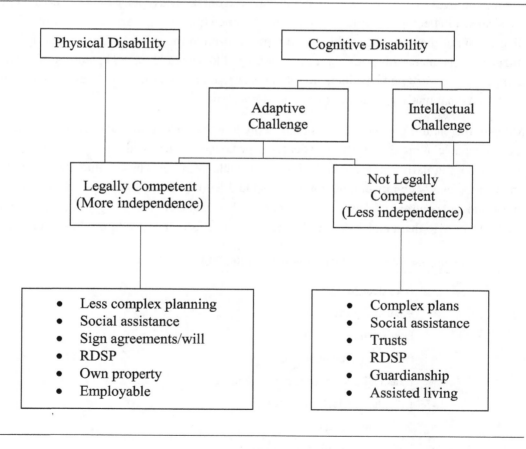

The chart in Figure 1.3 is an oversimplification of disability. Its only purpose is to show the different facets of disability to financial planning. Disability, whether physical or cognitive, is a continuum, and that adds to the complexity.

It's also important to understand that individuals with disabilities such as Asperger's or Tourette syndrome who function at a high level may be quite capable in managing their own financial affairs. The level of disability is on a continuum so making a judgement about legal capacity as it relates to disability is not wise.

Vulnerability

When we think of individuals with a disability, we often think of people with cognitive or physical challenges who meet the definitions outlined earlier in this chapter. However, from my perspective, there are other individuals for whom many of the planning ideas within a family context could apply. They are the individuals in need of protection or guidance because of their vulnerabilities. They could be teenagers, young adults, or seniors. They too require assistance so they can live normal lives without being deprived or taken advantage of. They do not have a physical or intellectual disability as commonly defined (perhaps in part because of insufficient diagnosis) but they are vulnerable and often fall through the cracks as far as qualifying for financial assistance. This does not reduce their need for special financial planning. Generally, there are fewer programs available to them because their issues do not always fit the precise definitions that qualify a person for financial assistance.

Many of the planning insights in this book apply to vulnerable individuals, such as those who are not capable of making life's basic decisions, who are careless with their personal finances, who are not regularly employed and who have trouble fitting in. These vulnerable individuals are usually legally competent, but therein lies the dilemma. Since courts are reluctant to limit their legal and contractual rights, caregivers should be cautious in deciding how much property they turn over to them and should utilize legal structures that help address this issue.

Figure 1.4   Common Attributes of the Vulnerable

- Poor decision-makers ✓
- Financially irresponsible ✓
- Don't want to face issues ✓
- Easily taken advantage of ✓
- Financial assistance is not structured ✓
- Life plan difficult to work with ✓
- Poor communicators ✓
- Fight back or refuse to act ✓

As a society, we need to take more responsibility in helping vulnerable individuals. Why are they so left out?

Disability and the Family

Some individuals can carry out life's daily activities even with their disability and live in a somewhat conventional way. They may own a home, have a job and take care of their personal affairs. Others are less capable and therefore live with family or in some kind of assisted accommodation. For the most part, this book speaks to the latter situation. The reason is simple: planning in the family setting is the more likely situation. My hope is that information in this book is transferable to situations involving independent individuals with disabilities.

Disability can strain personal and family relationships and sometimes original families evolve into new families because of divorce, estrangement or other changes in circumstances. The meaning of family can and does go beyond the original biological family. This book treats family in the broader context.

Disability as a Continuum

Individuals with a disability can have difficulties in one or several areas of daily living. Each challenge will manifest itself differently, but fundamentally these individuals will have either a cognitive or a physical disability, or both. Their cumulative effect correlates to the level of challenge that life brings.

At the lower end of the continuum are individuals who are functional at almost the same level as everyone else, but there is something holding them back. It may be hard for them to keep a job, make friends or just fit in. Their issues are difficult to identify usually due to their adaptive challenges, nevertheless they often need financial assistance.

At the other end of the spectrum are people with significant challenges. Taking care of them in a home setting may become impossible and they will require assisted living or supervised accommodation. It's often too stressful and exhausting for family to keep them at home, and the family home doesn't provide the necessary medical and protective devices that are required. In the middle of the spectrum are individuals who may be able to function in a home setting with assistance, but their disabilities inhibit their ability to live on their own.

Figure 1.5   The Disability and Lifestyle Continuum

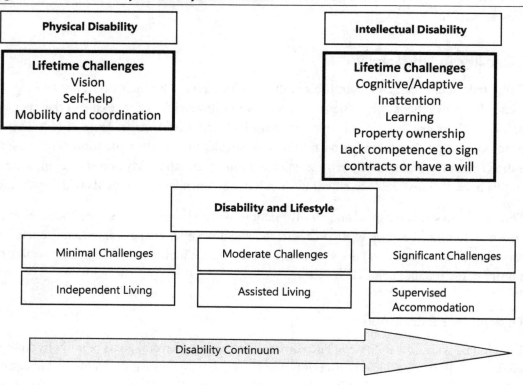

If the situation requires an assisted care accommodation, then government or not-for-profit organizations are usually the provider. Families of individuals with a disability must identify where their loved one fits on the spectrum. Once that decision has been made, it is easier to design a lifestyle and financial plan that suits the person. Sorting out long-term housing is without a doubt the most difficult issue to address and usually represents the highest cost of disability.

The cost to families to support a loved one with a disability is sometimes inversely related to the complexity of the disability. In other words, the more complex the disability, the more government programs that are available (including assisted living) and the less the family's cost. Some individuals may be employable and able to live by themselves but are eligible for government assistance such as the disability tax credit, RDSPs and other tax credits.

Developmental Assessment

Disability is a continuum and can range from mild to chronic (see Figure 1.5). In some cases, a person's placement on the continuum can change as they grow older. This means that the level of care and financial needs will also vary.

Admission to the many types of home care and other community programs will require a developmental assessment by a qualified practitioner to identify skill levels in the following areas.

- Adaptive behaviour (everyday skills)
- Intellectual/cognitive ability
- Verbal ability
- Non-verbal ability (spatial processing, working memory, qualitative reasoning, fluid reasoning)
- Visual ability (perception and motor integration)
- Social/emotional competence
- Academic ability (reading, oral languages, spelling, calculation)

The Challenges of Disability

Structuring the overall finances of an individual with a disability is a difficult job. Planning for individuals with intellectual challenges is quite different from planning for people who are physically challenged. A significant problem for those with learning disabilities is that the individual is unlikely to be able to own property, make a will or manage their own finances. Ownership of assets must vest in a trust, with a public guardian, or in someone else. Trusts need to be structured so that trust assets eventually pass to a charity or other family members as tax efficiently as possible when they are no longer needed.

As Figure 1.6 shows, intellectual challenges are usually harder to deal with than physical impairments. A physically challenged person, in many cases, can live independently and control their financial and legal affairs. This is generally not possible for cognitively challenged individuals, so more complicated financial and legal solutions must be found.

Figure 1.6   The Levels of Challenge

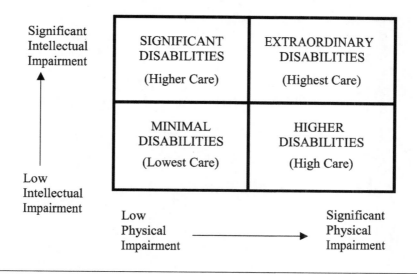

Figure 1.6 can help families identify constraints of their situation in developing a long term financial plan, as discussed in chapter 11.

Great strides have been made in assisting physically disabled individuals. Simple things like sloped curbs, automatic door access and motorized wheelchairs have vastly improved life for individuals with a physical disability. Given such assistance, people with physical disabilities can now live more independently and with more freedom than was previously possible.

Individuals with developmental challenges have also seen improvements as well. The use of computers and other electronic devices have taken these individuals to levels that they previously could not have achieved. Furthermore, both physically and developmentally challenged individuals are receiving more community support than they once did.

The Income Tax Act has many benefits available to individuals with disabilities and their families. The addition of the Registered Disability Savings Plan in 2008 is one of the most significant tax advances for individuals with disabilities. RDSPs have been of great benefit to individuals with disabilities and their families. However, the complexity of this savings plan has limited its use.

Most individuals with significant disabilities will qualify for social assistance. Some will choose to take these benefits and some must take them to meet their financial needs. Others will choose not to receive social assistance because they don't really need it and, if taken, the program benefit restrictions will constrain their quality of life.

The inability of individuals with an intellectual disability to own property or sign contracts presents special difficulties. In these cases, a family must take special steps to overcome these challenges through the creation of trusts for property ownership and income distribution.

PART 2 – FINANCES

Financial Betterment is Your Right

While this book is about financial planning for individuals with disabilities and their families, life planning and addressing family dynamics must also be part of the process. Families should search for financial assistance but avoid ways that negate better results using other methods.

From a personal financial planning perspective, the book's objectives are

- to let you know about the many programs that can provide financial assistance for you—both directly or indirectly;
- to tell you about the conditions you need to meet to get financial help; and
- to help you see the many ways that are possible so you can choose the ones that maximize financial assistance.

This book does not judge who should seek financial assistance because of a disability. Whether you are struggling to make ends meet, trying to improve your finances to make life more bearable or structuring the complicated finances of a high wealth family, you are entitled to everything that's available. This book does not offer an opinion on who should receive assistance; its only purpose is to help you discover your options and let you move forward no matter what your financial situation.

Family Life Cycle and Personal Finance

If your loved one has a developmental disability, then your financial responsibilities will last for years and possibly well beyond your lifetime. This is one of the main reasons planning for family members with disabilities is so difficult—the responsibility lasts a long time. Figure 1.7 provides an illustration of a family life cycle with regard to family finances.

The main components in determining the cost to support a loved one with a disability are as follows:

- the level and type of the disability;
- the length of time your financial support will be required;
- the type of care and accommodations your loved one will require; and
- the enhancements you choose to provide.

It is important to know where your loved one will live at their various stages of life. Accommodation and care costs are usually the biggest costs.

Figure 1.7   Family Life Cycle and Personal Finances

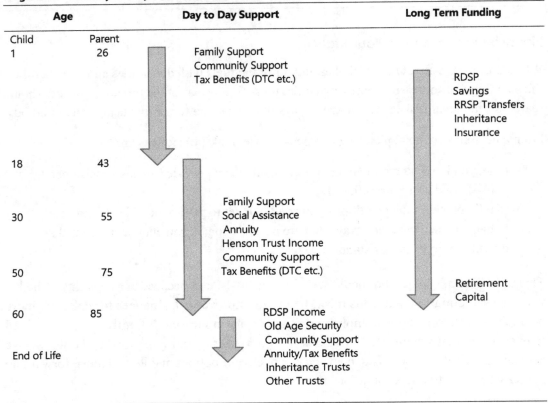

Age		Day to Day Support	Long Term Funding
Child	Parent		
1	26	Family Support Community Support Tax Benefits (DTC etc.)	RDSP Savings RRSP Transfers Inheritance Insurance
18	43		
30	55	Family Support Social Assistance Annuity Henson Trust Income Community Support	
50	75	Tax Benefits (DTC etc.)	Retirement Capital
60	85	RDSP Income Old Age Security Community Support	
End of Life		Annuity/Tax Benefits Inheritance Trusts Other Trusts	

Try plotting your own ages on this chart to see what support might be available at different stages of family life and how you must plan accordingly.

Financial Assistance Changes with Age

Parents and family want to do as much as possible for their loved one, but as an individual with disabilities grows older, the rules change because relationships change.

There is a shift in the criteria for financial support as individuals with disabilities move from adolescence to adulthood. Young adults eventually become legally independent and the courts support and respect that; when this happens, family influence becomes less. At the age of 18, in most provinces, an individual with disabilities is legally responsible for him or herself. The difficulty, of course, is determining when they are able to take on responsibility for life's decisions.

At the age of majority, decisions have to be made about how the family is going to carry out living arrangements, financial support and long-term involvement. In other words, a life plan is needed. Developing this life plan is a careful balance between protecting an individual with disabilities and giving them their freedom to make their own decisions.

As time moves on, children in the family may move to new communities and new relationships. Consequently, it becomes more difficult to figure out who will take the lead in supporting an individual with disabilities. This change in family relationships can lead to conflict. Sometimes, family members want to move in different directions regarding care needs, housing or necessities of life. One family member may have an idea, but others may disagree. This can cause family friction and sometimes result in legal battles between family members or between family members and community organizations.

Personal Finances Aren't Just About Growth of Capital

Without a doubt, the growth of financial capital is the one area of personal finances that gets the most attention. This is an appealing notion, but there is more to personal finances than capital growth, especially when losses of capital may have little ability to be recovered through a conservative portfolio for an individual with a disability. When disability of a loved one is involved, three other factors stand out as being highly important:

- security of capital for the life of your loved one;
- guaranteed income, possibly for many years; and
- inflation protection.

Growing savings is important in the wealth accumulation stage of investing, but it does add risk. Individuals with disabilities in your family will need a guaranteed income for many years beyond your lifetime, so risk must be reduced in favour of guaranteed income.

When it comes to securing an income stream for an individual with a disability, the focus shifts away from capital growth to income security and inflation protection. So choosing financial products that protect capital from eroding and have a guaranteed income stream become priority. Also, because you are planning for a loved one who may live perhaps twenty-five years longer than you, inflation protection is important.

Factor in Inflation and Life Expectancy

Unfortunately, people often overlook inflation and life expectancy when making financial plans. A reasonable cost of living increase for projections over time is about 2.5%. If the cost of living for a loved one with a disability is $20,000 a year, in ten years the amount needed would be $25,000, and in twenty years it would be almost $33,000. Therefore, increases in the cost of living always need to be considered.

In addition to inflation, you also need to consider how long your savings for a loved one must last. If, for example, your loved one is 20 years old today, you may need to take care of expenses for another 50 years in many cases. In this case you would require significantly more funds than if your loved one were 45 years old and only needed the funds for another 25 years.

The Four Pillars of Financial Support

The four pillars of financial support are social assistance, community support, tax benefits and family support. More recently, the RDSP funding has become a major component as well. Support through other tax benefits are helpful, but unfortunately are usually not a major contributor to financial support.

Until individuals reach the age of majority, financial responsibility primarily rests with parents. Social assistance usually starts at the age of 18 and ends when RDSP income and government pensions take over, around the age of 60. RDSPs funded early on start to pay out later in life. If RDSP income starts earlier, there is sometimes a penalty applied to these earlier withdrawals.

Figure 1.8 shows how each of four important contributors to financial support relates to day-to-day income, long-term savings and property ownership. The matching of needs and resources is confusing, so long-term plans need to be well thought out to be effective.

Figure 1.8   Four Financial Contributors

	Social Assistance	Community	Tax Benefits/ RDSP	Family Support
Children				
Day-to-day income				✓
Long-term savings			✓	✓
Accommodation		✓		✓
Adults				
Day-to-day income	✓		✓	✓
Long-term savings			✓	✓
Accommodation	✓	✓		✓
Retirees				
Day-to-day income			✓	✓
Long-term savings			✓	✓
Accommodation		✓		✓

Community support provides many services to individuals with disabilities including housing, home care, therapies, life skills training, education and transportation. The level of family support is based on the availability of extra income. For some it's very limited, but for others income may be sufficient to support the extensive cost of disability.

Family support to pay immediate expenses or fund long-term savings plans may include the following.

- Cash gifts
- Bequests
- Transfers of property to trusts
- Transfers of registered plans
  - RDSPs
  - RRSPs
  - RESPs
- Contribution of other property
  - Accommodation – sometimes by using trust
  - Life insurance products
  - Personal property (vehicles, furnishings, etc.)

The contribution of funds to benefit a loved one and the co-ordination of that process from many sources is more extensively dealt with in chapter 11, Financial Planning and Investing – Some Guiding Principles.

Transfer of Financial Assistance

In planning the finances of a person with a disability, it's important to maximize financial support. To do this, you must first know the rules of each support program and make sure you stay within them.

For example, financial assistance can be maximized in the following two ways.

- Do not exceed the asset, income or other limitations. For example, obtaining social assistance usually requires keeping the assets of the person with a disability and income below a certain level.
- If a tax benefit is not applicable, determine if it can be transferred to someone else in the family where it can be utilized. For instance, it may be possible to transfer non-refundable tax credits from a person with a disability who cannot use them to a family member who can.

Trusts for More Than a Single Reason

Holding property in a trust is usually an important part of financial planning for people with disabilities. And yet, trusts tend to be underutilized. Some practitioners who do not specialize in trusts may lack the experience to navigate this difficult area.

Trusts serve three basic uses for people with disabilities: tax planning, social assistance planning, and property ownership.

- Tax planning – Trusts can be used to minimize income tax in various ways and with the transfer of assets to final beneficiaries when the trust is no longer needed.

- Social assistance planning - A discretionary, such as a Henson trust, can be used to maintain social assistance and still provide some income without disqualification.
- Property ownership and transfers - Individuals with disabilities are often not legally able to own property, so using a trust is a way to move property from parents for use by a loved one without the person acquiring legal title. Also, a trust enables property ownership to be moved at a later point to siblings or other family members with certain tax benefits and fewer legal complications.

PART 3 – PLANNING

Setting Priorities

Financial issues relating to disability can be placed in ten categories, as depicted in Figure 1.10 at the end of this chapter. Some of these issues will be very important to you, some less so and some not at all. Review Figure 1.11 and write down your rating (1 – 10) for each of the ten points. It's a simple exercise, but it may help you understand where there is work to be done and where there is not. Disability covers so many issues that it's helpful to get your bearings at the beginning.

Agreement, Confirmation and Understanding

Readers of this book will have different levels of knowledge in terms of their understanding of personal finances. They may not have a clear understanding of their financial picture and why planning options relate to the level of disability. For example, social assistance and certain tax benefits will depend on meeting specific criteria that may be very complex.

The problem, of course, is to determine if and how your loved one fits onto the complicated spectrum of disability and personal finances. Members of a family may be at different levels of understanding from each other and this can lead to conflict. Hopefully this book will help all members of a family address the many facets of financial planning for disability shown in Figure 1.10 near the end of this chapter.

Written Records

Written documentation is so important when trying to navigate the many levels of approval that change from program to program. As someone with a disability gets older, documentation that you once needed may be required years later. You may be requested to produce documents such as birth certificates, medical reports and psychological assessments, to name a few.

As you sort this out, you will accumulate a pile of letters, several kinds of approvals, test results and other documentation. Hold onto them, file them and know where to locate them on short notice. Why? When you go to the next step you will no doubt be asked for something you had in your possession not long ago; good organization can save you a lot time and move you to the next stage more quickly. Organization of documents may seem unimportant, but this may be the best advice this book offers.

Planned Savings are Vital to Long-term Cash Flow

There is always a balance between accumulating savings for your own retirement and additionally saving for a family member with a disability. For individuals with higher incomes, this may not be a problem. But for others with more modest means, setting aside additional funds to support someone in your family years into the future can be difficult without good planning.

If there is an individual with a disability in your family, your cost of living will be higher and money needs to last longer - your lifetime and theirs. You must plan with as much certainty as possible so there will be enough funds to last for your generation and some of the next. Given this, savings plans such as annuities, life insurance and RDSPs are better in this situation because of their certainty and the tax benefits that a traditional stock market portfolio does not offer.

Pooling Family Resources

Most often, it is the parents who provide the leadership in planning the financial future for their loved one. However, they should not assume that others in the family will not want to help – now or perhaps in their wills. Often grandparents or aunts and uncles want to contribute. This is an important planning dynamic and is often overlooked. If you open up the conversation on this, not only might this lead to a more coordinated effort but it could also minimize income tax and maximize social assistance and other benefits. In the end, this can help in accumulating more resources than might otherwise be available.

Customize Your Planning

There are many variables involved with financial planning for a family with a loved one with a disability. It is impossible to say which techniques make the most sense without examining the particular circumstance. No matter how good a financial tool may look on paper, one size does not fit all. Here are some of the important influences that can impact your financial planning choices:

- the legal competency of your loved one;
- appropriate housing options;
- the tax and legal options for different structures; and
- the financial resources available within the family.

Legal competency should be addressed before you make other decisions. If your loved one is not capable of functioning independently, it is unlikely you will purchase a home for him or her even if you have the funds to do so. It is important to consider the total picture of disability financial planning by putting together a life plan and a financial plan, as discussed in part 4 of this chapter and summarized in Figure 1.10. A life plan which identifies the quality of life that you want for your loved one should come before a financial plan. It's good to know your destination before you figure out how to get there.

PART 4 – ESSENTIAL FINANCIAL ISSUES AND CONCERNS

Before embarking on the journey of personal financial planning for a loved one, you first need to have a map to make sure you know how to get where you're going. For example, one of the hottest topics related to disability is the Henson trust. From what you hear, you might think that every family must have one - and maybe that is true. But how much money should be in the trust so it can last for how long? Who will be the financial person establishing the trust? What other needs could the trust serve beyond preserving social assistance? And so on. You need to look at the road map and the ten essential issues before you start driving. Figure 1.11 provides a list of these issues.

Life Plan

Before families consider financial issues, they should first have a life plan. A life plan looks at what it is that you are trying to accomplish. Of course, your goal is to provide the best quality of life for your loved one. In many cases, government and non-profit sector support provide the basic necessities of life, but then you must decide if you are going to add to this to improve the quality of life for your loved one.

Figure 1.9 outlines the points to take into consideration when developing a life plan.

Figure 1.9   Life Plan Considerations

- Ability of the person with a disability to live alone or with others
- Financial assistance available to support independent living or shared accommodations
- Financial ability of family to provide funds to support a better lifestyle

---

The financial path is not easy and will take hours of time for fact-finding before you can settle on a proper life plan. Here are some questions you should ask yourself.

- Is it better to arrange for personal living accommodations rather than using community housing and is it financially possible?

- Is it possible to give up social assistance by contributing more finances in order to improve lifestyle?
- How do you keep family personally involved in the life of your loved one with a disability?
- What issues are important to your loved one and should be considered in the life plan?

Always keep the overall goal of quality of life for your loved one in mind when you answer the above questions as you develop a life plan.

Housing and Attendant Care

Understanding the housing options available to your loved one and which ones you favour is fundamental. If you want to upgrade housing, you need to ask yourself the following: What will it cost? Am I able to afford this? Does the complexity of the disability make this option possible? In some cases, attendant care may be a significant part of housing cost.

Long-term Money Plan

Many families do not take enough time to determine money needs for the long term. More often than not, they simply look at the first option available and move forward with plans based on the financial outcome. Your loved one's financial needs will depend on their type of disability. It's sometimes the case that the more complex the disability the less need there is for personal funds. This is because disability may reduce life's options that cost more money and basic needs will be supported by less expensive community facilities. Chapter 11 deals with this quite extensively.

The Constraints of Our Laws

Deciding where to establish the line between allowing people to act independently and protecting them from themselves is a challenging problem. For the most part, all of us have good intentions when it comes to the care of dependents, but we still need a legal framework to set reasonable boundaries and protect personal freedoms. This is particularly true for vulnerable individuals with cognitive disabilities. Laws exist to guide caregivers in making decisions that meet appropriate standards. The Law Commission of Ontario recently completed a study called, *Legal Capacity, Decision-making and Guardianship,* which is well worth reading and is cited in Appendix B.

Parents are legally responsible to look after their children until they reach the age of majority—either 18 or 19 years of age, depending on the province. However, in most provinces, this does not give parents authority over a child's finances. Parental responsibility to care for and provide necessities for their children can sometimes extend beyond the age of majority when there is a financially dependent relationship.

When individuals reach the age of majority they are presumed to be capable of entering into contracts. However, this may not always be the case. The capacity to enter into a contract is not necessarily the same as being able to manage one's financial affairs. Therefore, when an adult is incapable of managing their financial affairs or supporting themselves, a new set of rules under the law take effect compared to those for minors or capable adults.

Competency, Guardianship and Legal Issues

The competency of your loved one will legally impact the way you will structure their financial plan. If your loved one has a significant intellectual disability, trusts will almost certainly be used. Competency tests vary depending on the financial transaction—owning a property, making a will, or getting married.

Competency is by no means a straightforward issue and may result in disagreements between family members. This was tested recently in the province of Nova Scotia where the Nova Scotia Supreme Court required the province to enact a new law to align with the Charter of Rights and Freedoms. The new law includes a presumption of capacity clause. However, the new law also allows someone to apply to the court to represent another adult in making decisions. Any action or decision made for the adult should be done in the least restrictive and least intrusive manner possible.

Financial Caregiver Continuity

As you age and your involvement with a loved one with a disability changes, you must seriously consider who will take your place as caregiver. The individual must, of course, want to take on this responsibility and have the time and skills to do so.

Trusts – Property Ownership, Taxation and Income Distribution

Trusts are highly important structures for property ownership and controlling income flow to a person with a disability. This is especially the case for those who lack intellectual capacity. Trusts are discussed in chapter 5.

Social Assistance

If your loved one is eligible for social assistance, then you certainly must determine it if it's needed. In some cases, families do have the financial resources to forgo income assistance to give their loved one a better quality of life at a higher cost. Unfortunately, social assistance can be reduced when the personal assets of a person with a disability or family gifts exceed certain limits. In such cases, social assistance is reduced or eliminated. Income assistance is discussed in detail in chapter 3.

Community Resources

Community resources from municipalities, health care services and community not-for profits are one of the bedrocks of support for individuals with disabilities. These resources range from therapy and training, to life skills training, to special transportation. Not only do communities provide many necessary services, they usually do so at an affordable price. Community resources are discussed in chapter 2.

Tax Planning and Incentives

The Income Tax Act contains many benefits for individuals with disabilities and their families. Find out what they are and how to qualify. Non-refundable tax credits and registered plans such as the Registered Disability Savings Plan (RDSP) are the most prominent. A variety of benefits using trusts is discussed in chapter 5. They can be very helpful for their beneficial tax provisions and their advantageous legal frameworks.

A great deal of progress in improving tax benefits for disability was made when Jim Flaherty was Canada's Minister of Finance during the years 2006 - 2014. The most notable change he made was the introduction of the RDSP.

In the last five years, however, the federal government has become more restrictive in terms of benefits for individuals with disabilities. For instance, the following changes have been made.

- The principal residence exemption has been removed from inter vivos trusts.
- Only one qualified disability trust (QDT) is allowed for each individual with a disability even though trust funds could be established by different family members through their wills.
- The registration of an RDSP for an adult by a family member is only allowed as an interim measure.
- The beneficiary of a QDT (who must also qualify for the DTC) must also sign each year to qualify the trust as a QDT. This will necessitate the need for a guardian for QDT beneficiaries who are not legally competent to sign.

In some respects, recent changes to some tax rules have been limiting for individuals with a disability. Tax planning is discussed in chapter 6.

Estate Planning and Wealth Continuity

Estate planning is perhaps the most neglected area of all in planning for disability of a loved one in the family. The passing of assets and income to a loved one with a disability and then siblings through integrated legal and tax structures requires extraordinary attention to family dynamics. Professional assistance is a must and is discussed in chapter 8.

Key Areas of Disability and Financial Planning

Figure 1.10 Disability - The Ten Most Important Components of Financial Planning

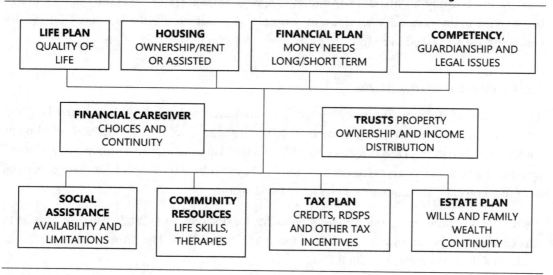

Figure 1.10 provides a summary of the areas that need consideration when planning for a loved one with a disability. The figure should get you seriously thinking about all of the components of financial planning before you dive into any one financial planning strategy. Too often, families design their financial planning structures without considering every area. For example, while an RDSP is good product, a family should first ask how much money is really needed in the future and whether or not the funds might eventually fall into the hands of the Public Trustee. Should an application for personal guardianship be considered and later recommended in a will? The Disability and Financial Life Plan Questionnaire on our website, www.thefamilyguide.ca, uses the same ten categories outlined here.

A brief description of the ten categories is provided in Figure 1.11.

Figure 1.11 Core Financial Issues and Concerns

It is important to know the financial landscape so you can plan the future for your family and a loved one with a disability—so you can look at the big picture and know how the pieces fit together. Think hard about the areas that concern you the most. These big picture areas, shown below, will help you get started. Assign a rating to each area and then consider where you should go from there.

- **Life Plan** (health and safety, personal care, transportation, community involvement, recreation, education and life skills, employment, government assistance limitations)

- **Housing** (home, apartment, assisted living, supervised accommodation, attendant care, rent vs own, family pooling)

- **Financial Plan** (long-term savings planning, budgeting, annuities, RDSPs, final beneficiaries)

- **Competency** (legal competence, tax structures, property ownership, investments, legal structures, guardianship)

- **Financial Caregiver** (continuity, financial assistance, cost and compensation, long-term continuity)

- **Trusts –** (property ownership and income distribution, compliance with laws, tax compliance, changing needs and costs, wealth continuity)

- **Social Assistance** (Henson trusts, medical benefits, quality of living, asset and income limitations, exempt assets and income)

- **Community Resources** (meeting program qualifications, availability, cost, funding assistance)

- **Tax Plan** (non-refundable tax credits, disability tax credit, other tax benefits, tax implications of change of ownership)

- **Estate Plan** (wealth continuity, wills, powers of attorney, executors, guardianship, beneficiary designations, trusts, qualified disability trusts, charitable giving)

Summing Up

Ultimately, families want to maximize financial resources for their loved one with a disability and maintain a structure that allows a proper balance between financial control and effective decision-making. A good financial plan should also consider wealth continuity in a family context. The plan becomes more difficult to execute if your loved one is intellectually challenged and cannot own property, sign contracts, or commit to binding agreements.

Chapter 1 has outlined the broader issues relating to personal finances and disability. The remaining chapters focus more on specific financial and tax issues and how they relate to disability.

CHAPTER 2

Communities – The Glue That Binds

Many communities are blessed with a multitude of service organizations that work behind the scenes. When someone in the family is confronted with a disability, community organizations do their part and are usually the first responders. There are many volunteer organizations that contribute to our health and wellbeing. At the core of these organizations are local volunteers who give countless hours to building community services and to making sure they are relevant as times change.

Government also contributes substantially, either directly or indirectly, to provide volunteer organizations with their funding—capital funding and program support. Government-sponsored programs help bring discipline and structure to local service agencies. School boards are also taking on an enhanced role by providing special education services to children with disabilities.

Community organizations, either through health care or social service avenues, get the first knock on the door when families are in crisis and must reach out. Not all community service organizations have resources for marketing, so it can take some searching to find services that you need. And if you do, then you must be able to show that the needs for your loved one meet their criteria as a service recipient.

To find out what is available, community directories can be a helpful tool. Documentation of your situation must be asked for by community organizations, so build up an organized file of information. And remember that many services will come under new providers as age changes so retain information from the past because it can often be recycled to meet today's needs.

PART 1 – THE ORGANIZATIONS

Community Services

There are many community organizations to offer assistance to individuals and their families for the many kinds of disabilities. Some communities will have more resources than others so it may be necessary to travel a distance to access certain services. However, more than likely, the travel is worth it.

Community services fall into a few major categories, as follows.

- Advocacy and support
- Counselling
- Diagnostic and personal care
- Education
- Health care
- Respite care
- Social integration and community activities
- Transportation
- Housing
- Residential Care

Health care, diagnosis and therapies are obviously of high importance to individuals with disabilities. But the availability of information and knowledge for all areas important to families about community services is also important. Families will have a significant need for knowledge and understanding about community services because, in all likelihood, this is all new to them.

The cost of some services is expensive and beyond the financial resources of some families. Community resources can help by putting families on a path to services they might otherwise not be able to afford. Many not-for-profits offer services at affordable rates on a fee-for-service basis because they are partially funded by government.

Canada is a caring country with a good federal and provincial social assistance network that functions reasonably well. Set out below is a sample of the types of community-based services that you may find in your community or somewhere close by.

- Adult day care
- Caregiver respite
- Caregiver support
- Community health centres
- Community information centres
- Counselling services
- Day programs
- Drop-in centres
- Family counselling
- Family support services
- Hospices
- Impaired vision services

- In-home services
- Life skills training
- Literacy instruction
- Meals on wheels
- Respite support

- Recreational facilities
- Self-help groups
- Assisted housing
- Support groups
- Transportation services

The difficulty many families have is finding organizations that meet their needs and figuring out how to contact them. Often you will be able to find a community services directory that will become a bible of information to seek out organizations that can help you. In general, community service providers can be diveded into four areas, as shown in Figure 2.1.

Figure 2.1   Community Service Organizations

- Not-For-Profits (registerd and non-registered)
- Provincial Government Agencies
- Municipal Services
- Private Organizations

In many provinces, governments can sometimes provide services directly to community residents but more often expertise available through community registered charities which they might fund. For example, a registered is charity providing development services may be getting significant provincial funding as direct grants or as fee-for-service cost sharing.

The Work of Governments Behind the Scenes

We put a lot of trust in our volunteer organizations, and rightfully so. They tend to be run by people who live locally and give their time and expertise at no charge. This model makes these organizations more locally driven and efficient and therefore their services can be better matched with the local needs of the community where they are situated. Provincial governments are increasingly funding locally managed organizations because governments see the opportunity to piggyback on the strengths of local volunteers.

As the scope of local assistance to people with disabilities has expanded, the size of such organizations has also increased. So too has the amount of funding provided by federal, provincial and municipal levels of government. Today many health-care organizations run by not-for-profit organizations are significantly funded by government. We should give government their due: they have increasingly adapted to using local organizations to fund local care needs.

While the increasing amount of disability funding is welcome, navigating the system to obtain needed services can be challenging. When a family explores social service agencies they enter a system that is much more complex than it sometimes should be. This can happen because they must provide services within their own capability and rules for eligibility of their services, but they may also have to live within the criteria of the particular ministry helping to fund the service. Here are some of the main criteria that can dictate patient eligibility.

- Complexity of the disability
- Age
- Assessment and testing results
- Conformity to admission standards

This is not a long list, but within each of the qualifications can be conditions that can be complex and restrictive. So, if you show even a small exception to the rules, you may not qualify. And then, as your age changes or your disability needs change you may be disqualified from a program and will need to seek another service provider.

There can be a high level of local people management skills and financial support that drive a wide array of community resources. Not only do people in the community provide financial support through many charities and non-profits, they also provide their skills on boards of directors and through their own personal involvement. Although provincial governments provide financial backing for non-profits and provincial organizations, local input is often present.

Not-For-Profit Organizations

There are many organizations to help people with disabilities and their families. Some of them are registered charities and some are unregistered charitable organizations. They both make a significant contribution to the life and well-being of a loved one with a disability. The community organizations that have a charitable registration are easy to identify. They include such organizations as Community Living, the Canadian Cancer Society, the Down Syndrome Association and other organizations that provide life skills training, therapies and medical treatments to people with disabilities.

There are also numerous organizations that are not registered charities and include such organizations as sports teams and service clubs driven by volunteers. They too do their share in providing needed services for individuals and families and add to the quality of life of individuals with a disability through their community work.

Funding of Community Services

Each year the Fraser Institute publishes a Generosity Index which compares charitable giving in Canada. In addition to making cash or in-kind donations, 44% of Canadians volunteer time to charitable and not-for-profit organizations. It's encouraging that Canadian charities provide community-based social, health, housing, educational, cultural and recreational services and work with strong partnerships with government. The funding of charities providing much needed community services breaks down as follows.

Figure 2.2 Charity Funding

Households	12%
Government (mainly provincial)	20%
Sales of goods and services	40%
Investments and memberships	22%

Governments like to support community services through contracts with charities and not-for-profits, in part because this gives these governments input into identifying local needs. Government, not-for-profits and charitable partnerships seem to be working well. This is comforting for those who draw heavily on their services.

PART 2 – HOUSING

Traditional Housing Options

When it comes to housing for a person with a disability, families need to think outside the box. Many options are available, although some are much more expensive than others. Out-of-pocket costs can, in some cases, be reduced by disability related tax credits, social assistance, and other assistance.

For people without disabilities, the type of accommodation needed at different life stages is fairly conventional and goes along the following lines, often related to age.

Housing	Facility
Independent Living	Home or rented accommodation
Assisted Living	Retirement home
Supportive Accommodation	Nursing home

Housing Options for Individuals with Disabilities

There are more housing options available for people with disabilities now than in the past. Shared independent residences are becoming more numerous but are still not enough to meet the increasing need encountered by a greater emphasis for independent living. The Passport Program in Ontario provides funds to make community living and involvement a more certain option. This area is changing at a fast pace, so families need to keep investigating options that might better suit them or their loved one.

Figure 2.3 shows the housing options for individuals with disabilities.

Figure 2.3   Housing Options for Individuals with Disabilities

Facility
Living with Family
Family Home
Attached Personal Residence (Granny Flat)
Independent Living
Rented or Owned Personal Residence
Shared Independent Living
Geared to Income Housing
Assisted Living
Group Residences
Retirement Homes
Nursing Home (Long Term Care)

Trends in living are changing rapidly. There is a new thrust to encourage people to live on their own or with others in community rather than in supportive accommodations. They can, in some cases, be provided extra financial assistance to do so. The new Passport Program in Ontario is a good example of this new trend.

Housing Choices and Their Effects on the Cost of Living

Beyond health care in certain situation, housing is perhaps the biggest financial issue of all. It can be the most expensive item in a personal budget or the least expensive, depending on the person's ability to care for him or herself and live independently.

In general, the out-of-pocket cost of living can be quite low for some high-needs individuals because infrastructure costs may be paid for by government. Some individuals will live in an assisted living setting that is largely paid for by government or is subsidized with social assistance income turned over to the facility as rent. An individual who has comparably low needs may be able to live alone or with others, but the cost can be much higher because their accommodations are not likely subsidized. Sometimes parents get together to form partnership arrangements to share costs with other parents, as discussed below.

A Private Home is Possible

Increasingly, parents from different families are coming together to provide a home for their children. They combine their monetary resources and can take advantage of economy of scale.

In Ontario, parents can apply for Passport funding of up to $35,000 a year which adds even more options for getting their loved ones involved in the community, which is as an added bonus.

Some families have the financial ability to purchase a home for a loved one who is disabled. In some cases, this is an option, but in other cases intellectual disability will make this unworkable. Even if ownership of a home is financially feasible for a person with a disability, it may not be a good idea if there are cognitive issues.

Social Assistance and Housing

Ownership of a home does not affect eligibility for social assistance in most provinces. This allows for some good options for home ownership. Should the individual with a disability not be capable of legally owning a home, ownership can be placed in a trust and, in some cases, be eligible for the principal residence tax exemption. At the death of the individual with a disability, the trust agreement would likely dictate that home ownership pass to another family member or to a charity and that the trust be wound up.

Home Care

Each province has an agency that assists with home care as shown in Figure 2.4

Figure 2.4   Provincial Home Care

Province	Agency	Website
Alberta	Regional Health Authorities	www.seniors.alberta.ca
British Columbia	BC Health Authorities	www.healthservices.gov.bc.ca/socsec
Manitoba	Regional Health Authorities	www.gov.mb.ca/health/homecare/index.html
New Brunswick	Family and Community Services (Extra Mural Program)	www.gnb.ca/0051/0384/index-e.asp
Newfoundland	Regional Integrated Health Authorities	http://www.health.gov.nl.ca/health/persons disabilities/fundingprogram_hcs.html#phs
Northwest Territories	Health and Social Services Authorities	www.hlthss.gov.nt.ca/english/our_system/ about_us/default/htm
Nova Scotia	Continuing Care	www.gov.ns.ca/health/ccs/homecare.asp
Nunavut	Health and Social Services	www.gov.nu.ca/health
Ontario	Local Health Initiatives Network	
Prince Edward Island	Home Care and Support	www.healthpei.ca/homecare
Quebec	Sante et Services Sociaux Quebec	http://msss.gouv.qc.ca/en/regions/index.php
Saskatchewan	Regional Health Authorities	www.health.gov.sk.ca/home-care
Yukon	Yukon Home Care Program	www.hss.gov.yk.ca/homecare.php

The home care option is an excellent way to go. Usually parents get involved as volunteers and board members so they have some hands-on control and participation. This is a great example of individuals and government working together.

Home Ownership or Renting

If a family can afford it, home ownership for their loved one with a disability is financially better than renting for three reasons. First, if a person with a disability rents a home, the rent is usually paid for by the family. Payment of rent is likely to come out of the supporting family's income, which may reduce or disqualify the individual with a disability from receiving social assistance. Alternatively, if the home is owned by the family or a trust and the person with a disability lives there, the provincial social assistance rules of most provinces state that the rent-free benefit does not reduce social assistance. And finally, if the home is owned by a trust, the principal residence exemption could be available and no tax will be payable on the capital gain on the home when it is eventually sold.

PART 3 – COMMUNITY SERVICES

Social, Recreational and Community Activities

When disability is an issue, socialization and integration in the community for the loved one with a disability is extremely important. Sometimes individuals with disabilities are not included as fully as they should be. For children especially, recreation needs to be part of their lives just as it is for children without disabilities. Seeing a youngster having fun and doing his or her best at an activity is a tonic for families. Most communities have organized recreational activities for children and adults with disabilities run by either the school system or not-for-profit organizations. The Ontario Passport Program was designed for this reason. Damon plays for the Cambridge Ice Hounds.

Education and Life Skills Training

In Ontario, the school system is required to offer programs for children with disabilities. The resources are significant and designed to assist life skills training for children with disabilities. There are also many not-for-profit organizations that offer life skills training for individuals with disabilities. This training increases social skills and self-esteem and allows individuals with disabilities to participate more fully in their communities. Food chains and other retailers are increasingly providing job opportunities for people with disabilities – a life skills gold mine.

Local Health Initiatives Network (LHIN)

LHIN centres in Ontario provide home services in the community; they receive provincial funding, but are largely managed in the community. They usually have staff at hospitals and have drop-in centres throughout their catchment area.

LHINs offer in-home care services, long-term care home placement, palliative care, and community resource information and referrals which fill the following needs.

- Arranging for health and personal support service visits in people's homes
- Authorizing services for children with disabilities in schools
- Managing admissions to long-term care homes
- Connecting people who have no physician with a primary health care provider
- Providing direct nursing care as well as rapid response, mental health and other specialty nursing

When you don't know where to turn, call a LHIN. They may not provide the services you need, but they can point you to other organizations that can.

Hospitals

There is no doubt that hospitals have deep roots in many communities. Despite their extraordinarily long history in health care, they are amazingly modern in their openness to patients and their patient-first attitudes.

Specialized medical services, such as those required by patients with disabilities, are sometimes only provided in regional hospitals. While they may not be located in your own community, they do make an extra effort to reach out to all of their patients no matter where they come from.

From time to time, Damon still travels to McMaster Children's Hospital and to Holland Bloorview Kids Rehabilitation Hospital for further treatment and assessment. The personal warmth is amazing. The last time at Holland Bloorview, there were lots of high-fives from everyone.

In writing this book, Bruce and Shirley passed on their deep gratitude and respect for the outstanding care and personal friendliness they received at McMaster Children's Hospital. Here is what they said to me.

Dr. Brandon Meaney, Division Head of Pediatric Neurology, has been an outstanding doctor in Damon's treatment and development. Damon saw him regularly in the first few years of his life and continues to have an annual monitoring visit with him. Dr. Meaney is a brilliant and thoughtful individual. He expresses carefully considered opinions and diagnoses and has an excellent rapport with his patients and their parents. It was Dr. Meaney who recommended Damon as the Poster Child for the 2006 McMaster Kids Telethon.

Dr. Jan Gorter, head of the Child Health Research Institute, has seen Damon regularly over the past few years, working to correct Damon's walking, his gait and getting him fitted with braces to assist in his walking and coordination development. Dr. Gorter has been a huge help in improving Damon's walking and overall coordination.

We worked with Dr. Saroj Saigel, head of the Growth and Development clinic, and Dr. Peter Rosenbaum almost immediately after Damon was born in order to secure necessary services. They put us in touch with organizations such as KidsAbility, the Brantford School for the Blind, and Community Care Access to start the next step in our journey.

Dr. Peter Steer had a lot of involvement in the first few months of Damon's life. He was very supportive and realistic about Damon's diagnosis and also offered a positive perspective on how to manage Damon's challenges.

There were many other doctors at McMaster who helped Damon succeed. The Neo-Natal Intensive Care Unit was invaluable in the first month of Damon's life. We owe a lot to McMaster and are extremely lucky to have had access to a world class hospital that provided such exemplary care for our son.

Specialized Programs – Therapies and Counselling

The not-for-profit sector does an excellent job of offering specialized programs in therapy and counselling. These organizations are usually financed in part by the municipal, provincial or even federal government. They are great services and are growing in number and scope.

In Town Public Transportation

No matter where you live, you need to get around town. People with disabilities may not be able to drive a car so they rely on public transportation. Fortunately, people with disabilities are often issued free or discounted public transit fares. Sometimes municipalities give passes to charities to distribute to those with low income.

Services in the Next Town

People who live in larger cities will likely find the services they need there. Usually, social and medical services, special housing, therapies and recreational facilities are available in larger centres. However, for those who live in smaller towns and cities, it may be necessary to travel quite a distance to get special medical treatment or the supportive accommodation needed for people with disabilities. Unfortunately, inter-city travel is not always available or easy; there is no clear solution for this for small town Canada.

Passport Program

Ontario offers the Passport Program to help individuals with disabilities better integrate into the community. This is a program for individuals with developmental disabilities over the age of 18. It has two main mandates:

- To support participation of individuals with developmental disabilities in daily activities; and
- To provide respite to primary caregivers.

In summary, the goals of the Passport Program, as shown in a brochure of Developmental Services Ontario, are as follows.

- Foster independence by building on individuals' abilities and developing community participation, social and daily living skills.
- Increase opportunities for participation in community with supports that respect personal choices and decision-making, and help people achieve their goals.
- Promote social inclusion and broaden social relationships through the use of community resources and services available to everyone in the community.
- Help young people make the transition from school to life as an adult in the community.
- Support families and caregivers of an adult with a developmental disability so they can continue in their supportive role.

The program is limited to improving the daily living and building related skills of a person with a disability. The Passport Program brochure indicates that this program does not support the following services and supports.

- Cleaning, food, meal preparation, snow removal, care of other family members and similar household expenses
- Tuition for post-secondary education for those who are eligible for certain government student assistance programs
- Allowances from the Ontario Disability Support Program (ODSP)
- Housing and home maintenance

- Clothing
- Holiday travel
- Dental care
- Fees for therapies/specialized services such as physiotherapy, occupational therapy and nurses
- Assistive devices and special equipment
- Vehicle purchases

The above list is not exhaustive but does outline most of the disallowed expenses.

The program reimburses primary caregivers up to $35,000 for expenses that meet either of the program's primary objectives. In addition, for individuals who do not have the financial resources to prepay the expenses, the program offers a brokerage arrangement where pre-approved organizations will pay the costs.

As the Passport Program brochure indicates, *Passport is a program that helps adults with a developmental disability be involved in their communities and live as independently as possible by providing funding for community participation services and supports, activities of daily living and person-directed planning. The program also provides funding for caregiver respite services and supports for primary caregivers of an adult with a developmental disability.* This program is part of an initiative that lets individuals control and direct their own lives as opposed to putting them in pre-selected programs and services over which they have little choice.

Summing Up

Communities offer so much to assist with disability. Smaller communities may not have as many services, but there are always volunteers willing to help. The combination of community leadership and provincial assistance with funding is a winning combination.

CHAPTER 3

Provincial Income Assistance

Social assistance for individuals with disabilities is a provincial responsibility. Provinces across the country each have their own distinct disability support programs. If families also create a Henson trust, it may be able to be used as a mechanism to maximize social assistance by holding income earning assets in a trust and limiting trust distributions to a loved one with a disability within social assistance income limitations.

Families take on a big challenge in structuring their own affairs in order to financially assist a loved one with a disability. However, unless this financial support is carefully planned it could eliminate social assistance. It is important for families to integrate social assistance with the other aspects of their personal finances to maximize financial help. Some families will have the financial resources to bypass income assistance, but the information discussed in this chapter may still be of value because it is worth taking these benefits into consideration at the very least.

PART 1 – INCOME ASSISTANCE

Income Assistance Across Canada

Provinces are charged with providing social assistance under financial arrangements between the provinces and the federal government. The province's mandate to its residents is set out in various provincial acts.

Figure 3.1   Provincial Disability Support Acts and Regulations

Alberta – Assured Income for the Severely Handicapped Act

British Columbia – Employment and Assistance for Persons with Disabilities Act

Manitoba – The Employment and Income Assistance Act

New Brunswick – Family Income Security Act

Newfoundland and Labrador – Income and Employment Regulation

Northwest Territories – The Social Assistance Act

Nova Scotia – Employment Support and Income Assistance Act

Nunavut – The Social Assistance Act

Ontario – Ontario Disability Support Program Act (ODSP)

Prince Edward Island – Social Assistance Regulations

Quebec – Quebec Pension Plan

Saskatchewan – Saskatchewan Assistance Act

Yukon – Social Assistance Act

Social assistance can cover income support, housing costs and medical care costs. This assistance is usually dependent on the assets and income of the person with a disability; the criteria define a person's eligibility for benefits.

Asset Limits

A person with a disability can own certain assets, generally referred to as exempt assets, and still receive social assistance (depending on the rules of the province in which they live).

In Ontario, the most common types of exempt assets are shown in Figure 3.2.

Figure 3.2   ODSP Exempt Assets

There is a long list of assets which are exempt under ODSP. Some of the major ones are as follows. In some cases the scope of the exemption is narrowed by the wording of the regulation.

- Personal assets of less than $40,000
- Principal residence
- Motor vehicle
- Tools of the trade related to employment
- Assets necessary for the operation of a business up to $20,000
- Prepaid funeral
- Inheritance trusts
- RESP funds
- RDSP funds

The above assets are usually, but not always, fully exempt assets based on provincial rules. Other assets such as the following are limited to a maximum amount.

- Non-discretionary trusts
- Cash value of life insurance

In Ontario, individuals with disabilities who own assets that disqualify them from social assistance are not allowed to give these assets away to get onside, but it is often possible to sell non-qualifying assets and purchase qualifying assets with the proceeds. This situation can often arise when an inheritance is received by a person with a disability.

The rules are very different from province to province, as outlined in Figure 3.3.

Figure 3.3   Provincial Social Assistance – Exempt Assets and Their Limits

	Exempt Asset Limits	Henson Trusts	Non-discretionary Trusts	Home
Alberta	$100,000	No		Yes
British Columbia	100,000	Yes	$200,000	Yes
Manitoba	4,000	Yes	200,000	Yes
New Brunswick	10,000	Yes	200,000	No
Newfoundland and Labrador	3,000	Yes	200,000	No
Northwest Territories	50,000	Yes		Yes
Nova Scotia	1,000	Yes		Yes
Nunavut	5,000	Yes		Yes
Ontario	40,000	Yes	100,000	Yes
PEI	900	Yes		Yes
Quebec		Yes		
Saskatchewan		Yes		Yes
Yukon	1,500	Yes		Yes

The rules regarding trusts exemptions can change frequently and readers should confirm rules in their own provinces when planning. RDSP plan balances are exempt assets in all provinces. In most provinces, RDSP income is also exempt when determining eligibility for social assistant.

Income Limits

Provinces have different rules that limit the income a person with a disability can receive while maintaining social assistance. The definition of income may not be restricted to salaries and investment income but can include gifts, inheritances and other amounts that do not show up on a tax return. Figure 3.9 provides a helpful picture of the effect of income and assets on social assistance support in the province of Ontario.

The rules will vary considerably from province to province, so it is important that you understand the rules for your province.

PART 2 - ONTARIO DISABILITY SUPPORT PROGRAM (ODSP)

Qualifying For ODSP

The ODSP Act provides a definition of a person with a disability to determine who is eligible to receive benefits. In general, the qualifications are as follows.

- The person has a substantial physical or developmental challenge that is continuous or recurrent and expected to last one year or more
- The direct and cumulative effect of the disability on the person's ability to attend to his or her personal care, function in the community and function in a workplace that results in a substantial restriction in one or more of these activities of daily living
- The disability, its likely duration and the restriction to the person's activities of daily living have been verified

The Disability Mandate Under the ODSP

A review of social assistance rules of all provinces and territories is beyond the scope of this book. This book does, however, review ODSP rules in some detail and, where possible, comment on rules in other provinces.

The ODSP Act spells out the broad framework under which support will be provided to individuals. Section I of the Act defines its mandate as follows.

- To provide income and employment support to persons with disabilities
- To recognize that government, communities, families and individuals share the responsibility of providing such support
- To serve people with disabilities who need assistance
- To be accountable to the taxpayers

It's clear that Ontario does provide income support, but the adequacy of that support is often debated. Support of about $1,100 a month for single recipients with no dependent for general living expenses and housing seems woefully inadequate. Support under ODSP starts after age 18 and typically ends at age 65 when federal retirement benefits negate social assistance.

Government assistance in Ontario is adjusted upwards from time to time based on assets and income levels of individuals with disabilities, but the thresholds are low today and require individuals to live at or below the poverty line.

ODSP Legal Structure

ODSP is administered by the ODSP Act, Regulations and Policy Directives. An outline of the Act, Regulations and Policy Directives is shown in Figure 3.10 at the end of this chapter.

The ODSP Act is relatively short, the Regulations section is somewhat larger, and the more than 70 Policy Directives dwarf both the Act and Regulations. The Policy Directives are by far the best source of ODSP information.

The ODSP Policy provides directives over the following areas.

- Applying for Income Support
- Eligibility Requirements: Who is Eligible
- Document Requirements Section
- Assets
- Income
- Calculation of Income Support
- Exclusion of Income Support
- Recipients in Institutional Settings
- Benefits
- Trustees and Pay Direct
- Receipt of Funds
- Fraud and Information Sharing
- Internal Reviewer and Appeals

ODSP Information Sources

Many organizations provide helpful information about ODSP rules. Should you want to drill down on the law itself, reviewing the ODSP regulations and policy directives can be extremely helpful. Although the ODSP regulations are detailed and complex, they also provide important information about rules, exempt assets, exempt miscellaneous cash incentives, and other important matters. The policy directives are helpful in explaining the government's interpretation of the act and its regulations.

ODSP Monthly Benefits

It is helpful to have some knowledge of the most common ODSP monthly benefits (budgetary requirements) for basic needs, shelter allowances and the Ontario Child Benefit (OCB). These benefit amounts are detailed, as of September 1, 2017, in Figure 3.4.

Figure 3.4   ODSP Monthly Benefits – Single Person

	Basic Needs	Shelter Allowance	OCB	Total
Single	$662	$489	$0	$1,151
Single Parent – one child	$805	$769	$114	$1,688
Single Parent – two children	$805	$833	$229	$1,867
Couple	$1,025	$769	$0	$1,794
Couple – one child	$1,025	$833	$114	$1,972
Couple – two children	$1,025	$904	$229	$2,158

- Shelter allowance amounts shown are maximums and may not apply in every situation. If actual housing costs are less than the maximum shelter allowance, recipients will only receive the amount they actually spend.
- OCB (Ontario Child Benefit) amounts may be lower than the maximum shown above, depending on the net income of the family. Families must file their income tax returns in order to receive the OCB.
- People on ODSP may be eligible for other provincial and federal benefits such as the GST/HST credit, the Ontario Trillium Benefit, or the Canada Child Benefit which are generally exempt income under ODSP.
- The benefit amount shown for a couple is increased where both individuals have a disability.

Other ODSP Benefits

In addition to monthly payments to ODSP recipients for basic needs and shelter, ODSP offers other benefits which are paid to ODSP recipients for certain disability-related expenses, as prescribed by regulation. Payments cover the following expenses of ODSP recipients listed under Section 9 of the Policy Directives.

Figure 3.5   ODSP Prescribed Benefits

9.1 Employment and Training Start Up Benefit and Up Front Child Care Costs

9.2 Community Start Up and Maintenance Benefit

9.3 Heating Costs

9.4 Home Repairs

9.5 Utilities

9.6 Assistive Devices

9.7 Dental Benefits

9.8 Drug Benefits

9.9 Guide Dog Benefit

9.10 Extended Health Benefit

9.11 Hearing Aids

9.12 Mandatory Special Necessities

9.13 Mobility Devices Batteries and Repairs

9.14 Vision Care Benefits

9.15 Back-to-School and Winter Clothing Allowance

9.16 Discretionary Benefit for Low-Cost Energy Conservation Measures

Many of these benefits have maximum payment limits. Nevertheless, they can be extremely helpful to individuals with disabilities in meeting the cost of certain payments that might not otherwise be affordable.

ODSP Income

Social assistance income and related benefits can be lost or reduced when the income of the ODSP recipient exceeds a certain level called the budgetary requirement. Income is calculated after determining the various exemptions that are allowed. Figure 3.6 shows how income limits social assistance in the province of Ontario.

Figure 3.6   Ontario Disability Support Program and Incomes

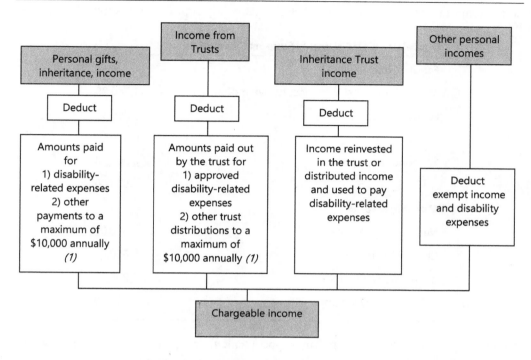

(1)   The $10,000 annual exemption is combined for the two sources shown above.
(2)   Budgetary Requirements are defined as the dollar value of assistance approved by ODSP.
(3)   Chargeable income reduces ODSP benefits.

Income of an ODSP recipient is based on the total income of the benefit unit (Regulation 37.1) which means that the income of a spouse (as defined by Policy Directive 2.3) is included in making the support calculation. A spouse includes someone who the applicant has been living with for at least three months and meets certain other tests.

Chargeable Income and Budgetary Requirements

Chargeable income is income received after adjusting for any exemptions and income directed to pay disability-related expenses. The amount is calculated monthly.

Budgetary requirements, as defined by ODSP, is income provided by ODSP. Essentially, the Ontario government is saying that this is what you require to live, and that is what they are going to give you. The current amount for monthly budgetary requirement for a single person in Ontario is approximately $660 for basic needs and $490 for shelter, or approximately $1150 in total. If an individual is provided with room and board, the shelter amount is reduced. There are a few other items that can increase budgetary requirements such as dietary and pregnancy allowances.

Figure 3.7 provides an illustration of how income support from ODSP is determined. Each dollar of non-exempt income directly reduces the budgeted requirement until support disappears.

Figure 3.7   ODSP Monthly Support Calculation

Family Gifts	
Amounts received in the last twelve months	11,700.00
Funds used for disability expenses	<u>1,200.00</u>
	10,500.00
12 month exemption	<u>10,000.00</u>
	500.00
Monthly income	
Net monthly income	<u>350.00</u>
Chargeable income	850.00
Budgetary requirements	<u>1,200.00</u>
ODSP monthly support	$ 350.00

The above Figure helps show how family support (calculated on a twelve-month basis) affects ODSP income support as compared with personal income of an ODSP recipient.

This can be a difficult calculation if gifts are involved, as shown in Figure 3.7. Some families overlook disability expenses or exemptions for certain types of income. While income may reduce monthly ODSP support, it does not necessarily eliminate other ODSP benefits unless such benefits are tied to the calculation of budgetary requirements.

Maximizing Social Assistance

As indicated earlier, social assistance can be reduced or eliminated should the person with a disability reach defined thresholds of either assets or income. If the asset threshold is exceeded, benefits will likely be cut off. If the annual income level (budgetary income) exceeds the limit, then social assistance will be reduced dollar for dollar by the chargeable income. In the case of employment and self-employment income, the income amount after government withholdings is reduced by another $200 monthly exemption and only half of the remaining amount reduces social assistance.

Certain types of income and assets may be exempt from the calculation, such as income used to pay medical expenses or purchase a home for a person with a disability. The most common way to limit these assets and income thresholds is by holding the property in a trust (Henson trust). The trust allows the trustee to limit the transfer of funds (capital or income) to the person with a disability.

Also, if assets are inherited by a person with a disability, this beneficiary may be able to invest the inheritance in exempt assets such as insurance products like segregated funds or an RDSP. Unless the ODSP recipient has the intellectual capacity to manage their own finances or guardianship exists, this may be difficult unless a legal decision maker is involved.

The amount of funds that can be transferred to a person with a disability might also be greater than one would expect because families are allowed deductions for amounts spent on disability-related expenses.

Exempt Income

The list of exempt income is also very long. Figure 3.8 shows some of the important exemptions listed in the ODSP regulations.

Figure 3.8   ODSP Exempt Income

- A variety of payments received from the province of Ontario
- Certain payments received under the Income Tax Act
- One half of monthly net employment income after a $200 reduction
- Certain amounts received as damages or compensation
- Certain amounts received from the sale or disposition of assets and applied towards approved purchases
- Payments from a trust, a life insurance policy, gifts or other receipts to a maximum of $10,000 in any 12-month period
- Gifts received for contributions to an RESP
- Gifts received for contributions to an RDSP

The list of exempt income is extensive and changes from time to time. If in doubt, individuals should consult ODSP Policy Directives for this information.

Reduction in Income Assistance – Assets and Income

Social assistance for an individual with a disability in Ontario is reduced and sometimes eliminated entirely when they have a certain level of assets or monthly income. If their assets (other than exempt assets) exceed $40,000, social assistance will be denied. If personal income, with some exceptions, family gifts and other voluntary payments exceed $10,000 for any continuous twelve-month period, that excess amount is counted as income and will reduce social assistance dollar for dollar. Income in excess of budgetary income requirements under ODSP will take away health, dental and other assistance.

Financial support by family members is usually made available to improve the quality of life of an individual with a disability beyond social assistance support. Under ODSP rules, voluntary payments include money from trusts, honorariums and windfalls but do not include casual gifts of insignificant value such as basic clothing, meals and basic food purchases.

ODSP support can be lost if a person with a disability owns more than $40,000 in assets or has more than $10,000 of family gifts and certain other income on a revolving twelve-month basis. An overview of the ODSP support qualifications is outlined in Figure 3.9.

Figure 3.9   Qualification for ODSP Support

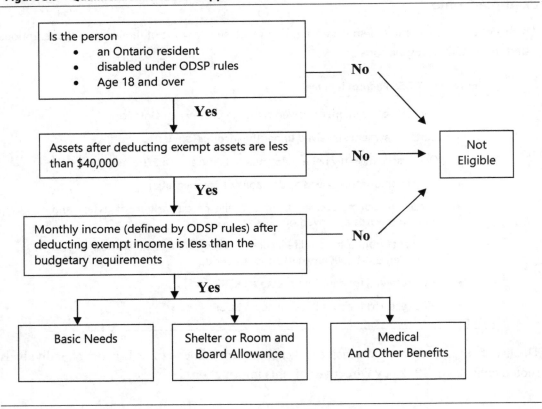

Canada Pension Disability Benefits

Sometimes disability occurs in the midlife stage of life—possibly because of health challenges or because of an unforunate accident. Until that time, the individual may have been employed and paid Canada pension premiums in order to receive pension benefits at retirement. Because of the disability before normal retirement age at 65, it may mean that a CPP disability pension will start because of a cognitive or physical disability of a long-term or indefinite duration.

If an individual qualifies for both the ODSP and a CPP disability pension, they are still required to apply for the CPP disability pension. Unfortunately, any CPP disability pension will reduce

ODSP income dollar for dollar. Not only that, if CPP income exceeds ODSP income, other ODSP benefits may disappear. There doesn't seem to be any way around this unfortunate outcome.

Disability Related Expenses

ODSP Policy Directive 5.9 allows an ODSP recipient to deduct certain expenses from income in order to determine eligibility for ODSP support payments. Examples of such expenses that may be deducted are as follows.

- Activities of daily living
- Social involvement or community activities
- Education and training
- Housing
- Health maintenance, health care and safety
- Religious observances
- Transportation
- Communication
- Employment

The expenses cover: 1) payments for items and services designed for people with disabilities; 2) enhancement for items and services for people with disabilities; and 3) items and services not specifically designed for people with disabilities but nonetheless compensate for or accommodate their disability limitations.

If these deductions are overlooked, income for ODSP purposes is overstated resulting in a reduction of ODSP monthly income.

Retirement Income for Persons with Disabilities

When an individual with a disability reaches age 65, pension income usually starts. At a minimum, individuals receive old age security, currently at about $600/month, and possibly the guaranteed income supplement for a total of over $1,000 a month. This may disqualify a person with a disability from social assistance.

Inheritance Trusts

Policy Directive 4.7, Funds Held in Trusts, deals with trusts under ODSP rules including trusts arising from inheritances and proceeds of life insurance which are both available for the maintenance and support of a person with a disability. Such trusts are exempt assets subject to a $100,000 limit for the capital value of such trusts. This $100,000 exemption is a combined exemption for inheritance trusts and the cash value of life insurance contracts such as segregated funds. Payments out of the inheritance trust are treated as exempt income provided that the amount is used for disability-related items, services, education or training, or the purchase of exempt assets such as RDSPs.

While Henson trusts are usually a preferred option over inheritance trusts, inheritance trusts have application in certain situations. For instance, they may be used by a person with a disability who inherited property and could lose ODSP benefits if the inheritance is not moved to an inheritance trust or some other exempt asset.

Segregated Funds and Annuities

Policy Directive 4.8 to ODSP rules deals with the rules regarding life insurance. Life insurance is an exempt asset, provided it does not exceed $100,000. Any amount in an inheritance trust is added to the segregated funds and annuities amounts so the total limit for all of these assets is $100,000.

Segregated funds, annuities and deferred annuities are insurance products. This means they are exempt assets and can top up the $40,000 liquid asset limitation by another $100,000. Segregated funds are complex, so getting professional advice in this area is recommended. Annuities are less popular than segregated funds because they are less flexible and the income they generate may reduce ODSP eligibility. Part 3 of chapter 11 provides further commentary on segregated funds.

Avoiding Income Disqualification

As already mentioned, ODSP will be denied if the person's assets exceed $40,000. This could happen for a few reasons:

- the individual receives significant gifts or bequests from a relative;
- the individual receives proceeds of an RRSP; or
- the individual receives RDSP income beyond current needs and generates significant savings.

If or when an ODSP applicant fails to meet or comply with the conditions of eligibility set out above, one of the following penalties will likely happen with respect to support:

- support will not be granted;
- support will be withdrawn for a period of time; or
- support will be reduced, cancelled or suspended.

This is an area that requires much advanced planning. There are options to choose from—some better than others.

The excess asset problem of an individual with a disability cannot be easily avoided and certainly can't be sidestepped by giving away property to a family member. Here are some solutions.

- Purchase exempt assets such as home or disability equipment
- Invest in segregated funds up to $100,000
- Transfer an inheritance to an inheritance trust on death (not exceeding $100,000)
- Deposit all or part of the gifts and inheritances in an RDSP account

A family member supporting a loved one should consider the following techniques to reduce income.

- Use a Henson trust to limit income and avoid asset ownership by the individual with a disability.
- Carefully review the expenses of the person with a disability to determine if some of them are disability-related expenses and can be paid for by family.
- Carefully review the income sources of the person with a disability to determine if any of them are exempt income.
- If the person with a disability has accumulated assets over the allowable limit, seek out ways to move the assets to exempt assets. You cannot simply sell them or give them away.

ODSP Case Worker

It is crucial for families to keep in contact with the ODSP case worker. This person is their personal connection to ODSP and their lifeline for help and guidance. An open and honest relationship is necessary to establish a condition of trust. The case worker can invoke or revoke benefits.

Giving Up on Social Assistance

Social assistance of monthly cash payment amounts and medical benefits, drug plans and dental care are necessary for many people with disabilities. But accepting social assistance usually requires that the income of the person with a disability not exceed the monthly benefits, or the benefit will be lost.

A family supporting a loved one with a disability may want to provide a higher quality of life, but if they do, the individual may risk losing ODSP monthly income and possibly benefits. That's a difficult decision to make.

The length of time for which social assistance benefits may be lost is a factor for families in deciding whether or not to provide additional support. If a parent is, for example, 85 years old, and their child with a disability is, for example, 55 years old, social assistance may only last for another ten years. So, keeping up social assistance compared with increased family support is a difficult decision. There are many factors in planning when it comes to accepting or rejecting social assistance. It's important to spend some time thinking about the consequences of your decisions and the effect on the lifestyle of a loved one.

PART 3 – ADDING A HENSON TRUST

What is a Henson Trust?

The most well-known trust involving disabilities is the absolute discretionary trust, often called the Henson trust. The Henson trust is used as part of financial planning for a person with a disability. The use of trusts in planning, including the Henson trust, is discussed in chapter 5.

The will of a man named Leonard Henson of Guelph, Ontario made landmark history in changing Ontario law (followed by other provinces). The new law allowed assets to exist in a trust for individuals with disabilities without violating social support conditions. The Henson trust is so often talked about but its planning possibilities beyond maximizing social assistance are seldom utilized.

The history is as follows. Leonard Henson wanted to provide a fund to assist his daughter, Audrey, so he set up a trust for her in his will. The terms of the trust gave the trustees complete discretion on the amount and timing of any payments to Audrey. Audrey could not demand payments from the trust because she was a discretionary beneficiary. That seemed to assure Leonard that his daughter would not be disqualified from ODSP because trust assets did not belong to her and trustees controlled the income flow to meet her needs. Despite these restrictions, the Ontario government said that the assets of the trust were assets available to Audrey and disqualified her from ODSP. To make a long story short, Ontario lost its case and the Henson trust was born. The clause used by Leonard Henson in his will is included below.

> **NOTE   Leonard Henson Will – Trust Clause**
>
> *To pay so much of the income therefrom, or the whole of the income therefrom, together with so much of the capital thereof to or for the benefit of my daughter AUDREY JOAN HENSON as my Trustees shall in the exercise of their absolute and unfettered discretion consider advisable from time to time. Any income not so paid in any year shall be accumulated by my Trustees and added to the capital of the residue of my estate, provided, however, that if it becomes unlawful for my Trustees to continue such accumulation of income, then the income not so paid in any year to or for the benefit of my said daughter shall be paid to the Guelph and District Association for the Mentally Retarded Incorporated.*
>
> *The residue of my estate and the income therefrom shall not vest in my said daughter and the only interest she shall have therein shall be the payments actually made to her, or on her behalf, and received by her or for her benefit therefrom. Without in any way binding the discretion of my Trustees, it is my wish that in exercising the discretion in accordance with the provisions of this paragraph, my Trustees take account of and in so far as they may consider it advisable take such steps as will maximize the benefits which my said daughter would receive from other sources if payments from the income and capital of the residue of my estate were not paid to her for her own benefit, or if such payments were limited to an amount or time. In order to maximize such benefits, I specifically authorize my Trustees to make payments varying in amounts and at such time, or times, as my Trustees in the exercise of their absolute discretion may consider in the best interests of my said daughter.*

Leonard Henson's will established a number of important rules for the trust in successfully holding assets for a beneficiary that the person could neither own or control with the following provisions. For instance, Henson's will:

- restricted income payments to or for the benefit of Audrey at the discretion of the trustee;
- allowed the trustees to pay income to an alternative beneficiary—a charity;
- assured that Audrey had no direct interest in trust assets and that they were not available to her;
- allowed the trustee to consider restrictions to Audrey's income to maximize social assistance benefits that she would not otherwise receive; and
- authorized the trustee to make payments on behalf of Audrey in amounts and at such time as the trustees considered to be in her best interest.

It is important to note that the payments were not to be made directly to Audrey, but were instead made for her benefit. This is an important part of Henson trust wording because, in many cases, the beneficiary is not legally competent and therefore cannot deal with payments received. Personal guardianship may be an option.

Henson trusts are sometimes referred to as absolute discretionary trusts. In other words, the trustees have absolute discretion in regard to the management of trust funds and payments to beneficiaries. On the death of the beneficiary with a disability, the assets remaining in the trust are usually disbursed to family members or sometimes to a charity.

Henson trusts should be prepared by lawyers who specialize in this area, or at least have experience in the complexities of trust law and disability planning. The Henson trust also needs to fit into the financial and tax planning objectives of the individual and his or her family.

Henson trusts are permitted in British Columbia, Manitoba, Saskatchewan, Ontario, New Brunswick, Nova Scotia, PEI and, with some limitations, in Newfoundland and Labrador and Quebec. Alberta is the only province with no enabling legislation.

Trusts are extremely helpful vehicles in planning for individuals with disabilities, especially the absolute discretionary trust (Henson trust) and the inheritance trust allowed by social assistance rules in some provinces. Other trusts are important and are discussed in this book in chapter 5. Although the focus is often on the relationship between trusts and social assistance, there is an equally important interplay between trusts and income tax rules that apply to them.

There are many reasons why individuals should be leaving assets in trust for a child with disabilities Maximizing social assistance is only one of them - a Henson trust can incorporate many other advantages, as discussed in chapter 5. The use of a Henson trust to only preserve social assistance is important but sometimes overemphasized.

Trust Distributions Affect Social Assistance

It has sometimes been suggested that payments made by a Henson trust to third parties for an individual with disabilities do not count as income that reduces ODSP support. That is incorrect. Section 37(1) of the ODSP regulations provides that income is calculated by adding together the total amount of all payments of any nature paid to or on behalf of or for the benefit of the individual with a disability. One exception to this rule is pre-approved payments by a trust, related items, or services which are exempt as income that would otherwise reduce ODSP support.

ODSP reporting requirements for Henson trusts are found in Policy Directive 4.7. Essentially, a trustee has a duty to report trust finances to the beneficiary, who in turn must report to ODSP. The policy directive points out that the government's demand for such information is based on section 5 of the ODSP Act. The section states that a person is not eligible for ODSP unless they provide information and the verification of information required to determine their eligibility.

Henson Trusts – Now or Later

Consider an example in which social assistance ends at age 65 because of government pension income and a testamentary Henson trust is in the will of the parents. The duration of a Henson trust will, in large part, depend on the age difference between the parent and the child with disabilities. For example, if a child is born when the parent is age 25, and the parent passes away at age 80, the child would be 55 years old at that time. Therefore, the Henson trust would only have ten years to maximize social assistance. That is a relatively short period of time. It's possible that other, less complicated ways can be found to maximize social assistance, or the Henson trust can incorporate other important tax and estate planning ideas. In order to make it worthwhile, it is important to remember that almost all trusts pay tax at top tax rates, except qualified disability trusts arising on death. A preferred beneficiary election could help with this.

There are advantages to setting up a Henson trust during a parent's lifetime rather than waiting until a parent dies, particularly if the trust serves other purposes beyond income support. Such uses might include the owning of a residence for the loved one with a disability, income splitting with family members, or paying income of the trust directly to the person with a disability in a low tax bracket.

Trusts – Complying With Ontario Law

The Accumulations Act in Ontario is another hurdle to overcome. This legislation provides that after 21 years, trust income cannot be added to the capital and must be paid out. Normally this is not a problem because the trust will usually provide that annual income and can be divided among more than one of the beneficiaries and distributed as the trustees determine. Since the ODSP benefit recipient does not have any enforceable right to income or capital of the trust, the Henson trust would allow that part or all of the income be paid to another beneficiary satisfying the Accumulations Act.

Choosing a Trustee

The trustees of a Henson trust, or any trust for that matter, are taking on significant responsibility for the individual with a disability and they should be prepared to take this on. Some of the responsibilities involved for both trustees and members of the family are:

- involvement in the life of the individual on an ongoing basis;
- a sensitivity to the financial requirements of the individual;
- a good understanding of the terms of the trust and expectations of the settlor;
- a good understanding of provincial social assistance laws;
- competent legal and financial advisors.

Finding someone in the family to take on the financial caregiver role and to take responsibility for the financial affairs of an individual with a disability is a big concern of aging parents. A corporate trustee may be a possible solution if the size of the trust relative to fees charged makes it possible.

Talk to Your Family

Henson trusts are designed to limit ownership of assets by individuals with disabilities and restrict their income so they can get social assistance. Parents of a child with a disability need to explain the implications of a Henson trust to other members of the family. Consider the case where Uncle Bill wants to leave something in his will to his niece, Kimberly. Kimberly's mom and dad have previously set up a Henson trust to maximize ODSP but if Uncle Bill gives Kimberly a bequest, he will most surely undo everything. Ask Uncle Bill to make his bequest to a Henson trust established in his will and mom and dad will alter their planning accordingly.

Henson trusts fill a special niche with respect to maximizing ODSP benefits. In addition, trusts in general are excellent vehicles, perhaps the only vehicle, for those who cannot or should not own property or cannot have a will. The trust becomes a holding tank for distributing funds to individuals with disabilities—even if the individual does not receive social assistance.

Summing Up

Complying with the rules for provincial income assistance is difficult. Low income families with limited resources have the most need for income and are at a significant disadvantage in their attempt to navigate the system entirely on their own. They often don't have lawyers and financial advisors at their disposal.

For many, the receipt of social assistance is important not only for the monthly income but also for the added benefits that the assistance provides. However, there is lots of work to be done to make the rules easier to navigate and the outcomes fairer based on the particular circumstances.

Figure 3.10 Ontario Disability Support Program - Act, Regulations and Policy Statements

Act

	Section
Part I – Eligibility for and Payments of Support	2-18
Part II – Effective Date of Income Support Decisions and Internal Review and Appeals of the Decision	19-31
Part III – Employment Supports	32-36
Part IV – Administration of the Act	37-48
Part V – General	49-59

Regulations

	Section
Part I –Eligibility for Income Support	3-13
Part II – Application for Income Support	14-21
Part III – Refusal, Cancellation or Reduction of Income Support	22-26
Part IV – Assets	27-28
Part V – Calculation of Payment of Income Support	29-43.1
Part VI – Benefits	44-45.3
Part VII – General	46-55
Part VIII – Reviews and Appeals	56-71
Part IX – Transition	72-73

Policy Directives

	Policies
1. Applying for Income Support	1.1-1.4
2. Eligibility Requirements – Who is Eligible	2.1-2.7
3. Documentation Requirements	3.1-3.2
4. Assets	4.1-4.9
5. Income	5.1-5.7
6. Calculation of Income Support	6.1-6.5
7. Extension of Income Support	7.1-7.2

Figure 3.11 Ontario Disability Support Program – Important Definitions (Not a complete list)

Disability-related Items

Assistive devices

Health care and safety items, such as prosthetics or life-alert systems

Disability-related support services, such as attendant care, sign-language interpreting or specialized equipment

Renovations or alterations to a home to improve accessibility or to maintain health and safety standards

Education and training costs related to a disability

Income

CPP/OAS/EI

Guaranteed Income Supplement (GIS)

Guaranteed Annual Income Supplement (GAINS)

WSIB benefits

Earnings from job, training program (50%)

Profit from a farm or business, including self-employment

Loans

Child or spousal support

Exempt Income

Family gifts – to a maximum of $10,000 annually

Trust fund income – to purchase (approved) disability-related items and services

Compensation awards (maximum $100,000) – for pain and suffering. Amount can be used for any purpose. Awards over $100,000 must be used for care expenses arising from the injury

Loans – to purchase disability-related items and services approved in advance by the Director

Liquid Assets

Cash

Money in bank accounts

Stocks and bonds

RRSP

Vehicles (other than primary)

Property (other than principal residence)

Trust fund

Exempt Assets

Home and shared residence

Car

Insurance – Life, Segregated funds, Annuities

Budgetary Requirements

The total value of assistance provided by ODSP

CHAPTER 4

Family - Support and Communication

Individuals with disabilities require both financial and emotional support. Some families have significant financial resources, while others do not. In either case, it is important that finances be structured to make a complete financial plan so well-intentioned actions by some members of a family do not negate participation by others.

Disability can cause family stress, often resulting in hard feelings and conflict. However, provincial laws may require the family of a person with a disability to apply a level of fairness in dividing finances amongst members which can allow individuals with a disability to challenge the support or asset distributions they are receiving in certain situation.

Grandparents and others may want to help out financially by adding something now or later in their wills. They may need guidance so they know how best to contribute through an RDSP or a Henson trust, for instance. Tax laws can allow the tax-free transfers by family members from their RRSPs, RRIFs and RESPs to RDSPs and other plans for the individual with a disability. Failing to understand the process can produce income or assets that will result in the loss of government assistance that would otherwise be available.

It's best to be transparent in developing integrated family support plans. The Financial and Life Plan Questionnaire on my website, www.thefamilyguide.ca, provides a helpful checklist for doing this. It can help establish an understanding of where things are now so you can move forward with a plan for the future.

PART 1 – FINANCIAL SUPPORT

Ways for the Family to Offer Financial Help

Until recently, the Henson trust and family gifts stood almost alone as the major income vehicles for a family in supporting an individual with a disability. Now, family support is available through other funding sources as well, as illustrated in Figure 4.1.

Figure 4.1   Family Support for Individuals with a Disability

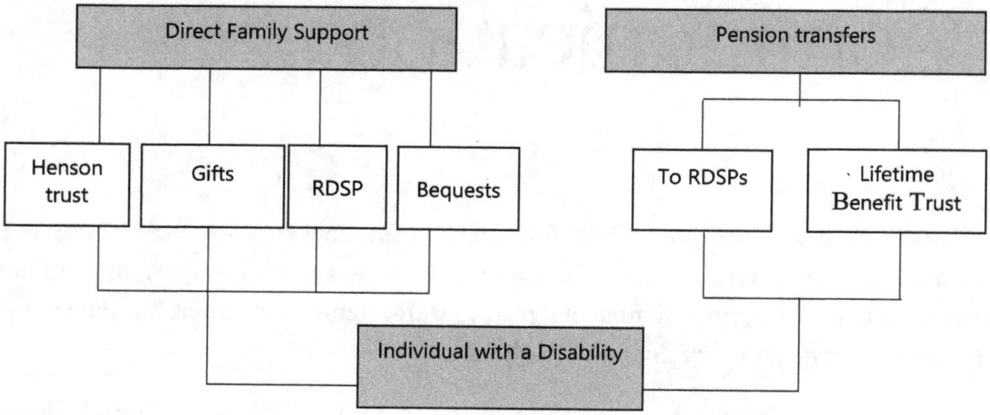

When individuals with disabilities are minors, their financial well-being is the responsibility of their parents. When children reach the age of majority, a family's financial responsibility usually decreases or may even stop. In the case of individuals with a disability, family support usually continues and may even increase. As the chart in Figure 4.1 above indicates, support can come directly from family or from pension transfers. For families with high disposable income, social assistance may not be necessary; but for many, it is mandatory.

In the end, a family will need to decide whether or not financial support is sufficient or whether they will forgo social assistance and provide more funds giving their loved one a higher standard of living.

Some individuals with disabilities are capable of providing for themselves. An individual with physical disabilities, for example, may be able to earn a living and family support may not be needed. These individuals are still entitled to most benefits directed towards individuals with disabilities.

Financial Support

Financial support is dependent on available financial resources. But a complex disability may mean that assisted living accommodation may be necessary, which is largely funded by government, so there may be less need for family financial assistance. Financial support can be maximized with knowledge, smart planning and the right structures.

When disability does not exist, financial assistance does not end at life's end. If an individual with a disability is part of the family, financial planning has to reach much further into the future. For instance, if you were 25 years old when your child was born and you live until the age of 85, your child will be 60 when you die. If your child is financially independent, you will only need to plan finances for your lifetime. But if your child is not capable of providing personal finances at the age of 60, you will need to add another 25 years onto your financial planning cycle.

Accommodation Support

At the end of the day, the level of financial help and personal care that family, government and the non-profit sector provide will be significantly influenced by personal choice and by an individual's level of disability. Figure 4.2 shows the relationship between family and government support based on the levels of accommodation.

Figure 4.2   Living Arrangements and Family Support

	Family Accommodation	Independent Living	Assisted Living
Accommodation Support:			
Family	Moderate	Significant	Minimal
Government and Not-for-Profit	Minimal	Minimal	Significant
Care Support:			
Family	Significant	Moderate	Minimal
Government and Not-for-Profit	Minimal	Moderate	Significant

Family accommodation allows an individual to live on his or her own but with a high degree of assistance from family and less from government and not-for-profit. It might mean an individual lives in a granny flat or an apartment in their parents' home.

As the complexity of disability increases, care shifts from family accommodation to assisted living. More government funds and more care support are required, but the cost to family significantly decreases.

If the individual has a less complex disability, then independent accommodation may be possible; this comes at a very high cost to families and a low cost to government and not-for profits. Disability is on a continuum and independent living is more likely to be an option for an individual with a physical disability than it is for someone with a cognitive disability.

Some families are able to pay the costs involved with independent living. And sometimes there is financial support to foster independent living and community involvement, so the playing field is getting better.

Care Support

If the complexity of disability is high, there is usually a greater need for special care, perhaps with assisted living. Family can be involved as they wish depending on their age, their other demands in life and their ability to provide financial assistance.

When a disability is severe, government and non-profit organizations usually have a bigger role to play and the individual with a disability and their families have a smaller (nevertheless important) role. This changes over time depending on the health and age of the person with a disability, and on the kinds of accommodations available where they live.

Employment of Individuals With Disabilities

A 2013 report by Employment and Social Development Canada outlines the following statistics.

- Canada's labour force has 2.4 million individuals with disabilities
- Only one million of these people with disabilities are employed
- 53% of Canadians either have a disability or are related to a close family member with a disability
- There are 1.3 billion people worldwide with disabilities

Participation in the workplace of individuals with disabilities is improving. This trend is noticeable in the retail sector and is becoming more apparent in the technology and manufacturing sectors. That is certainly positive, but hopefully there are still greater improvements ahead.

Inheritances - Equal Treatment by Family

Parents can face a dilemma as to whether to treat their children equally in their inheritances or to make an uneven distribution. In some situations, equal treatment may be appropriate, but in other cases, perhaps not.

A child with a disability may need more than an equal share of the family financial resources if their needs are high. This is a difficult area to deal with and one that everyone in the family needs to have some input into or it can create family friction. Henson trusts, RDSPs and other planning tools can provide financial benefits that will help mitigate the problem.

Reach Out for Help and Advice

Planning for the financial needs of a loved one with a disability can be a difficult job. Disability is complex and costs are often hard to determine. It is therefore important to reach out to family, community, social service agencies and advisors for financial advice.

Furthermore, it is important that everyone works together going forward. If not, there can be overlap and loss of government benefits if family funding exceeds permitted levels. Also, there may be family members such as aunts, uncles and grandparents who intend to contribute financially and through their wills.

Money Management

Individuals with disabilities may have money available to them through RDSPs, trusts or other savings vehicles—and these funds will increase as time passes. It is imperative to prevent significant losses of capital through conservative investing, as discussed in chapter 1.

Funds accumulated for a family member with a disability can become substantial and can usually be found in the following places.

- RDSPs
- A Henson trust
- A Lifetime Benefit trust
- Other trusts

There may come a time when you should consider whether you should be managing these funds yourself or whether you should be employing a professional money manager. Chapter 11 discusses this in some detail.

Balancing Things Out With a Life Plan

It's one thing to deal with the financial issues of disability, and yet another to deal with the life issues. As previously mentioned, life issue decisions will drive financial planning. But so often people push ahead and contribute to an RDSP or set up a Henson trust before determining their needs based on the life plan of the individual.

A life plan looks at questions such as: Where will our loved one with a disability live? What level of recreational activities can and do we wish them to be involved in? Do we plan to purchase a house or will they live in a specialized residential setting? You need to cover every aspect of how you see their life unfolding. Only then can you determine what it will cost and where the money will come from. Part 4 of chapter 1 deals with these questions and issues.

PART 2 – LEGAL STRUCTURES

Property Ownership and Control

It's important for families to understand the legal considerations if a loved one is developmentally challenged and not competent to make good legal decisions. Such individuals are not able to own property or enter into binding agreements.

If an individual does not have the legal capacity to own property, then when property comes into their hands it will come under the control of the Public Trustee. When this happens, a more complicated and limiting structure will result. This could happen, for example, if a person with an intellectual disability receives gifts or bequests or is entitled to pension plans. Most of this can be avoided with advanced planning. For example, if your loved one will someday become the recipient of income from an RDSP, those proceeds will probably come under the control of a legal decision maker such as the public trustee.

In carrying out planning, families will usually prevent assets from coming under the control of the Public Trustee by establishing trusts. In these cases, siblings of the person with a disability or other members of the family usually become trustees of the trust. This also allows these assets to be paid out by the trust to family members or a charity when they are no longer needed by the person with a disability.

Should property find its way to the Public Trustee, someone in the family may wish to apply to the courts to obtain personal guardianship of the individual's assets in order to take on financial decision-making.

There are several possibilities for the ownership and control of property—Public Trustee, personal guardian and the use of a combination of trusts and financial products. If the disability is a physical one, then guardianship is not an issue, but if it is a cognitive one, then control could come under a Public Trustee or personal guardian unless planning is done by the use of trusts to avoid this. If the cognitive issue is an adaptive disability and not an intellectual one, then it is more likely that the Public Trustee will not be involved. These possibilities are shown in Figure 4.3.

Figure 4.3   Property Ownership/Contract Ability and Disability

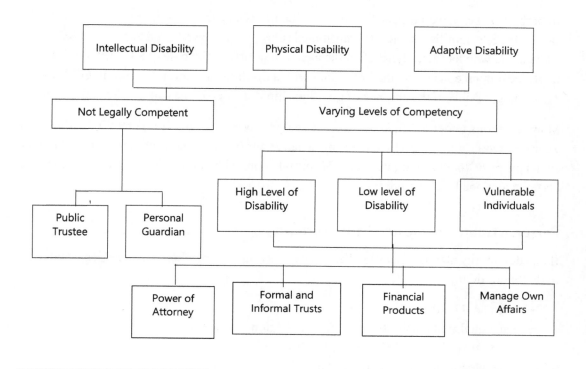

Guardianship can be held by the Public Trustee or personal guardianship can be applied for. Ownership of assets by a trust probably provide more input into personal decision-making.

Families are likely to understand the needs of a loved one with a disability better than a Public Trustee. Nevertheless, a Public Trustee does have its place in certain situations to protect the finances of an individual with an intellectual disability. A personal trustee has even more discretion in making appropriate choices to meet the needs of a person with a disability.

Generally speaking, if a family has the required skills to manage property and finances through trusts and a good choice of financial products, this is a better route than letting substantial assets fall into the hands of the Public Trustee. However, if this does happen, an application for personal guardianship may be a route that takes you at least part of the way to improved financial control.

Personal Guardianship and Taxation

Two recent tax structures have increased the likelihood that guardianship will be playing a larger role in the lives of families involved with disability. They relate to the following financial structures.

- Registered Disability Savings Plan

- Qualified Disability Trusts

In both of these, personal guardianship may be necessary to allow the plans to exist. In the case of RDSPs, families (subject to transitional rules) will not be allowed to set up an RDSP for a loved one who has already reached the age of majority. In the case of a Qualifed Disability trust, the annual consent by the individual with a disability is required to retain QDT status. This is not possible in the absence of guardianship if the person has an intellectual disability.

Many elections under the Income Tax Act can only be made by a competent individual or a guardian who signs the particular form. Because our tax laws have an increasingly broader social purpose, there is a greater need for formal approval by all parties for authority to make certain elections legally binding.

Personal Guardianship and Legal Authority

If an adult family member lacks intellectual capacity, family members will need legal authority to do the following.

- Open an RDSP
- Make qualified disability trust annual election
- Open other plans (RRSP, TFSA, RESP)
- Make elections under the Income Tax Act
- Sign leases
- Direct the use of funds coming from RDSPS, inheritances, gifts, annuities and other income sources

A personal guardian must keep records and account for the use of funds. The personal guardian must also follow a management plan that has been approved by the courts.

Financial Caregivers

Financial caregivers are those who, in one way or another, have financially supported a person with a disability. They may have done so through gifts or bequests. Those who take a deep interest in the financial issues of a person with a disability also fulfill this function by starting a coherent financial plan through the use of trusts, registered plans and other vehicles.

Summing Up

Family support comes from the heart. Yet sometimes difficult family relationships or inadequate communication can stand in the way of good outcomes. Ongoing family conversations are the key. And yet, a loved one with a disability can be a uniting force for family togetherness. It is up to us.

CHAPTER 5

Trusts – Fundamental to Planning for Disability

Trust law, developed centuries ago, has since evolved into the modern-day trust—an arrangement whereby someone (the settlor) transfers property to someone else (the trustee) for the benefit of a third party (the beneficiary). Today, a trust is an excellent estate and financial planning tool allowing a parent to have assets managed through a trust by someone in the family or maybe even a corporate trustee for a loved one with a disability. In many respects, tax rules for trusts accommodate interim property ownership. This chapter does not deal with graduated rate estates.

While trusts can be effective in managing the legal and financial affairs of a person with a disability, in some ways, recent tax changes have made their use more complicated with some added, but restricted benefits. Since an individual lacking intellectual capacity cannot usually own property or enter into legal agreements, trusts continue to be an ideal vehicle for accomplishing otherwise impossible objectives. A trust is an effective tool in resolving financial, legal, tax and income assistance issues.

This chapter discusses six types of trusts designed to solve disability-related financial problems and related compliance issues. Other chapters, particularly chapter 8 on estate planning, deal with the use and limitations of trusts in financial and tax planning for disability. Because of the complexity of tax, legal and social assistance rules and their interplay, you should be relying on professional advisors skilled in these areas and preferably with some background in disability. The material in this chapter is quite technical in nature, but understanding the concepts is important.

PART 1 – THE LEGALITIES OF TRUSTS

Use of Trusts in Disability

Trusts have several purposes when it comes to disability, as shown in Figure 5.1.

Figure 5.1   The Purpose of Trusts Relating to Disability

Trusts

- To retain social assistance benefits (Henson trusts)
- To manage ownership of property for a person who is not legally able to do so
- To make distributions to a beneficiary for day to day living costs
- To accommodate favourable tax treatment including the transfer trust assets to others when the trust is no longer needed
- To hold a residence for a person with a disability in a trust
- To receive RRSP and RRIF plan proceeds on the death of a parent or grandparent (Lifetime Benefit trust)
- To hold inherited assets as exempt assets under provincial social assistance rules (inheritance trust)
- To receive life insurance proceeds on death (Life insurance trust)
- To have access to graduated tax rates (Qualified Disability trust)

There is a serious lack of knowledge about trusts by families involved with disability. In the end, trusts are flexible vehicles for holding property that will be managed by trustees under rules in the trust document as dictated by the person who established the trust (settlor). Beneficiaries enjoy the assets of the trust through distributions they receive from the trust. Trusts are effective vehicles for managing the distribution of your wealth according to your rules when you are unable or no longer wish to do so or after you die.

In disability planning, trusts are usually discretionary—this means that trustees have full power to decide, if, when and how much will be distributed to a beneficiary. The beneficiaries have no absolute rights to distributions nor are any trust assets set aside for them. Once the trust has fulfilled its mandate to supplement the income of a beneficiary with a disability, the trust is usually terminated and any remaining trust assets are distributed to surviving family members or sometimes to a charity.

It is sometimes thought that a Henson is unique to disability, but this is not the case. A Henson trust is simply a discretionary trust with the core purpose of preserving social assistance for a beneficiary. Although a Henson trust is primarily used to fulfill that mandate, it can be used for many other purposes such as owning a home, avoiding the Public Trustee or getting better tax treatment.

What Is A Trust?

The law does not recognize a trust as a legal entity even though it has legal standing under our laws. There must be intention by the settlor to establish a trust, identifiable property that will be held in the trust and beneficiaries who will receive property from the trust. And finally, a settlor must settle property on the trustees giving them the legal authority to carry out the terms of the trust. The end result is a separation of the legal ownership of the trust property held by the trustees from the beneficial ownership held by the beneficiaries. Figure 5.2 shows the trust structure and its financial relationships.

Figure 5.2   Trust Property and Distributions

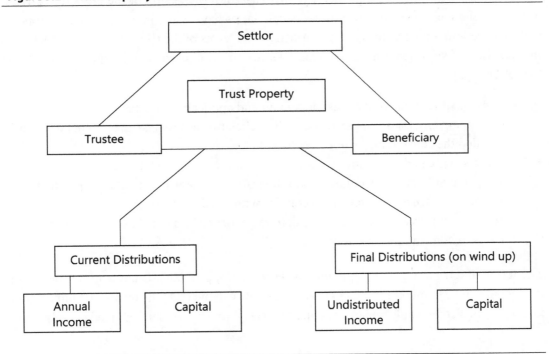

Testamentary and Inter Vivos Trusts

Trusts established during one's lifetime are known as inter vivos trusts. Trusts arising on death are known as testamentary trusts and are generally established through a will.

Until the end of 2017, inter vivos trusts were the only trusts taxed at the top rate whereas all testamentary trusts were taxed at graduated rates. Testamentary trusts are now taxed at the top marginal rate except for a few special kinds of trusts including qualified disability trusts and graduated rate estates for the first thirty-six months after death.

Inter vivos trusts should not necessarily be discarded because of their high tax rate. For example, they are still useful in distributing income on a tax deferred basis, can serve an asset holding function and can manage property. They also facilitate the tax-free transfer of trust assets to final beneficiaries when the trust is no longer needed.

Trustees

A trust is not a legal entity but does have legal standing, so it must be managed by the trustees. The trust document dictates the rules for holding, transferring and distributing property of the trust which is carried out by the trustees. Hence, any reference to a trust is really a reference to its trustees.

Trustees hold legal title to the property in the trust until ownership of the property is transferred to beneficiaries. In the meantime, beneficiaries have entitlement to the trust property at the discretion of the trustees as determined by the terms of the trust. This puts the trustees in a position of significant fiduciary responsibilty to beneficiaries and requires them to do the following.

- Obey the directions of the trust document and applicable trust law
- Act impartially for all of the classes of beneficiaries unless instructed otherwise (this is called the "even hand" rule)
- Exercise care and prudence
- Not personally profit through the administration of the trust beyond its specific terms
- Not permit a trustee's interests to conflict with those of the trust
- Be ready to provide a full accounting to the beneficiaries with respect to the trust's assets, income and distributions

The terms of a trust, together with applicable trust law, provide a framework for managing the income and capital of a trust. However, trust law can override the terms. It's important to know how this could apply and to structure the trust terms to avoid unintended consequences.

Trust Distributions

A trustee can distribute all or part of trust income each year reducing its own income as allowed by the trust document. For example, when a settlor puts $50,000 in a trust, this money is the trust capital. Supposing the trust earns a 5% return on the capital, or $2,500. After a year it would have $52,500. If the trustee wishes to distribute $2,000 to a beneficiary, the trustee could either distribute all capital, leaving $48,000 of capital, or distribute trust income from the year, leaving $500 of taxable income in the trust. This after tax income is then added to the capital of the trust.

A capital distribution is not taxable to a beneficiary but the income distributions are taxed in the beneficiary's hands but reduce the trust income to avoid double taxation. An income distribution would probably create little tax on beneficiaries with disabilities because they are usually in low tax brackets. Distributions escape social assistance clawbacks if they are kept within the allowed exemption. Trustees will also be guided as to whether to distribute income or capital based on the tax rate that applies to the beneficiary and to the trust. Professional advice may be needed to sort this out.

When a beneficiary dies, there is likely to be some property remaining in the trust. The trust document will indicate who gets this capital. These recipients are known as remainder beneficiaries. The remainder beneficiaries are usually family or a charity or both. The settlor of the trust will certainly want to think about who he or she names as the final beneficiaries because this is fundamental to property ownership continuing throughout trust planning in the first place.

Letter of Wishes

Anyone setting up a discretionary trust is empowering the trustees with significant authority. Diligent trustees will always want the trust income and property to be used for the beneficiary with a disability and for other beneficiaries as the settlor directs. And yet, how are the trustees supposed to know what to do when the intention in a particular situation is unclear within the terms of the trust?

One solution is for the settlor to write a non-legally binding letter of wishes giving the trustees guidance as to his intentions and the latitude trustees should use in coming to their decisions. A letter of wishes would do the following.

- Provide an understanding of the reasons for the trust and its broad goals and objectives
- Provide guidance of any special needs of the beneficiary that are to be satisfied
- Give direction to the trustee on whether or not to confer with others for guidance in decision-making
- Provide instructions on whether or not the letter of wishes should be kept confidential

This is a difficult document to write, but it can be extremely helpful. Anyone considering writing a letter of wishes should get help from a lawyer to ensure that it does not override trustee powers. A letter of wishes might also be used in connection with wills and financial powers of attorney to assist attorneys and executors in their decision-making.

Trusts and Taxation

The Income Tax Act outlines the tax consequences of certain financial transactions of trusts in several main areas.

- Transfer of property to the trust
- Transfer of property from the trust
- Tax rate on income earned by the trust (maximum or graduated)

- Flow through of tax characteristics of property distributions
- Other rules for the tax treatment different than trust law would dictate

In general, tax consequences of trusts also depend on whether transactions involve a spouse or partner and whether the trust arose during the lifetime of the settlor or after death.

Control of a Trust for Tax Purposes

There is a provision in the Income Tax Act (subsection 75(2)) that can have unfortunate tax implications if the disposition of property transferred to a trust can effectively be controlled by the settlor or someone of his or her choice.

The provision is more technical than described above and can deem income to be taxable to the trustee, destroying a main use of a trust. Therefore, it is important in all trusts that the settlor not be the sole or controlling trustee of a trust. If the settlor is one of several trustees, the settlor should always be outnumbered by other trustees and is usually restricted from naming a replacement trustee.

Tax Features of a Trust

Tax laws for trusts are complex and careful thought is needed for drafting their terms. Some of the rules common to discretionary trusts for avoiding adverse tax consequences are outlined in Figure 5.3.

Figure 5.3   Features for Inclusion in a Family Trust

Features of a discretionary trust, designed to avoid adverse income tax and legal consequences, are listed below. Discretionary trusts...

- Prohibit anyone other than the settlor from gifting property to the trust if that property has a fair market value greater than the fair market value of the property gifted by the settlor.

- Prohibit the settlor from subsequently changing terms of the trust, or controlling assets held by the trust.

- Prohibit trust assets from reverting to the settlor under the terms of the trust.

- Clearly describe the property received as the initial property settlement.

- Require that a majority of the trustees are residents of Canada.

- Give the trustees the power to alter the terms of the trust to better achieve the original purposes of the trust but not to change those purposes in any material way. This can provide flexibility to adapt to changing tax laws. Care must be taken to not make changes that will be considered by the tax authorities to constitute a new trust.

- Provide the trustee with the general authority to make any elections, designations, etc. under the Income Tax Act.

- Make provisions to ensure they have the power to make such distributions immediately before the expiration of the 21 years from the date the trust was created, unless the trust deed allows the trustees to make capital distributions at any time.

- Include a clause in the trust to deal with perpetuities under provincial law.

- Prohibit beneficiaries from receiving or otherwise obtaining the use of any of the income or capital of the trust until reaching the age of majority.

This is a long list of do's and don'ts to consider for tax and legal reasons.

New Trust Tax Rules in 2016

Many new tax rules for 2016 and later years can have a significant effect on the way trusts are structured for tax planning. For example, these new tax rules abolish graduated tax rates for trusts except for qualified disability trusts and for estates for their first thirty-six months (graduated rate estates).

The tax rates that apply to individuals and trusts in disability are shown in Figure 5.4.

Figure 5.4   Tax Rate Comparison

• Individuals	Graduated rates
• Qualified disability	Graduated rates
• Other trusts	Top rate
• Registered disability savings plan	Income not taxable until distributed

If you are using a trust and avoiding the high tax rate is an issue, one of the following options may be helpful.

- Use a QDT
- Distribute trust income to beneficiaries, preferably in a low tax bracket
- Make the preferred beneficiary election for trust income taxed at the beneficiary's tax rate
- Select trust investments that have income taxed at lower rates
- Select investments that distribute little or no income

Few good options are available to reduce tax on a trust for individuals who can't qualify for the disability tax credit with resulting QDT tax treatment. Income on all trusts for them will be taxed at the top rate. While this is unfortunate, trusts still have valuable purposes such as holding assets for a person with a disability or avoiding the cost and complexity of guardianship. The use of trusts in disability planning has been hurt by these new high tax rates, but trusts are still important for other planning reasons. The high tax rate problem could possibly be solved by use of the preferred beneficiary election discussed in part 8 of this chapter.

Trusts and Property Ownership

In most cases, it is not wise or even lawful to transfer the ownership of property to intellectually challenged or vulnerable individuals. They will usually have trouble managing or owning property due to their vulnerability or they may not be legally competent to do so. Instead, property may be put in a trust and distributions from the trust can be managed and controlled through the trustees. When the trust is no longer needed, trustees will distribute the remaining property under the terms of the trust.

Trusts and Disability

There are six kinds of trusts used in disability, as shown in Figure 5.5. The Henson trust can be put in place during the lifetime of the settlor or upon death. Other trusts that can come into existence at either time are principal residence trusts, insurance trusts and, more commonly, testamentary trusts. All other trusts described in Figure 5.5 are testamentary trusts arising upon death.

Figure 5.5   Trusts for Persons with Disabilities

TRUST	PURPOSE
• Henson Trust	Primarily to maximize social assistance
• Principal Residence Trust	To hold a home
• Inheritance Trust	To hold inherited assets so they will be exempt assets under some provincial social assistance rules
• Lifetime Benefit Trust (LBT)	To receive RRSP/RRIF proceeds from a supporting individual as a tax-free rollover for the benefit of an impaired child or grandchild
• Life Insurance Trust	To hold an insurance policy or more often to receive the proceeds of insurance on death
• Qualified Disability Trust (QDT)	A testamentary trust for a family member with a disability

The use of trusts in financial planning for an individual with a disability is complex and far reaching but particularly important in planning for intellectual disability. Families will need assistance from an experienced professional with an understanding of disability and the use of trusts if they are considering using any of them. Each of these trusts is discussed in more detail in part 2 of this chapter.

Corporate Trustees

Family members may be ideal candidates to act as trustees because they know the beneficiary better than anyone. However, situations often arise where there are no other family members or none of the family members have the necessary financial and legal background to act as trustees. A corporate trustee, in addition to personal trustees, might help balance out personal and business skills among the trustees.

If a trust arises from a parent's will, there may be no one to act as a trustee. Perhaps siblings of the child with a disability have moved away or perhaps they don't want the responsibility either because they don't have the necessary skills or time to as act as trustees. At that point, it would seem necessary to provide a corporate trustee.

Before deciding on a corporate trustee, you should interview one or two of them to become more familiar with what they bring to the table. They may be able to add input into the creation of the trust documents in consultation with your lawyer. Fees of corporate trustees should be reviewed to see if they are affordable – especially for smaller trusts.

Rules Against Accumulations and Perpetuities

The opening paragraph of this chapter refers to the evolution of trust law from centuries ago to present day. Two rules that can still apply today from the 1600s are the rule against accumulations and the rule against perpetuities. Some provinces have either modified or abolished the rules, so you should find out the status of the rules in the province in which you live. A brief description of the rules follows.

The rule against accumulations prohibits the accumulation of income in a trust beyond a specified period of time, usually twenty-one years. At that time, the annual income of a trust must be distributed each year by the trust. In disability, the distribution of income may create problems such as loss of social assistance or the need for guardianship of a beneficiary who is not legally competent to own significant property distributed by the trust.

The rule against perpetuities provides that property of a trust must vest within a certain period of time—this is usually expressed as being within the lifetimes of the beneficiaries plus twenty-one years. Some provinces and territories have amended this rule, and some have abandoned it. The rule against perpetuities should not be confused with the twenty-one-year disposition rule under the Income Tax Act.

Individuals should review the possible impact of these rules in their province if they have set up a trust for a family member with a disability that may last several years.

PART 2 – HENSON TRUSTS

A Henson trust is a discretionary trust similar to any discretionary trust, but its primary function is to maximize social assistance. The trustees have full discretion to control the trust assets and their distribution to beneficiaries. Henson trusts, or absolute discretionary trusts as they are sometimes called, are recognized in all provinces except Alberta. Beyond that, Henson trusts can combine their main purpose with other uses.

- To supplement the income of a person with disabilities based on the settlor's wishes
- To hold property for a person with disabilities who cannot or should not own property
- To prevent ownership of assets from falling under the control of the Public Trustee
- To facilitate the transfer of property to final beneficiaries
- To minimize income tax if the trust is a QDT

Henson trusts help families arrange their financial affairs over the long term, despite the difficulties brought about by disability. The trustees become a kind of property manager when personal ownership is not a good choice or even a possibility.

However, if a Henson trust is only used to assure social assistance, the need for such a trust is becoming more questionable for the following reasons.

- Income from RDSPs does not reduce social assistance in most provinces. If RDSP income is planned so that is becomes a major component of the income of an individual with a disability, then income becomes less relevant. With good planning, RDSP income can start at about age 45 without the repayment of bonds and grants.

- Social assistance rules in some provinces allow higher exempt asset limits than they once did. Therefore, asset limits may not be a factor in limiting social assistance. RDSPs are becoming more popular to provide income to individuals on social assistance.

Henson trusts can also be useful to manage the personal finances of vulnerable individuals who do not qualify for social assistance but who cannot or should not own significant personal assets. If structured properly, a principal residence trust, an Inheritance trust and a Qualified Disability trust can all qualify as Henson trusts and combine their specific uses with the Henson trust use.

If you are contemplating using a Henson trust now or in your estate planning, think beyond the narrow use of the standard Henson trust and consider broader uses as well.

PART 3 – PRINCIPAL RESIDENCE TRUSTS

Although the principal residence tax benefit for trusts has been reduced, they can still be used for ownership for an individual with a disability; such planning might be considered when trust ownership is also a good idea for other reasons. The Income Tax Act restricts the use of the principal residence exemption for trusts to a spouse, common-law partner, former spouse or a child. Unfortunately, this narrow rule prevents other family members, such as grandparents, from creating principal residence trusts.

No taxable benefit is received for maintenance of the home by the beneficiary occupying the home unless the trust pays for the upkeep and maintenance of the property out of the income of the trust. Given the beneficiary's low taxable income in most cases, this may not be a problem. But if it is, this problem can be avoided by paying such expenses out of trust capital. Use of a trust to own a residence also reduces future growth of a parent's estate and should reduce their income taxes upon death.

Tax laws have changed to limit the use of the principal residence exemption in a trust. As discussed in part 7 in this chapter, one of the few trusts that allows someone to claim exemption under the principal residence rules is a qualified disability trust. This is a trust arising on death that has at least one beneficiary entitled to the disability tax credit. The beneficiary of the trust must be named in the will.

The new rules exclude the principal residence exemption if a trust beneficiary does not qualify for the DTC. For situations where a home held by a trust qualified as a principal residence under the old rules but not under the new rules, the principal residence exemption ended at the end of 2016.

Under ODSP rules, income must essentially be a cash receipt in order to reduce ODSP benefits. The advantage to a person with a disability living in a home held in a trust is that it does not reduce ODSP.

PART 4 – INHERITANCE TRUSTS PROTECT INCOME ASSISTANCE

Leaving a bequest to an individual with disabilities could increase assets beyond the maximum amount of exempt assets and cause social assistance to stop. However, in some provinces there are options for avoiding this by transferring an inheritance or the proceeds of insurance to an inheritance trust even after it is received. Alternatively, an Inheritance trust could be established in the will of a person leaving an inheritance in a trust for a loved one with a disability. By doing that, the inheritance would not be income for social assistance in the month it is received and therefore not reduce income benefits.

Some provinces allow bequests and/or insurance proceeds paid to a person with a disability to be moved to an inheritance trust after being received. In Ontario, the amount in the trust cannot exceed $100,000. However, payments received from such a trust, other than those for approved disability items and services, count as income. Therefore, careful management of the trust funds is important so that they never exceed the limit. Ontario Policy Directive 4.7 provides some helpful advice.

Ontario also allows insurance cash value of up to $100,000 as an exempt asset for a person with a disability. This cash value of the insurance is not in addition to the Inheritance Trust exemption so the sum of the two cannot exceed $100,000.

PART 5 – LIFETIME BENEFIT TRUSTS

A Lifetime Benefit trust is an excellent vehicle to transfer RRSP or RRIF balances in your will to a spouse, common-law partner, child or grandchild (beneficiary) if the individual has an intellectual impairment (the Income Tax Act uses the word infirm). In the case of a child or grandchild, the individual also must be dependent on the parent or grandparent because of the vulnerability. CRA views that a child or grandchild is dependent if their income is less than the sum of their personal exemption plus the disability tax credit, or about $20,000 in total.

The trust would be set up in the will of the taxpayer and must meet the following conditions.

- Personal trust
- No person other than the beneficiary can receive income or capital of the trust during the lifetime of the beneficiary
- The trustees are allowed to pay amounts to the beneficiary from the trust of their discretion

- In determining whether to pay an amount to a beneficiary, the trustees must consider the needs of the beneficiary including their comfort, care and maintenance

Inheritance trusts came into existence because intellectually challenged individuals are seldom able to personally own a RRSP/RRIF, so the Public Trustee would become involved.

A Lifetime Benefit trust must use the funds received to purchase an annuity - either a life annuity or a term certain annuity to age 90. The Income Tax Act attributes the annuity income to the beneficiary, but in many cases the tax payable could be negligible. In any event, the tax can be paid by the trust.

The advantages of lifetime benefit trusts are many, as follows.

- Avoids the necessity of guardianship
- Avoids significant tax on a RRSP or RRIF proceeds by a parent or grandparent
- Allows the trustees to limit payments to the beneficiary to maximize social assistance as a Henson trust
- Allows any annuity balance to be paid to other family members on the death of the lifetime beneficiary as the trust provides

In Ontario, the trust would be required to distribute all of its income each year to the beneficiary once the trust was in existence for twenty-one years because of the law against accumulations. This might mean that the beneficiary could lose social assistance benefits. In practice, this may not be a problem because after the twenty-one years, many beneficiaries would no longer be collecting social assistance.

The Lifetime Benefit trust rules are complex and can discourage families or even their advisors from using them. That is unfortunate because the benefits given up can be substantial and definitely should be worked into planning more often than they are. Figure 5.6 below may be helpful in understanding the Lifetime Benefit trust.

Figure 5.6   Lifetime Benefit Trusts

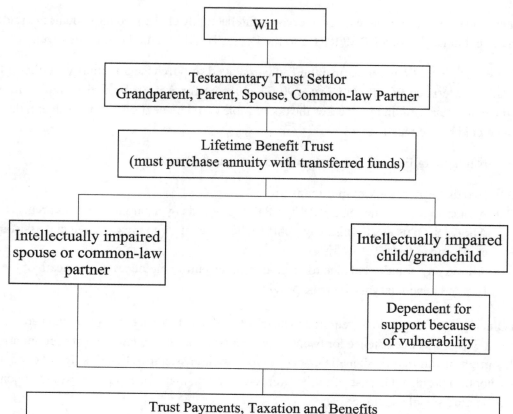

Will

Testamentary Trust Settlor
Grandparent, Parent, Spouse, Common-law Partner

Lifetime Benefit Trust
(must purchase annuity with transferred funds)

Intellectually impaired spouse or common-law partner

Intellectually impaired child/grandchild

Dependent for support because of vulnerability

Trust Payments, Taxation and Benefits

- Payments to beneficiary by trustee must consider needs including comfort, care and maintenance
- Payments only to beneficiary during his/her life
- Annuity income is attributed to beneficiary for tax purposes
- Annuity is owned by the trust – annuity can be life annuity or annuity to age 90
- Annuity can have a guarantee period which may provide a lump sum payment on death
- Annuity income does not have to be paid out
- Trust could qualify as a Henson trust
- Must elect to have tax deferral apply
- Trust provides a way to name remainder beneficiaries not available if beneficiary is not legally competent

PART 6 – LIFE INSURANCE TRUSTS

Insurance trusts are useful in handling large sums of money received from an insurance policy. They can be set up so that a trust either owns the policy from the outset or receives insurance proceeds when the insured individual dies. The latter situation is more relevant with regard to disability. Insurance trusts for individuals with disabilities can qualify as qualified disability trusts and even fill the function of a Henson trust. This is a great way of providing long-term income for your beneficiary after your death and balancing out estate distributions to family members.

Although they can be created within a will or outside a will, it is generally advisable to create the trust outside of the will. An added bonus to insurance trusts is that they can be structured to allow for the elimination of estate administration tax (also known as probate fees) on the insurance proceeds.

Insurance trusts must be properly structured to meet the criteria of the Income Tax Act and provincial insurance laws. You will definitely need professional assistance from both an insurance specialist and a trust professional if you want to go down this path. The possibilities for your estate planning are significant, especially for high wealth individuals.

PART 7 – QUALIFIED DISABILITY TRUSTS (QDT)

QDT Defined

The federal government believed that the graduated tax rates for testamentary trusts were being used unfairly and often resulted in the creation of multiple trusts to significantly reduce income tax. Therefore, the government has abolished the graduated rates for virtually all testamentary trusts. However, they have continued the graduated rates for the first thirty-six months of an estate (graduated rate estate) and for testamentary trusts established for an individual with disabilities if the person qualifies for the disability tax credit. This new trust is called a qualified disability trust (QDT).

Here are some of the important qualifications for a QDT.

- Only testamentary trusts will qualify as a QDT
- At least one of the beneficiaries of the trust must qualify for the disability tax credit
- The trustee and the beneficiary with a disability (electing beneficiary) must jointly elect on an annual basis that the trust be a QDT
- There can only be one QDT for each person with a disability
- Existing testamentary trusts eligible for graduated tax rates will cease to be eligible for QDT status if they fail to qualify under these new rules

Unfortunately, QDTs leave out vulnerable people who do not qualify for the disability tax credit.

There have been significant changes to the tax rates for trusts recently enacted into law by the government of Canada. Starting in 2016, these new laws affect all trusts by taxing most of them at the highest tax rate on all income unless the trust fits under one of the few exceptions. Trusts not eligible for graduated rates will pay tax at the approximate top rates noted below, which will vary depending on the province.

- Interest   53%
- Dividends   40%
- Capital Gains   27%

The QDT has some complicated rules to recapture the low tax rate benefit from the use of graduated tax rates if someone other than the eligible beneficiary (EB) receives a distribution from the QDT. This book does not discuss this in detail. It is important that only the EB receive trust distributions to avoid this problem.

Existing Testamentary Trusts

Many testamentary trusts have been created for family members with disabilities since 2016. If the beneficiary does not qualify for the disability tax credit, the trust cannot be a QDT and will not qualify for graduated tax rates. Also, if guardianship does not exist for people with intellectual incapacity, thereby not allowing a valid annual election, these trusts will not qualify as QDTs and their tax rates will move to the top rate. This is unfortunate.

PART 8 – TAX PLANNING AND COMPLIANCE FOR TRUSTS

Trusts as Tax Free Conduits

As a general rule, property cannot be transferred into a trust without paying tax on the appreciation in the value of the asset. On the other hand, any unrealized gain on assets passing out of the trust to a beneficiary is not taxed in the trust except for certain trusts. Instead, the unrealized gain on distributed property is deferred and taxed to the beneficiary when they sell the asset. This makes trusts extremely valuable in cases where assets transferred into a trust have appreciated in value at the time these assets are transferred to final beneficiaries.

Preferred Beneficiary Election (PBE)

The Income Tax Act contains a provision that, under certain cases, allows the income of a trust to be taxed in the hands of beneficiaries and not the trust, even if the income is not paid to the beneficiary. The tax advantage can be significant if the beneficiary is a person with a disability and in a low tax bracket. The preferred beneficiary election is one situation where this is available if either of the following conditions apply.

- The beneficiary qualifies for the disability tax credit
- The individual is at least 18 years old and a dependent on another person because of a cognitive or physical impairment

In order for the person with a disability to be considered a dependent, his or her income cannot exceed the federal Infirm Dependent tax credit amount, currently at $6,883. The beneficiary must be the settlor of the trust or a spouse or partner, former spouse, child, or grandchild of the settlor. Other individuals including a parent, grandparent, sibling, aunt/uncle, niece/nephew, spouse or partner of the settlor if the person is a resident of Canada may also qualify. And finally, another condition of the preferred beneficiary election (PBE) is that an election to make the PBE must be made by the trustee of the trust as well as by the beneficiary.

Use of the PBE will not be possible if the person with a disability has an intellectual disability and does not have a legal decision maker. Use of the PBE should not reduce social assistance since no income is actually paid to the preferred beneficiary. To qualify for the PBE, the election must be filed within 90 days of the end of the trust's year in prescribed form. The election may designate all or any portion of the accumulated income of the trust to the preferred beneficiary. The PBE can certainly be used to minimize income tax that would otherwise be based on the trust's tax rate as would apply to an inter vivos Henson trust. Also, since only one QDT is allowed for each individual, the PBE could probably be used by other trusts not qualifying as a QDT.

21-Year Disposition

Under the Income Tax Act, most trusts are deemed to dispose of their assets every 21 years and must pay tax on any deemed gains on unrealized assets at that time. This could be a problem when a trust retains assets for the long term without periodic sale of assets to reduce annual income. This 21-year disposition is not a problem if there are no unrealized gains in the trust or trust assets are entitled to a tax or exemption such as a principal residence. Careful tax planning is important.

Winding up of a Trust

In most, but not all cases, the assets of a trust are transferred to capital beneficiaries on a tax-deferred basis (roll over) when a trust is wound up.

Should the trust document provide that an amount be given to charity, a charitable donation tax credit will be available to reduce any tax payable by the trust. Since the assets are transferred at cost and no tax applies, the charitable donation tax credit would not be used. In this case, the trustee is allowed to make an election under the Income Tax Act to deem that proceeds of the assets are realized at fair market value. Then, of course, the donation tax credit could be used.

Summing Up

Before recent changes to the tax rules for trusts, this area was complex but manageable. Now it is more complex and less manageable. Nevertheless, for families who should be using trusts to hold property for a loved one with a disability, the effort to abide by the new rules is worth the struggle. Perhaps things will never be as easy as they once were, but for those wanting to make a loved one with a disability as financially secure as possible, a trust is still a worthy objective.

The 2018 federal budget added to this complexity by requiring the reporting of the identity of all trustees, beneficiaries and settlors of a trust. Trusts would also have to file annual tax returns even if the trust had no income in the year.

On a final note, it seems incredibly unfair that an inter vivos trust for an individual with a disability is not entitled to graduated tax rates or the principal residence exemption. That certainly is not fair treatment for an individual with a cognitive disability who has no ability to own property or administer investments on their own.

CHAPTER 6

Tax Planning – Navigating the Tax System

Tax planning is critically important and yet often neglected. Getting your taxes done each year, even by a qualified tax advisor, is just not enough. And yet, that's exactly what most people do. At one time, income tax was mostly about collecting taxes to pay the country's bills. It still is—but now there is more emphasis on social policy and fairness in taxation. Consequently, more provisions recognize special situations that reduce or delay taxes and make the system more equitable—as where disability exists, for example.

Not that long ago, there were more tax deductions than tax credits. Tax deductions disproportionally benefit taxpayers in higher tax brackets. To improve fairness, there has been a shift away from tax deductions and towards non-refundable tax credits in order to give the same tax advantage to everyone, regardless of income level.

Beyond maximizing tax credits, there are other ways to reduce, delay or transfer income or tax credits to someone else in the family. These options can lower the tax burden and may even result in a tax refund that might otherwise not be possible.

The Income Tax Act describes certain tax incentives that are available to individuals who are dependent on others because of a "mental infirmity". In this chapter and particularly in chapter 5 dealing with trusts, I have chosen to use the term "cognitive impairment" as a more appropriate description. I still use the Income Tax Act term for clarity when quoting or referring directly to that document.

This chapter explores tax planning options for families with a loved one with a disability. This area is quite complicated, so you should obtain professional advice once you know the basics outlined here. For readers who want to dig deeper, references to section numbers in the Income Tax Act and line numbers on your tax return are sometimes included here. A few of the charts and diagrams are lengthy, so they have been put at the end of the chapter.

Taxation – The Big Picture

Before you try to lower your tax bill, knowledge of how tax rules are structured is important. In simple terms, here are some concepts you should understand.

- When your income moves higher, tax rates increase and you pay more tax.
- Some types of income get special treatment and are taxed at lower rates than others. For example, dividends and capital gains are taxed at lower rates than salary, pensions or interest income.
- Tax rules are designed to prevent you from moving income to someone else in your family in a lower tax bracket. However, there are some legitimate ways to do this.
- You are allowed to lower your taxes by claiming non-refundable credits, but these credits on their own will not give you a tax refund. There is some opportunity for individuals to move these credits to other family members to reduce their tax burden.
- You can often defer taxes to future years by using tax structures such as RDSPs.

Tax planning is not easy. It takes time to become knowledgeable about this. Appendix C provides a list of Canada Revenue Agency publications related to disability that should help you.

Here are some tax planning techniques to help you reduce taxes.

- Delay taxes using RDSPs, RESPs, or RRSPs
- Spread income through family loans
- Don't miss tax credits such as dependent support, medical expenses and the DTC
- Challenge the CRA and formally object if necessary – they sometimes get it wrong
- Get advice – taxation is complicated

Figure 6.1 provides a listing of the sections of the Income Tax Act by subject areas for provisions that may apply to disability.

Figure 6.1   Income Tax Act References

	Section
Lifetime Benefit Trust	60.011
Disability supports deduction	64
Trusts and their beneficiaries	104 to 108
Personal and other credits	118 to 118.1
Medical Expense credit	118.2
Mental or physical impairment (DTC)	118.3 to 118.4
Tuition credit	118.5
Registered Retirement Savings Plan (RRSP)	146
Home Buyers Plan (HBP)	146.01
Lifelong Learning Plan (LLP)	146.02
Registered Education Savings Plan (RESP)	146.1
Tax Free Savings Account (TFSA)	146.2
Registered Retirement Income Fund (RRIF)	146.3
Registered Disability Savings Plan (RDSP)	146.4

Income Tax Rates

Canadian taxpayers are taxed at graduated rates which increase as income increases. Both the federal and provincial governments apply taxes to your income. The provincial brackets and rates are different in every province and different than the federal brackets. A taxpayer's total tax is simply the sum of federal and provincial taxes applied to your income in the province in which you live.

Figure 6.2 shows actual taxes for Ontario residents payable at various levels up to an income level of $140,000.

Figure 6.2   Total Taxes Payable (Ontario resident)

Actual Income	Tax	Rate
$ 20,000	1,751	8.75%
40,000	5,761	14.40%
60,000	11,275	18.80%
80,000	17,310	21.64%
100,000	24,931	24.93%
120,000	33,613	28.00%
$140,000	46,865	31.24%

Non-Refundable Tax Credits

Tax rates vary with income levels, whereas tax credit rates are the same no matter what the income level. This is fair because the same credit rate amount applies to everyone. Provincial tax credits vary from province to province and sometimes certain credits are not available provincially even though there is a federal credit. Figure 6.3 depicts an illustration of the categories of non-refundable tax credits.

Figure 6.3   The Sources of Non-Refundable Tax Credits

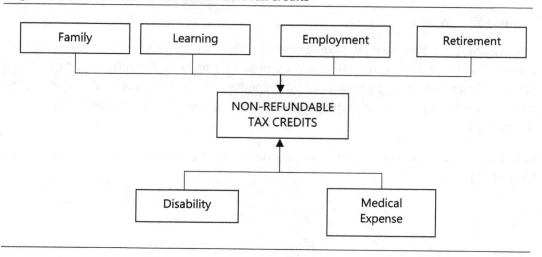

As can be seen in Figure 6.3 and, in more detail, Figure 6.11, non-refundable tax credits are divided into six different categories for better understanding.

The four categories at the top of the chart are more general tax categories, whereas the two categories at the bottom apply more specifically to disability. These disability-related tax credits are discussed in parts 2 to 7 of this chapter. Figure 6.11 at the end of this chapter provides an analysis of non-refundable tax credits.

Non-refundable tax credits that reduce taxes because of non-discretionary health-related expenses are often of limited help. These tax credits would be significantly improved from a policy sense if they were fully refundable, especially for low income taxpayers.

Vulnerable or Markedly Restricted

While some tax credits and tax benefits are available to individuals who are vulnerable, other benefits require that a person have a severe disability (markedly restricted) and qualify for the disability tax credit (DTC). Disability is a much higher standard to meet than being vulnerable, as discussed in part 2 of this chapter. A vulnerable person is not defined in the Income Tax Act but is thought to be someone who is dependent on others for the long term because of limited capabilities. Further comments can be seen below under the heading Level of Restriction.

The Value of Tax Credits

After you know a credit amount, you will then need to know the tax rate that applies to the credit amount to determine your tax savings. While the tax rate applied to the non-refundable credit amount varies from province to province, this book will use a 20% combined federal and provincial rate to be conservative (see combined tax credit rates in Figure 6.4). The tax credit for donations over $200 is higher and calculated at the highest rate of approximately 45%. Some non-refundable tax credits are a fixed *credit amount*; some have a stated maximum amount and others are based on the cost involved, with some limitations. Figure 6.11 provides more details on the value of tax credits.

Figure 6.4 shows the tax savings in each province for a credit amount of $1,000.

Claiming Non-refundable Tax Credits

The claiming of non-refundable tax credits on your personal tax return (Schedule 1) is confusing to say the least. Fortunately, tax return schedules are provided and are of some help.

- Schedule 1 – Non-refundable tax credits
- Schedule 2 – Credit transfers
- Schedule 5 – Canada Caregiver calculation
- Schedule 6 – Working income tax benefit
- Schedule 12 – Home accessibility expenses

Figure 6.4   Provincial Tax Credit Rates

	Federal	Provincial Minimum	Combined	Tax Savings
British Columbia	15%	5.06%	20.06%	$200
Alberta	15%	10.00%	25.00%	$250
Saskatchewan	15%	10.75%	25.75%	$257
Manitoba	15%	10.80%	25.80%	$258
Ontario	15%	5.05%	20.05%	$205
Quebec	15%	16.00%	31.00%	$310
New Brunswick	15%	9.68%	24.68%	$247
PEI	15%	9.80%	24.80%	$248
Nova Scotia	15%	8.79%	23.79%	$238
Newfoundland and Labrador	15%	8.70%	23.70%	$237
Northwest Territories	15%	5.90%	20.90%	$209
Nunavut	15%	4.00%	19.00%	$190
Yukon	15%	6.40%	21.40%	$214

Tax Benefits for Individuals with Disabilities

Figure 6.5 illustrates tax benefits for individuals with disabilities based on different categories, as follows.

Disability Tax Credit	Part 2
Dependent Support	Part 3
Medical Expenses	Part 4
Refundable and Deductible Amounts	Part 5
Plans and Grants	Part 6
Other Benefits	Part 7

The tax benefits available in parts 2, 3, and 4 are (with one exception) non-refundable tax credits and are of no value unless tax is payable before applying these credits or the credit can be transferred to another family member. The benefits available in parts 5, 6 and 7 come in the form of refundable credits, tax deductions, tax refunds or tax benefits from plans and grants.

Figure 6.5   Disability-Related Tax Benefits

Disability Tax Credit and Child Supplement (Part 2)	Non-refundable credit
Dependent Support (Part 3)	
Eligible Dependent	Non-refundable credit
Canada Caregiver Credit	Non-refundable credit
Enhanced RESP Benefits	Expanded benefit
Medical Expenses (Part 4)	
Medical practitioner payments	Non-refundable credit
Attendant care	Non-refundable credit
Prescriptions and medications	Non-refundable credit
Medical devices	Non-refundable credit
Home modifications	Non-refundable credit
Travel and meal expenses	Non-refundable credit
Tuition fees as medical expenses	Non-refundable credit
Refundable and Deductible Amounts (Part 5)	
Refundable medical expenses supplement	Refundable credit
Disability supports deduction	Tax deduction
Enhanced child care expense deduction	Tax deduction
Working income tax benefit supplement	Refundable credit
Plans and Grants (Part 6)	
Study grants	Cash amount
Life-long learning credit	RRSP withdrawal for education
Home buyers plan	RRSP withdrawal for home ownership
Other Benefits (Part 7)	
Canada Child Benefit	Cash amount
Child Disability Benefit	Cash amount
Preferred Beneficiary Election	Trust income allocation
RRSP/RRIF Rollover to RDSP (1)	Tax free plan transfer on death
RESP Rollover to RDSP (1)	Tax free plan transfer on death
RRSP/RRIF Rollover to RRSP (1)	Tax free plan transfer on death

PART 2 – THE DISABILITY TAX CREDIT

Disability Tax Credit

The non-refundable disability tax credit ($8,113) can be claimed by an individual with a qualifying disability, or by the supporting person of that individual, no matter the age of the child. It is not classified as a medical expense and therefore has its own rules. An additional credit called the child disability supplement ($4,733) is available for children under age 18.

There are four criteria for qualification for the DTC as follows.

- The impairment must be severe and prolonged
- The impairment must result in a marked level of restriction or require significant therapy
- The impairment must affect the ability to perform certain basic activities of daily living
- The impairment must be certified by a medical practitioner on form T2201 and be approved by the CRA

CRA interprets markedly restricted to mean at least 90% of the time. This is very uncertain criteria and unsatisfactorily measured in come cases - particularly where the disability is a cognitive one. There are further comments below under Level of Restriction.

If a person requires fourteen hours per week of life sustaining therapy essential to sustain a vital function so that otherwise they would be markedly restricted, that too qualifies him or her for the disability tax credit. Life sustaining therapy includes the following.

- Essential to sustain vital functions of the individual
- Required to be administered at least three times a week, averaging not less than 14 hours
- Not of significant benefit to others

Qualification for the disability tax credit opens the way to many other tax benefits, as shown in Figure 6.12 near the end of this chapter.

Income Tax Folio S1-F1-C2, Disability Tax Credit, is an excellent source of information on the DTC. Figure 6.6 shows the structure for DTC eligibility.

Figure 6.6   Qualifications for the Disability Tax Credit

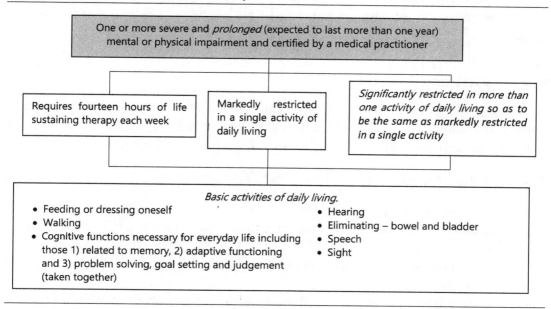

One or more severe and *prolonged* (expected to last more than one year) mental or physical impairment and certified by a medical practitioner

Requires fourteen hours of life sustaining therapy each week

Markedly restricted in a single activity of daily living

Significantly restricted in more than one activity of daily living so as to be the same as markedly restricted in a single activity

Basic activities of daily living.

- Feeding or dressing oneself
- Walking
- Cognitive functions necessary for everyday life including those 1) related to memory, 2) adaptive functioning and 3) problem solving, goal setting and judgement (taken together)
- Hearing
- Eliminating – bowel and bladder
- Speech
- Sight

Feeding excludes identifying, finding, shopping for or procuring food and normal food preparation. Dressing oneself does not include identifying, finding, shopping for or procuring clothing. A basic activity of daily living does not include working, housekeeping or a social or recreational activity. The DTC more restricted definition is very different than the one used in the Ontario Disability Support Program Act which defines a disability to be a restriction in activities of daily living to attend to personal care, function in the community or participate in the workplace. The CRA definition of disability based on an activity of daily living can be very limiting and negates the application of the DTC in some cases.

The wording used throughout the T2201 Information Guide and on the application form itself has recently improved. Each of the seven activities is accompanied with good examples and there is even a helpful self-assessment questionnaire. Form T2201 is now shorter and better laid out for medical practitioners to complete and applicants to understand.

Medical doctors and nurse practitioners are authorized to certify that an individual meets the markedly restricted test. In addition, the following specified practitioners are also allowed to complete the certification in certain areas.

- Sight – optometrist
- Speech – speech language pathologist
- Hearing – audiologist
- Feeding or dressing – occupational therapist
- Cognitive (adaptive and intellectual) functions – psychologist

Nurse practitioners were added recently to be able to provide certification in areas where a medical doctor or the specified practitioners are not usually available such as in Canada's far north.

Markedly Restricted

In order to qualify for the disability tax credit, an individual's performance of a basic activity must be markedly restricted in one area or in more than one area so that the combined result of these significant restrictions is the equivalent of being markedly restricted in one area.

If therapies are the criteria, they must meet the following three tests.

- Expected to sustain a vital function
- Required to be administered at least three times a week for a duration of averaging no less than 14 hours a week
- Could not be reasonably expected to be of significant benefit to others not so impaired

There is a great deal of public concern about the ability of individuals to meet this test, for example, for type I diabetes. And well there should be. The Income Tax Act defines the activities spent on therapies as follows.

- Time away from normal activities
- Time spent to determine dosage
- Time spent by a child's primary caregiver performing or supporting activities related to administration of the therapy

Cognitive Functions Definition and Eligibility for the DTC

The Income Tax Act provides a definition of cognitive functions necessary for everyday life for disability tax credit purposes.

Form T2201 describes the three types of cognitive functions as follows.

- *Adaptive Functioning* (abilities related to self-care, health and safety, initiating and responding to social interaction, and common, simple transactions)
- *Memory* (the ability to remember simple instructions, basic personal information such as name and address, or material of importance and interest)
- *Problem-solving*, goal-setting, and judgement, taken together (the ability to solve problems, set and keep goals, and make appropriate decisions and judgements)

The description of adaptive functioning shown on form T2201 is a source of significant controversy between the CRA and taxpayers. The Community Living Centre – British Columbia defines adaptive functioning as *how well a person handles common demands in life and how independent they are compared to others of a similar age and background.* Their material assesses adaptive functioning in three areas.

- Practical skills
- How you manage your home and personal care
- How you manage money
- How you use the telephone
- How you get from place to place
- How you stay safe and healthy
- How you follow schedules and routines
- How you work
- Social skills
- How you behave, talk to and understand others
- How you feel about yourself
- How you solve problems
- Whether you make your own mind up about things or whether other people influence you
- How you follow rules, obey the law and whether you are easily taken advantage of
- Conceptual skills
- Are you able to plan and organize?
- Can you use abstract concepts like time, money and numbers?

It is not at all clear how the CRA administers this adaptive functioning criteria. If adaptive functioning is an issue, then an adaptive functional assessment would be a helpful attachment to form T2201.

DTC Application

To support your DTC application, you should submit medical information such as copies of medical reports and diagnostic tests.

The criteria that an applicant must meet for a successful application are not easily shown in the case of mental functions for everyday living, and CRA policies in that regard are less clear. If an applicant has been rejected once, it is significantly more difficult to be successful through an appeal. Families are strongly advised to get help on the DTC application from advisors familiar with the process rather than trying a 'do-it-yourself' approach which is often not successful.

Child Disability Supplement

The child disability supplement of $4,733 is a non-refundable tax credit for children under age 18 that is in addition to the DTC. The amount of the credit is reduced by the amount of child care expenses or attendant care claimed as a medical expense for the child.

Transferability of the DTC

Individuals eligible for the DTC are often unable to use it because they have little or no taxable income. In such cases, the credit can be transferred to other family members (supporting persons) who provide support for the basic necessities of life and are the spouse, common-law partner, parent, grandparent, child or grandchild, brother or sister, aunt or uncle, or nephew or niece of the person qualifying for the disability tax credit. Illustration 6.11 provides more information on the transferability of the DTC.

Support includes supplying necessary maintenance or the basic necessities of life on a regular basis. If the individual with a disability receives social assistance, the supporting individual will have to show that the assistance was not sufficient to fully meet the basic needs of the person and that the person needs additional assistance. Income Tax Folio S1-F1-C2 contains helpful information in this regard.

Tax Savings from the DTC

The direct tax savings from the DTC is calculated by multiplying the federal and provincial credit amounts by the applicable federal and provincial tax rates, as shown in Figure 6.7.

Figure 6.7 Disability Tax Credit	
Disability Tax Credit	$8,113
Child Disability Supplement	$4,773
Tax credit rate	20%
Tax savings	$2,557

Since the credit is non-refundable, unfortunately it can only be used to offset taxes payable and cannot result in a tax refund. However, on the positive side, the credit is transferable to supporting family members who may be able to use it.

Prolonged Impairment

In order to qualify for the credit, the Income Tax Act provides that, "an individual has one or more severe and prolonged impairments." It is prolonged, "where it has lasted or may reasonably be expected to last, for a continuous period of at least 12 months." If the impairment doesn't continue in later years, the credit will be discontinued at that time.

CRA's Tax Folio S1-F1-C2 indicates that "a claim will not be denied solely because the person dies within the 12-month period." Individuals who are in long-term accommodation or who become bedridden because they are terminally ill will not be denied on this basis. Medical practitioners can sign DTC applications after death providing the necessary conditions were met before the individual died and providing the doctor could have made the decision about the disability at that time.

Level of Restriction

To qualify for the DTC as shown in Figure 6.6, the level of restriction needs to meet any one of three tests.

- The individual is *markedly* restricted in a basic activity of daily living
- The individual is significantly restricted in more than one activity of daily living so that the cumulative effect is the equivalent to being markedly restricted in a single activity of daily living
- The individual requires specified hours of life-sustaining therapy

According to CRA, to be markedly restricted, the CRA has determined that an individual must be restricted 90% of the time or more. This is fairly easy to show in six of the seven activities of daily living, but the cognitive functions are an exception. DTC applications are more likely to fail with respect to cognitive functioning simply because it is not possible to show. How can it be shown that an individual lacks certain cognitive functions necessary for daily living 90% of the time when they only manifest themselves periodically?

An individual is also markedly restricted where all or substantially all of the time, even with therapy and the use of support devices and medication, the individual is unable (or requires an inordinate amount of time) to perform a basic activity of daily living.

Justice D. G. Bowman in *Radage v. the Queen*, a Tax Court of Canada decision, made the following comment on the phrase *all or substantially all of the time* and CRA's 90% test when dealing with cognitive functioning.

> *To meet the criteria in paragraph 118.4(1)(b) he must all or substantially all of the time either be unable to perform that activity or require an inordinate amount of time in which to do so. I question the appropriateness of "all or substantially all of the time" or "requires an inordinate amount of time" when we are dealing with thought processes. Some quick and decisive thinkers facilely arrive at the wrong conclusion. Some slow and ponderous thinkers laboriously arrive at the right one. Which one has the problem, the tortoise or the hare?*

Let's think of an example. It is agreed that individuals with autism are on a spectrum – a continuum if you wish. How then is it possible to determine whether it is at 89% and doesn't meet the test or at 92% and does meet the test. The 90% test is flawed. Not only is the 90% test problematic in regard to cognitive function, but even the wording of the Income Tax Act needs a change.

A person receiving life-sustaining therapy must meet the following tests.

- The individual's ability to perform a basic activity would be markedly restricted except for the therapy
- The therapy is essential to sustain a vital function of the individual
- The therapy is required to be administered at least three times each week for a total of at least 14 hours a week

Retroactivity

CRA tax relief provisions allow taxpayers to retroactively file for tax credits that have been overlooked as far back as ten years. This includes unclaimed DTCs. This could provide a tax refund of up to approximately $20,000 for missed DTCs. Other overlooked credits could increase that amount even further. Once the DTC application has been approved by the CRA, a T1-ADJ Adjustment Request form must be filed with the CRA to claim the credit for the applicable years unless form T2201 authorizes the CRA to make the re-assessment.

Other Tax Benefits from the DTC

The DTC is a pivotal section of the Income Tax Act because it opens the door to many other tax benefits such as the following.

- Child disability supplement (for a child under the age 18)
- Registered disability savings plan
- Qualified disability trust (QDT)
- Tax free disability related employment benefits – transportation allowance to work and attendant for work assistance
- Enhanced tuition credit – tax credit as a full-time student is available even if the student is not enrolled full time
- Enhanced $10,000 child care expense deduction
- RESP contributions extended to 25 years and plan duration extended to 30 years
- RRSP funds may be withdrawn under the homebuyers plan to fund the purchase of a dwelling for a related person eligible for the DTC
- Preferred beneficiary election – trust income taxed to the trust beneficiary
- Medical expenses for an attendant, attendant or nursing home care, group home care or special therapy (see Figure 6.9)

Figure 6.12 at the end of this chapter shows a longer list of examples of situations where the DTC makes other tax benefits available. In a few cases, certain tax benefits related to disability can be claimed by an infirm individual even though they don't qualify for the DTC.

The Complexity of the DTC Provision

Section 118.3 and 118.4 of the Income Tax Act contain the rules regarding the disability tax credit. They are complex, confusing and in many ways unfair to taxpayers trying to qualify for the credit. The Honourable Donald G. H. Bowman had the following to say about the application of disability tax credit rules in *Radage v. The Queen* in the Tax Court of Canada.

> *"The legislative intent appears to be to provide a modest amount of tax relief to persons who fall within a relatively restricted category of markedly physically or mentally impaired persons... The court must, while recognizing the narrowness of the tests enumerated in sections 118.3 and 118.4, construe the provisions liberally, humanely and compassionately and not narrowly and technically."*

The comments of Justice Bowman are welcome and certainly relevant today. CRA should apply this more liberal thinking to their legislative interpretations. Perhaps the only change today is that the DTC no longer is of modest benefit to taxpayers given its pre-condition to qualify for so many tax benefits such as the qualified disability trust and the registered disability savings plans.

PART 3 – OTHER SUPPORT FOR DEPENDENTS

Eligible Dependent

To qualify for the wholly dependent person non-refundable tax credit (NRTC) of $11,135, the person claiming the credit must be related to the taxpayer as:

- the child or grandchild of the individual or the individual's spouse, or
- the parent, grandparent, brother, sister, uncle, aunt, niece or nephew of the individual or the individual's spouse and living in Canada at some time during the year.

Individuals who are not married or do not have a common-law partner may claim this credit for a child who is 18 years of age or older and dependent on the taxpayer due to a cognitive or physical impairment. This is the same credit as the eligible dependent credit for children under age 18 without a disability.

Your dependent must be wholly dependent on you for support at some time in the year and must live in Canada, unless the dependent is your child. If more than one person supports the individual, the individuals providing support can split the credit. If your dependent has income, the credit is reduced dollar for dollar by that income. You cannot claim this credit if you are married or in a partnership relationship, but you may claim the credit if you are separated, depending on the circumstances.

Canada Caregiver Credit

Until the end of 2016, three non-refundable tax credits provided tax relief for caregivers. They were the Infirm Dependent Credit, the Caregiver Credit and the Family Caregiver Tax Credit. Starting in 2017, these credits were replaced with the new caregiver amounts for dependent family members with a physical or cognitive impairment.

The new Canada Caregiver Credit (CCC) provides tax relief for certain family members who are dependent on others because of a physical or cognitive impairment.

- **$6,883**
  This credit applies to 1) a spouse/partner, 2) an eligible dependent age 18 or over, or 3) a family member age 18 or older and dependent on the individual for support – child, parents, grandparents, brothers/sisters, aunts/uncles, nieces/nephews. Under the old rules, all grandparents were included but this is no longer the case.

- **$2,150**
  This credit can be claimed for 1) a spouse/partner, 2) an eligible dependent 18 years of age or older, or 3) a child under age 18. The credit increases the married/partner and eligible dependent credit from $11,685 to $13,835.

The Canada Caregiver Credit of $6,883 will be reduced dollar-for-dollar by the dependent's net income above $16,163. The increased 13,835 credit for dependent spouses/partners and an eligible dependent will be reduced by their income over $11,635. Where the CCC applies, there is no longer a requirement for the dependent to live with the caregiver.

CRA has published a helpful commentary on this called *Consolidation of Caregiver Credits*. CRA defines a child as dependent for the CCC to be someone who is dependent on others for an indefinite duration requiring much more assistance for their personal needs and care compared to others of the same age.

RESPs for Persons with Disabilities – Expanded Benefit

RESPs provide an annual tax credit which can help finance a person's education. If a person with a disability can make use of RESPs and qualifies for the disability tax credit, both the contribution years and the plan distribution years increase, as shown in Figure 6.8.

Figure 6.8   RESP for Individuals with Disabilities

	Normal Period	Period for DTC
Contribution Period (years)	31	35
Maximum Distribution Period (years)	35	40

For RESP beneficiaries with disabilities there is no requirement to be enrolled in a post-secondary program on a full-time basis if a physical or mental disability prevents this. A doctor or certain other medical practitioners must certify this in writing.

PART 4 – MEDICAL EXPENSE CREDITS

Medical Expense Claim

A person may claim the medical expense tax credit for yourself, your spouse, your partner, or your children under age 18. There is no limit on the amount claimed providing it exceeds the lesser of 3% of your net income or $2,237.

In addition to this standard claim, a person may also claim the credit for a dependent relative which includes a child or grandchild age 18 or over of an individual or their partner, or a parent, grandparent, brother, sister, aunt, uncle, nephew or niece.

Whether someone is dependent is not determined in the Income Tax Act. A person qualifies as a dependent for support if the taxpayer is a supporting person and has supplied monetary support in terms of the basics of life such as food, shelter and clothing on a regular and consistent basis. If the individual was in receipt of other support, the taxpayer must be able to show that the other support was insufficient and the individual had to rely on the taxpayer to pay medical expenses.

Medical Expenses by Category

There is a long list of medical expenses in the Income Tax Act that qualify for refundable tax credits. In order to help readers understand them, this book had divided them into the following categories.

- Medical practitioner payments
- Attendant care
- Medications and other prescriptions
- Medical devices and equipment
- Home modification tax benefits
- Transportation and travel expenses

Medical Practitioner Payments

Most of us understand that payments to doctors, dentists, hospitals and other medical expenses paid to a medical practitioner are claimable medical expenses. In some provinces, certain practitioner payments qualify as a medical expense and in other provinces they do not. Each province has its own list of registered medical practitioners. There is a lengthy list of other medical practitioners in the Income Tax Act who qualify, including the following.

- Chiropractors
- Massage therapists
- Naturopaths
- Optometrists

Payments not covered by private health insurance can be claimed on your tax return. Expenses for cosmetic reasons, unless also necessary for health reasons, are not claimable. For medical practitioner payments as well as other medical expenses you can claim such payments made during any twelve-month period ending in a taxation year. The same is true in the following year so the twelve-month periods that are allowed may overlap.

Attendant Care

CRA defines attendant care as care provided by an attendant who does personal tasks that a person is unable to do himself or herself (CRA-RC4065). The following would be included

- Food preparation
- Housekeeping services for a resident's personal living space
- Laundry services for a resident's personal items
- Health care (registered nurse, practical nurse, certified health care aide, personal support worker)
- Activities (social programmer)
- Salon service (hairdresser, manicurist, pedicurist) is included in monthly fee
- Transportation (driver)
- Security for a secured unit

The medical expense tax credit allowed for attendant care is complex; it is described in the Income Tax Act in seven different subsections as follows.

- Full-time attendant (not at home)
- Full-time care in a nursing home (markedly restricted)
- Remuneration for attendant care (full or part time)
- Full-time attendant at home (self-contained domestic establishment)
- Nursing home care (lacking mental capacity)
- Group residence
- Schools (care and training)

CRA considers full-time care to be when a person needs constant care and attention. Claiming a tax credit for all types of attendant care except for Remuneration for Attendant Care, Group Home Care and Schools will result in the denial of a claim for the disability tax credit and vice versa. On the other hand, qualification for the disability tax credit is a necessary condition to claim all credits for attendant care except for Full-Time Attendant at Home, Nursing Home Care and Schools. If you are allowed either the DTC and the attendant care expenses, then you can choose whichever one is best for you. The attendant care criteria are outlined in Figure 6.9.

As discussed earlier, Figure 6.9 reflects wording used in the Income Tax Act in the reference to *mental or physical infirmity*, although it might be more appropriate to refer to *cognitive or physical impairment.*

Figure 6.9   Attendant Care Costs (Medical Expenses)

	Full-Time Attendant	Full-time Care in Nursing Home	Remuneration for Attendant Care	Full-Time Attendant at Home
Income Tax Act	118.2(2)(b)	118.2(2)(b)	118.2(2)(b.1)	118.2(2)(c)
Required Care Level	Remuneration for full-time care attendant	Full-time care	Remuneration for full or part-time attendant care	Remuneration for full-time attendant at home
Institution/Caregiver	Individual	Nursing home	Attendant care or Retirement home	Individual
Creditable Portion	Support wages	Fees paid	Support wages	Full-time attendant wages
Qualifications	Qualify for DTC	Qualify for DTC	Qualify for DTC	Certified by medical practitioner
Reason	Markedly restricted	Markedly restricted	Markedly restricted	Dependent because of physical or cognitive impairment
Amount Allowed	Expense amount or DTC	Expense amount or DTC	Expenses to $10,000 ($20,000 year of death) and DTC	Expense amount or DTC

	Nursing Home Care	Group Residence	Schools
Income Tax Act	118.2(2)(d)	118.2(2)(b.2)	118.2(2)(e)
Required Care Level	Full-time care due to cognitive incapacity	Remuneration for care or supervision of individuals with severe or prolonged challenges	Care and training due to lack of physical or cognitive capacity
Facility/Caregiver	Nursing home	Supportive Accommodation	Supportive Accommodation
Creditable Portion	Fees paid	Support wages	Care and training wages
Qualifications	Certified by medical practitioner as infirm	Qualify for DTC	Certified by appropriate person
Reason	Lacking cognitive capacity	Severe or prolonged impairment	Physical or intellectual incapacity requiring special equipment
Amount Allowed	Expense amount or DTC	Expense amount and DTC	Expense amount and DTC

Generally, attendant care costs are claimed rather than the DTC if they exceed the DTC amount.

The tax provisions allowing attendant care are both generous and complex. Since they are clustered as medical expenses, they often can be transferred to a supporting family member of an adult child, parent, grandparent and others that are dependent for support. CRA interprets dependent for support to be both financial and non-financial support. The attendant care provisions are complicated. A more logical way to look at these credits is to group them as follows.

Full-Time Attendant
- Full-time attendant not at home (qualify for DTC)
- Full-time attendant at home (vulnerable)

Nursing Home
- Full-time care in nursing home (qualify for DTC)
- Nursing home care (vulnerable)

Part-time Care (would also include full-time)
- Attendant care (qualify for DTC)
- Retirement home care (qualify for DTC)

In all cases except for part-time care, you must choose between the DTC and actual care costs. If only part-time care is required, then the amount allowed is care costs up to $10,000 plus the DTC amount.

Medications and Other Prescriptions

The cost of prescription drugs and medication used to diagnose, treat or prevent diseases or other health conditions are medical expenses. They must be lawfully acquired and be prescribed by a medical practitioner. The list of qualifying costs is pages long in the Income Tax Act and cannot be fully covered here.

Medical Devices and Equipment

Regulations to the Income Tax Act contain pages and pages of medical devices and equipment that qualify as medical expenses. Eye glasses, guide dogs, and wheelchairs are among the most common, but many others are available. The *Personal Tax Return Guide* written by Paula Ideias and published by Carswell contains an extensive summary of medical expense tax credits in Appendix A of that book.

Home Modification Tax Benefits

In general, certain expenses relating to the renovation or alteration of a residence is a medical expense for an individual who lacks normal physical development or has continuing mobility issues. The expense must allow the individual to gain access and to be mobile or functional within the home. Such expenses should not increase the value of the home or be an expense that would normally be incurred by a person without disabilities.

The tax benefits allowed fall into six categories and apply to landlords, home owners and home renters, as follows.

- Rental property incentives
  - Disability-related modifications to buildings
  - Disability-specific device or equipment
- Dwelling improvement incentives
  - Alterations or renovations to dwellings (medical expense)
  - Driveway modifications (medical expense)
  - Incremental construction costs of a principal place of residence (medical expense)
  - The home accessibility tax credit – starting in 2016

The rental property incentives give landlords a tax deduction for disability-related modifications to their properties or for the purchase of certain equipment that aids a home occupant with a disability. The dwelling improvement incentives allow taxpayers with disabilities and, in some cases, other family members, to claim non-refundable tax credits.

Transportation and Travel Expenses

If an individual must travel 40 kilometres or more each way to obtain medical expertise that is not available near their home, those costs are considered to be medical expenses. If it is necessary to have an attendant make the trip, those costs also qualify as medical expenses. $17 per meal per person and a rate per kilometre (currently 55.5 cents for Ontario residents) can be claimed with proof of a visit to a medical facility. Accommodation receipts are required, but gas and meal receipts are not.

PART 5 – REFUNDABLE AND DEDUCTIBLE AMOUNTS

There are five ways in which family support can be supplemented by enhanced tax benefits of various funds. The assistance comes in the form of refundable tax credits or through special or enhanced tax deductions. The supports are as follows.

- Refundable medical expense supplement (refundable credit)
- Disability supports deduction (tax deduction)
- Child care expenses (enhanced tax deduction)
- Working income tax benefit supplement (refundable credit)

Refundable Medical Expense Supplement

The medical expense supplement is a refundable tax credit, meaning that it will result in a tax refund even if no taxes are payable. It is designed to help pay for medical expenses of individuals with a disability over age 18. In order to qualify for the supplement, the taxpayer and spouse must earn at least $3,465 in employment or business income. The supplement is reduced by 5% of family income over $26,277. The maximum medical expense supplement is 25% of allowable medical expenses plus 25% of the disability support deduction (discussed in the next section) to a maximum of $1,187. Qualification for the disability tax credit is required.

Disability Supports Deduction

The disability supports deduction provides tax relief for certain medical expenses relating to education or employment and is tax deductable to the extent that it is not reimbursed. The individual does not have to be eligible for the disability tax credit but the claim must be supported by receipts and the taxpayer must file a prescribed form.

Qualifying expenses include sign language, interpretation services, teletypewriters, optical scanners, and a long list of other supports. The amount that can be claimed is limited to the lesser of expenses paid in the year or the amount earned from work or business. If the individual is attending a designated educational institution the expenses paid are limited to earned income for the year plus the least of 1) $15,000, 2) $375 times the number of weeks of attendance and 3) taxable income other than earned income. See Revenue Canada folio S1-F1-C3 for other detailed rules that apply.

Enhanced Child Care Expenses

Child care expenses are a tax deductable amount with some limitations. You can deduct up to $6,000 for each child age 6 and under and up to $5,000 for each child between the ages of 7 and 16. If one of your children qualifies for the disability tax credit, the deduction increases to $11,000 regardless of age.

The deduction is limited to two-thirds of the income of the parent with the lower income. Child care expenses must be supported by receipts.

Working Income Tax Benefit and Disability Supplement

The working income tax benefit is a refundable tax credit for low income families who earn employment or business income. Individuals under 65 must be eligible for the disability tax credit in order to receive a disability supplement. The rules are complicated and families who think they might qualify should seek professional advice. The credit was promoted by Jim Flaherty when he was Canada's finance minister as a way to enable individuals with disabilities to enter the workforce. The credit was expanded in the 2018 federal budget.

PART 6 – PLANS AND GRANTS

Study Grants

The study grant is available to provide financial assistance for post-secondary education for students with disabilities. There are two grants available—The Canada Student Grant for Service and Employment for students and The Canada Student Grant for students with permanent disabilities. The first grant provides assistance of up to $800 and pays for education expenses such as tutoring, note takers, and sign language interpreters. The second grant is worth up to $2,000 and pays for the cost of books, supplies and other education expenses for students with financial need.

Life-long Learning Credit

The life-long learning credit is a federal program which allows all individuals to withdraw up to $20,000 from an RRSP to pay for post-secondary education. Students must be enrolled in school on a full-time basis to receive this credit, but students who are attending school on a part-time basis and who have a disability can also use this program.

Home Buyer's Plan

The home buyer's plan allows home buyers to withdraw $25,000 from their RRSP to purchase a home without paying income tax providing they have not owned a home for at least five years.

However, individuals with disabilities do not have to wait the five-year period providing that the new home is more accessible or better suited in some way.

PART 7 – OTHER BENEFITS FOR PERSONS WITH DISABILITIES

Canada Child Benefit (CCB)

Until the end of 2016 there were a number of child tax benefits available to families with a child with a disability which could help with cash flow. They were as follows.

- Canada child tax benefit (CCTB)
- National child care benefit supplement (NCBS)
- Universal child care benefit (UCCB)
- Child fitness credit
- Child arts credit

These benefits have now been discontinued and replaced by the Canada child benefit (CCB). The CCB is a tax-free monthly payment to eligible families to help with raising children under 18 years of age.

The CCB is $6,400 a year for each eligible child under 6 years of age and $5,400 a year for each eligible child between ages 6 and 18 years of age. The benefit is reduced by a formula based on family income. The CCB income does not count as income that reduces social assistance.

Child Disability Benefit (CDB) (supplement to CCB)

The child disability benefit is a tax-free amount of up to $2,730 a year. It is available for families who care for a child under 18 years of age with a severe and prolonged physical or mental disability. It is paid to individuals who are entitled to the Canada child benefit. The child must be eligible for the disability tax credit.

Preferred Beneficiary Election (PBE)

The preferred beneficiary election is discussed in part 8 of chapter 5. Most trusts will now be taxed at the top tax rate, including trusts that are commonly used in disability planning, except for a QDT. The PBE will generally be used where the QDT is not available. Consequently, the QDT and the PBE will become widely used where multiple trusts exist, but only one can qualify as a QDT.

PART 8 – TAX PLANNING

Tax Planning – Show Me the Ways

Good tax planning can be summarized as follows.

- Minimize current income—defer income where possible.
- Claim all non-refundable tax credits for which you are eligible—the list keeps getting longer.
- Claim deductible expenses—so many are overlooked.
- Review your overall tax filing options—get some help.
- File tax returns even if you are not taxable—pick up your refundable credits.
- Revise prior returns if a benefit was overlooked—people rarely think of this.
- Seek out income that is taxed at preferred rates—dividends and capital gains.
- Split income among family members, if possible—count the ways.
- Allocate non-refundable tax credits to family members who can best use them.
- Use RDSPs.

Taxes Delayed are Taxes Saved

The magic of registered savings plans is the ability to put aside money today that will be taxable years into the future when funds are drawn out—usually on retirement. A tax delayed is a tax saved. Consider this simple example. Jones saves $1,000 each year for 20 years in an investment. Smith puts $1,000 each year into a registered plan. Both have a tax rate of 30% and both earn 6% on their investments. Who has accumulated the most in 20 years? Since Jones pays 30% of his income in tax, his non-registered investment can only get a return of 4.2% after taxes. Smith pays no current taxes on his registered plan investments, so he gets the full 6% return.

The chart in Figure 6.10 shows how Smith's accumulated investments in registered funds beat Jones' investments in non-registered funds.

Figure 6.10 Comparison of Non-Registered and Registered Fund Investments

	Non-Registered Funds	Registered Funds
5 years	$ 5,400	$ 5,600
10 years	12,100	13,200
20 years	30,400	36,800

Obtaining Tax Credits for Past Years

The CRA allows refunds for any tax year that ended within ten years of the calendar year when the taxpayer's request is filed. This ten-year limitation period rolls forward every January 1.

Refund claims are also often overlooked simply because a taxpayer has no tax payable and therefore does not file a tax return. Refundable tax credits such as the child tax credit or GST credit can be claimed even when no tax is payable, so returns should always be filed. Other credits such as the disability tax are also often overlooked and might be available for transfer to another family member. Ten years' worth of disability tax credits would amount to around $17,000 or more if a young child is involved.

The CRA allows a taxpayer to obtain tax refunds retroactively, but the procedures can be complicated. Obtain advice to see if you think you can benefit.

Credits for Family Members Age 18 and Over

It's important to know which credits are available to you once your dependent family member becomes 18 years of age and older. Information is provided in Figure 6.13 at the end of the chapter regarding the following.

- Dependent's medical expenses
- Disability tax credit transfer
- Wholly dependent person
- Canada caregiver

Figure 6.13 provides a brief summary of the terms and conditions for these credits.

Advocate for Tax Fairness

The Income Tax Act provides financial support for disability in five main ways.

- Non-refundable tax credits with some transferability to family members
- Registered disability savings plan (RDSP)
- Tax free transfer of registered plans (RRSPs and RRIFs) on death to plans for family members with a disability
- Special provisions regarding disability provisions in certain trusts, including QDTs (see chapter 5)
- Use of a QDT on death

Most of these tax provisions are complex and difficult for the average person to understand, let alone use in their tax filings. Without question, the RDSP offers the greatest tax benefit of all by providing adequate pensions for individuals with disabilities; but its complexity discourages qualified individuals from applying.

The tax provisions surrounding non-refundable tax credits are also complex, which no doubt means they too are under-utilized. Furthermore, most of these non-refundable credits have a relatively small monetary value to individuals with a disability although they can sometimes be transferred to supporting family members.

Some of the recent changes to the Income Tax Act have been financially unfortunate for those with disabilities. For example, an inter vivos trust can no longer own a principal residence for a person with a disability. This is an unfortunate narrowing of a legitimate use of trusts. Also, requiring an individual with a disability to annually elect that the trust be a QDT is another complexity and costly to solve by guardianship in the case of a beneficiary with an intellectual disability. Allowing only one QDT for a person with a disability limits broad family support and should be changed to include plans set up by grandparents or aunts and uncles even when one has already been put in place by a parent.

A few years ago, the CRA closed its district tax offices across Canada and effectively eliminated the opportunity for individuals to discuss their tax issues in person with the CRA. Their substitute helpline is largely ineffective and lacks the personal touch that gives confidence to taxpayers that their problems are getting a fair hearing. Taxpayers have loudly complained about the unwillingness of the CRA to deal with the disability tax credit in a more open and less arbitrary fashion. Doctors want to practice medicine and avoid administration which can sometimes make them less inclined to approve the complicated DTC rules. Despite these hurdles, families and caregivers must do everything they can to get as much benefit as possible for their loved ones out of the tax system.

Tax Credit Transfers

In many cases, individuals with a disability do not have significant income and therefore they may not be able to utilize non-refundable tax credits. However, many of these tax credits can be transferred to another family member who may be able to utilize the credits including parents/partners, grandparents, brothers/sisters and others. Set out below are some of the credits that can in certain cases be utilized by higher income family members.

- Disability Tax Credit
- Medical Expense Credit
- Attendant Care Costs Credit

If you add any of those credits that you claim on your tax return, it may give you more money to support a loved one with a disability – perhaps helping to fund DTC contributions, as an example. The recent enhancement of the Canada caregiver tax credit, working income tax benefit and disability supplement are certainly helpful.

Summing Up

Tax rules are difficult to understand and even more difficult to apply to a particular situation. It's not always what you know about taxes, it's more about what you don't know.

Non-refundable tax credits can be a large tax benefit for disability, but the application of these credits is complex. They are of no benefit to taxpayers unless they already have taxes payable and many don't. Perhaps non-refundable tax credits should be replaced by refundable credits, subject to income limitations. That would help make up for the lack of disposable income of low income individuals who often must pay medical and other disability related expenses out of income that is beyond their means.

The federal government recently re-instated the Disability Advisory Committee. The committee will be a way for stakeholders to provide their input into CRA in its decision making. The role of the advisory committee is as follows.

- The administration and interpretation of the laws and programs related to disability tax measures
- Ways in which the needs and expectations of the disability community can be better taken into consideration
- Increasing the awareness and take-up of measures for people living with disabilities
- How to better inform people living with disabilities and various stakeholders about tax measures and important administrative changes
- Current administrative practices and how to enhance the quality of services for people living with disabilities

Individuals with disabilities and their families and friends should make good use of the committee and provide their thoughts, ideas and comments to it. Earlier in this chapter, suggestions about the *all or substantially all of the time* should be at the top of its agenda.

Figure 6.11 Non-Refundable Tax Credit Amounts

	Schedules Line	Federal Credit Amount	Savings (Rounded)	Transferable
Family				
Basic – F (8)	300	$11,635	$2,330	
Spouse/partner – F, (C- $1)	303	11,635	2,330	
Charitable Donations (Schedule 9)	349	P		Either Spouse
Home Buyer - M	369	5,000	750	

The charitable donations tax credit can be carried forward for five years.

	Schedules Line	Federal Credit Amount	Savings (Rounded)	Transferable
Learning				
Tuition	323	P		Spouse, Parent, Grandparent
Student Loan Interest	319	P		Not transferable

The tuition credit can be carried forward indefinitely.

	Schedules Line	Federal Credit Amount	Savings (Rounded)	Transferable
Employment				
Employment - M	363	$1,178	$230	
CPP Contributions – M	308	2,564	510	
EI Premiums - M	312	836	170	

The credits cannot be carried forward.

	Schedules Line	Federal Credit Amount	Savings (Rounded)	Transferable
Retirement				
Age 65 – F (C – $36,430)	301	$7,225	$1,450	Either Spouse
Pension – M	314	2,000	400	Either Spouse
Medical Expense				
Medical Expenses (includes attendant care)	330	P		Either Spouse
Dependent's Medical (2)	331	P		
Disability				
Disability Tax Credit - F	316/318	$8,113	$1,620	(1)
Child Disability Supplement - F	316	4,733	950	(1)
Wholly Dependent Person -F (3) (C - $1) (8)	305	11,635	2,330	
Canada Caregiver Credit				
Schedule 5	307	6,883	1,380	
Schedule 5	303/305/307	2,150	430	
Home Accessibility – M	398	10,000	2,000	

NOTE 1 – *Amount is claimable by supporting spouse, parent, grandparent, child, grandchild, sibling, aunt, uncle, niece, or nephew*

    2 – *Medical expenses can be claimed for costs paid for dependent relative over age 17*

    3 – *Must reside with taxpayer, be over age 18 and vulnerable*

    4 – *Credit amounts are either fixed (F), subject to a maximum (M), or the amount paid (P). In some cases, the credit will be clawed back when income reaches a certain level (C)*

    5 – *The savings column is based on a 20% tax savings for all credits except for donations where a 45% rate is used. This is a conservative approximation for most provinces when federal and provincial rates are combined.*

    6 – *The March 2017 federal budget replaced the caregiver, infirm dependent and family caregiver credit with a new Canada Caregiver credit effective in 2017. See part 3 of this chapter.*

    7 – *These tax credits cannot be carried forward*

    8 – *This credit may be increased by $2,150 for infirm spouse or wholly dependent person*

Figure 6.12 Tax Benefits – Individuals Qualified for DTC and The Vulnerable

The disability tax credit (DTC) has become extremely broad in its reach for qualification for many tax benefits for non-refundable tax credits, tax deductions, tax refunds and tax plan transfers. And then there are tax benefits available where a person with a disability does not meet the DTC qualification but nevertheless has intellectual or physical vulnerabilities that still get special tax treatment.

QUALIFY FOR THE DISABILITY TAX CREDIT

Child Disability Supplement

Registered Disability Savings Plan (RDSP)

Child Disability Benefit

RRSP/RRIF/RESP Rollover to RDSP

Enhanced RESP Contribution Period and Plan Length

Preferred Beneficiary Election

RRSP Funds to purchase a home under HBP

Home Buyers Plan for Related Person

Home Accessibility Tax Credit

Enhanced Child care Expense Deduction

Child over 18 Claimed as a Dependent

Working Income Tax Benefit Supplement

Refundable Medical Expenses Supplement

Group Home Care Costs – Attendant Care

Remuneration for Attendant Care – Attendant Care

Full-time Care in a Nursing Home – Attendant Care

Full-time Attendant – Attendant Care

Relief from Health Premiums in Certain Provinces

Qualified Disability Trust (QDT)

VULNERABLE (NEED NOT QUALIFY FOR DTC)

Preferred Beneficiary Election – Over 18 and dependent

Lifetime Benefit Trust (RRSP/RRIF rollover on death of supporting individual)

Training Courses

Disability Supports Deduction

Figure 6.13 Tax Credits Available for Dependent Family Members Age 18 and older

	Dependent's Medical Expenses	Disability Tax Credit	Eligible Dependent	Canada Caregiver (Adult Dependent)
Income Tax Act	118.2 (1) D	118.3(2)	118(1)(b)	118(1)(d)
Tax Return Line	331	316 OR 318	305	307
Amount of Maximum Credit		$8,113	$11,635	$6,883
Canada Caregiver Credit Add-on			$2,150	
Tax Savings Based on 20% Rate (approximate)		$1,623	$2,758	$1,376
Income Threshold	$2,268	None	$13,785	$16,163
Medical Condition	None	DTC	Infirm	Infirm
Required Certification	None	DTC	DTC or doctor statement	DTC or doctor statement
Must Live with Taxpayer	No	No	Yes	No
Claimant Must Be Unmarried	No	No	Yes	No
Credit Can Be Shared	Yes	Yes	No	No

Dependent for support means both financial and non-financial support (Folio S1-F4-C1)

The determination of dependent is complex, so it will be necessary to carefully assess your particular situation to determine if the credit is available.

Generally, it means providing support such as food, clothing and cash for medical and health related services.

CHAPTER 7

RDSPs – A Generous Pension Plan for Disability

In 2007, then Minister of Finance, James Flaherty, introduced the Registered Disability Savings Plan (RDSP). It became law in 2008. RDSPs are essentially pension plans which allow individuals with disabilities and their families to save for the long-term by making non-deductible contributions to the plan. RDSPs accumulate income free of tax and the funds are partially taxed at age 60 when they are withdrawn as a pension. $90,000 of government assistance is available in the form of grants and bonds. Family members and others can contribute to the RDSP to support their loved one with a disability.

The RDSP benefits provide an astonishing hand up to individuals with disabilities with respect to their finances. The complexity of RDSPs, however, require a steep learning curve for plan holders that can be discouraging. That is why a separate chapter for RDSPs is necessary.

Almost everyone with a disability should have an RDSP—even those who can earn a living without financial assistance. The RDSP is by far the best financial tool available for individuals with disabilities, although it is not without a few shortcomings and limitations. The rules are complex and have changed several times, so make sure your understanding is up to date. You are advised to seek out qualified advisors who are experts in dealing with the unique financial issues of disability.

PART 1 – RDSP OVERVIEW

RDSP – The Basic Concept and Purpose

An RDSP is a pension plan for an individual with disabilities. It is, by far, one of the best programs ever developed to financially assist individuals with disabilities in their retirement.

Unlike an RRSP, contributions to a RDSP are not tax deductible, but income in the plan accumulates tax-free the same as it does in RRSPs. In addition, the government contributes to RDSPs (bonds and grants) which provides generous financial assistance to individuals with disabilities. The CRA's publication RC4460(E) is a helpful source of information.

When funds start to be paid out of the RDSP (usually in the year the individual turns 60) they are partially taxable (to account for plan growth) and partially non-taxable to allow for a tax-free return of funds contributed to the plan. The RDSP pension starts at age 60 and assumes life expectancy to be age 83. Many individuals with a disability may not reach age 60, let alone age 83. Consequently, RDSPs may not be a good planning vehicle in cases where life expectancy is shorter.

Qualifying as an RDSP

RDSPs can be opened for any individual until the end of the year in which they turn 59 if the person qualifies for the disability tax credit, is a resident of Canada and has a social insurance number. Contributions to an RDSP can be made by the plan holder or anyone approved in writing by the plan holder. The beneficiary (a person with a disability) or his estate must receive all RDSP funds and no amounts can be returned to contributors or anyone else.

If an individual has an intellectual disability, there are transitional rules which allow a family member to open the plan. This rule has been extended to 2023.

Loss of RDSP Eligibility

A loss of eligibility for the DTC means a loss of eligibility for the RDSP. The loss may be temporary, based on certification by a medical practitioner that the individual will likely be eligible again for the DTC in the foreseeable future. The RDSP may be retained in this situation by filing an election by the end of December of the year the DTC became ineligible to keep the RDSP open. The election is valid for the following five years.

The implications of a beneficiary becoming ineligible for the DTC are shown in Figure 7.1.

Figure 7.1   RDSP Loss of Eligibility

- No further contributions allowed
- No government contributions will be paid to the plan
- RDSP must be collapsed
- Grants and bonds received in the past ten years must be repaid
- Income of RDSP taxed to the beneficiary

RDSPs and Social Assistance

At one time, funds in an RDSP or the income from an RDSP could put individuals off side with respect to social assistance. Most provinces have changed their social assistance rules to exempt RDSPs, but families should check the latest status. This exemption has made RDSPs an even better savings plan for persons with disabilities.

Pension income from an RDSP must start by the end of the year that the beneficiary turns 60, and social assistance usually ends at age 65. Even though RDSP income may not reduce social assistance, the RDSP payment could cause the individual's cash on hand to exceed the asset threshold; families should beware that this can be a problem if cash flow is not deployed quickly.

The Savings Potential of RDSPs

Most people do not appreciate the significant financial benefits of RDSPs for long-term savings, so families should look at them very seriously. An RDSP, compared to investing, will significantly improve the long-term financial well-being of a loved one with a disability and mitigate the negative effects of inflation.

Suppose, for example, a family put $1,500 into an RDSP and received grants and bonds of $4,500 as compared to just investing $1,500. Assume that the interest rate is 3%. The difference in accumulated funds is striking as shown in Figure 7.2 below for different periods of time.

Figure 7.2 RDSP Savings Advantage

TIME	RDSP	Conventional Savings	RDSP Advantage
In 5 years	$34,800	$8,700	$26,100
In 10 years	$79,200	$19,800	$59,400
In 15 years	$136,000	$34,000	$102,000
In 20 years	$208,300	$52,000	$156,300

Figure 7.2 shows that an RDSP provides a much better return than conventional savings. Even if taxes are factored in (which they haven't been in this example), an RDSP comes out way ahead.

RDSP Timelines

After an individual qualifies for the disability tax credit under the Income Tax Act, contributions to the plan can begin. It is important to know the age levels at which contributions can be made, when bonds and grants can be received and when the RDSP pension begins. Otherwise, contributions could be disallowed and bonds and grants could be missed. Figure 7.3 depicts this timeline.

Figure 7.3   RDSP Life Cycle

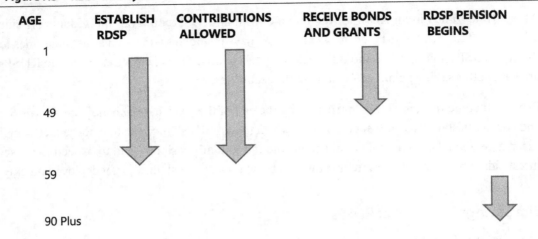

| AGE | ESTABLISH RDSP | CONTRIBUTIONS ALLOWED | RECEIVE BONDS AND GRANTS | RDSP PENSION BEGINS |

If plans permit, lump sum withdrawals (called disability assistance payments [DAPs]) are allowed, in addition to lifetime RDSP pension withdrawals (called LDAPs). However, DAPs and LDAPs taken early may result in repayment of bonds and grants.

If RDSPs start to pay out at age 60, then parents would likely be age 85 or older if they are still living. But if parents stopped personal support of their child with a disability on retirement, for example when they are age 65 and their child is age 40, there is a long period of time when no parental financial support is available to the individual with a disability. Somehow that gap needs to be filled through other financial support in the financial plan.

RDSP Beneficiary

An RDSP can have only one beneficiary and that must be an individual who qualifies for the disability tax credit. Consequently, there is only one person who can receive RDSP funds while the plan is in operation or after it is wound up.

If the beneficiary is not legally competent and RDSP withdrawals begin, it is very likely that the Public Trustee will take control of the plan unless someone secures personal guardianship through court application. Parents and others investing funds in an RDSP should be aware of this possibility. Early withdrawals are likely to be affected by this issue as well. The ability for an RDSP to accumulate funds is significant, but in some circumstances, control over these funds may eventually be lost. It may signal that applying for personal guardianship is a must.

RDSP Account Holder

The DTC issue presents a problem for setting up an RDSP for a beneficiary who is not legally competent. RDSP rules allow parents to set up an RDSP for an adult with an intellectual disability until the end of 2023 under transitional provisions.

Allowable Investments

Allowable investments for RDSP plans are essentially the same as allowable investments for other registered plans. For the most part, investments are restricted to publicly traded investments such as stocks, bonds, mutual funds, segregated funds and other similar financial products.

RDSP Budget Amendments

The federal government has continued to improve RDSP rules almost every year since RDSPs first became available. Withdrawal penalties have been softened, transfers from other tax plans have been allowed and carry over rules allow contributions for past years. Figure 7.4 outlines the RDSP budget changes as will be discussed throughout this chapter.

Figure 7.4   Important RDSP Budget Amendments

2010

Transfer of RRSP or RRIF to RDSP

Ten year carry-over rule to allow past year contributions

Relaxation of need for full guardianship

2011

Penalty elimination in case of shortened life expectancy

2012

Certain relatives and others can open an RDSP

New formula for maximum withdrawals where contributions are less than grants and bonds

RESP rollover to RDSP

RDSP kept open for four years if loss of DTC eligibility occurs

Repayment of grants and bonds limited to $3 of repayment for each $1 withdrawn

PART 2 – CONTRIBUTIONS AND OTHER RDSP FUNDING SOURCES

Rules and Limits

RDSPs have certain characteristics that need to be understood. Some of these features are as follows.

- An RDSP can only be for the benefit of the beneficiary.
- Distribution on death will be determined by the terms of the beneficiary's will or provincial laws concerning distribution of assets by someone who dies without a will.
- If a beneficiary is not legally competent there could be no will and estate distributions would be dictated by provincial intestacy laws.
- Withdrawals will be unavailable if grants and bonds in the previous ten years have exceeded personal contributions or they may also be limited by the value of grants/bonds themselves in the previous ten years.
- The RDSP plan holder must approve contributions to the plan by other parties and possibly even by the beneficiary.
- If an RDSP beneficiary reaches the age of majority but is not legally competent, parents will have to obtain guardianship in order to set up an RDSP after transitional rules expire at the end of 2018.
- Investments offered by financial institutions may be limited to their own funds and therefore discretionary management may not be available.
- It may not be impossible for a beneficiary to receive early payouts if needed by the beneficiary and he or she is not legally competent or guardianship is not in place.

Government Assistance – Bonds and Grants

Funds accumulated in an RDSP come from the following sources.

- Contributions including RRSP/RRIF/RESP transfers (maximum) $200,000
- Tax free grants and bonds (maximum)
  - Bonds $20,000
  - Grants $70,000
- Accumulated growth in the RDSP from accumulated income

Transfers from an RRSP/RRIF and RESP do not collect bonds and grants.

When you combine these three inputs, they are powerful wealth generators for an individual with a disability. Plan holders and family members who contribute only $1,500 a year over 20 years can potentially receive $70,000 (tax free) as a Canada Disability Savings Grant (CDSG) and another $20,000 (tax free) as a Canada Disability Savings Bond (CDSB), bringing the total benefit to $90,000. That's a three for one payoff. And then, of course, the plan will earn income on these funds.

Even if some contributions are not eligible for CDSGs, the funds will still accumulate tax free inside the plan, which is a significant advantage.

Calculation of Bonds and Grants

Entitlement to the amount of bonds and grants is dictated by the source of family income. Family income is based on the income of the parents until the beneficiary turns age 19, and after that on the income of the person with a disability and their spouse if they are married. Consequently, the receipt of bonds and grants is minimal until age 19.

The calculation for the Canada Disability Savings Bond (CDSB) for the 2017 entitlement is shown in Figure 7.5.

Figure 7.5   Bond Entitlements

Family Income	Bond
$30,000 or less	$1,000
From $30,000 to $45,916	Reduced to zero as income increases

The Canada Disability Savings Grant (CDSG) entitlement calculation is shown in Figure 7.6.

Figure 7.6 Grant Entitlement

Family Income	Grant	Yearly Maximum
Income of $91,831 or under		
First $500 contribution	$3 for each $1 contributed	$1,500
Next $1,000 contribution	$2 for each $1 contributed	$2,000
		$3,500
Income over $91,831		
First $1,000 contribution	$1 for each $1 contributed	$1,000

The grant is certainly the larger of the two amounts and is available to families beginning at birth, providing family income is less than $91,831. In most cases, the grant will be fully available when the child turns age 19 because it is then based on the child's income, which is likely to be minimal. This is different for the bond which, in most cases, is not available before age 18 is reached.

It is also important to remember that net income for bond/grant amounts is based on income of the second prior year. Therefore, income needs to be determined starting in the year they become 17 years of age. A large percentage of individuals may need to file past due returns.

Repayments of Bonds and Grants

RDSP bonds and grants can be repayable for several reasons. In some cases, a full repayment is required, and in other cases, only a partial repayment is required. Full repayment of bonds and grants within ten years is required if

- the RDSP is terminated;
- the RDSP is deregistered;
- the beneficiary is no longer eligible for the disability tax credit (DTC); or
- the beneficiary dies.

Partial repayment of bonds and grants is required if

- the RDSP withdrawals are made within ten years of receipt of the bonds or grants.

The original rules requiring the repayment of bonds and grants were onerous and required full repayment of all bond and grant amounts received within ten years when an amount was paid out. This rule has been modified and now requires a $3 repayment of government contributions for every $1 of payout to a maximum amount equal to the bonds/grants received in the ten years prior to the withdrawal. The penalty is still quite heavy and should be avoided, if possible, by making contributions early. The RDSP is a pension plan and early withdrawals are not advised unless absolutely necessary.

Since RDSP income starts to flow out at age 60 and RDSP contributions must end at age 49, no bond or grant repayments would apply to LDAP payments after retirement.

Ten Year Carryover Rule

RDSP rules allow you to go back and make contributions for the previous ten years based on the rules for family income for the year to which you are contributing. The maximum grant you can receive in any one year is limited to $10,500. If you do not understand that no more than $10,500 in grants can be received in any one year, it is easy to contribute more than you should for grant refunds. If carry forward grants are available, the government gives you the biggest possible advantage when you make a retroactive contribution because the government pays out the higher 3:1 grant ratio first before paying out the lower 2:1 ratio.

For example, assume that John is age 35 in 2017 and qualified for the DTC in 2012. In 2017 he has six eligible contribution years (five in back payments and one for the current year) because he qualified for the disability tax credit in those years. He contributes $3,750 to the RDSP in 2017. Figure 7.7 shows the calculation of the maximum entitlement.

Figure 7.7 Maximum Retroactive Contribution Entitlement

Contribution Entitlement - Prior Years

	Amount	Years	CDSB/CDSG Contribution Amount
300% Grant	$ 500	6	$ 3,000
200% Grant	1,000	6	6,000
Bond	$1,000	6	6,000
			$15,000

Figure 7.8   CDSB/CDSG Received

	Contribution	Factor	CDSD/CDSG Received
300% Grant	$3,000	3	$ 9,000
200% Grant	750	2	1,500
	$3,750		$10,500
Bond			6,000
			$16,500

As seen in Figure 7.7, in 2018 John will still have $5,250 ($6.000-$750) in a contribution entitlement for previous years towards the 200% grant amount. The 300% grant amount and the bond amounts for previous years have been used up.

Transfers from RRIFs and RRSPs

Tax rules allow transfers to RDSPs from the plans of parents who want to help provide capital to the RDSP. This rule change, introduced in 2010, allows money from an RRSP/RRIF holder to be transferred on death to the RDSP of a dependent child or grandchild. The amount of the transfer is limited to the available contribution room in the RDSP. This transfer into the RDSP does not obtain a RDSP grant and will be taxable when RDSP funds are distributed. Transfers from registered pension plans are also allowed under certain circumstances.

In order to make the transfer, the child or grandchild will be considered to be dependent on the deceased person if one of two conditions exist.

- There was a relationship of dependency between the child/grandchild and the parent/grandparent who provided care and financial support.
- The child/grandchild is financially dependent, meaning his or her income is less than the sum of the basic personal exemption of $11,635 and the disability tax credit amount of $8,113, for a total of almost $20,000.

RESP Transfers for Disability

There are times when RESPs have been set up for an individual with a disability and then later this person is unable to use the plan amounts for education due to their disability. The Income Tax Act allows for the tax-free transfer of RESP growth to an RDSP of a person with a disability if the conditions shown in Figure 7.9 exist.

Figure 7.9   Transfer of RESP Income to a RDSP

There are a number of required conditions for the transfer of RESP income to an RDSP, as follows.

- Plans must have a common beneficiary
- An RESP must allow accumulated income payments
- The beneficiary has a severe and prolonged mental disability preventing post-secondary education, or the RESP has been in existence for at least ten years and each of the RESP beneficiaries is at least 21 years old and not pursuing post-secondary education, or the RESP has been in existence for more than 35 years
- The transfer from the RESP will reduce RDSP contribution room and will not receive RDSP grants
- RESP contributed income to an RDSP is taxable on withdrawal
- RESP bonds and grants must be repaid to the government
- Private RESP contributions are returned to the contributor
- The RESP must be terminated by the end of February of the following year

If RESP contributions are refunded to the contributor, they can use them to make further contributions to an RDSP. This looks like a long list of conditions, but they are not difficult to meet in most situations – particularly for an RESP set up for a single person.

Early RDSP Funding

RDSPs are so much more effective if contributions are made as early in life as possible. By doing so, the funds in the plan can grow even larger given the longer years that they will be invested. Also, the earlier funds are invested in a RDSP, the earlier in life that funds can be withdrawn from a RDSP without repayment of bonds and grants. Since many RDSP beneficiaries may have shorter life expectancies than usual, starting the withdrawals before age 60 may be important. Planning to start withdrawals at about age 35 would be a reasonable objective.

For example, if RDSP contributions started at $1,000 a year for the first eighteen years of the beneficiary's life, there would be about $56,000 in the plan at age 18 based on a return rate of 5%. If $1,500 were then contributed to the plan through to age 34, there would be about $265,000 in the plan at that time and maximum bonds and grants would have been received. Finally, if we assume that no other contributions were made to the plan, the balance in the plan at age 60 would be about $900,000.

RDSPs are powerful savings vehicles that can be made even better if contributions start early.

PART 3 – RDSP WITHDRAWALS

The Pension (LDAP) Withdrawal Formula

Once a beneficiary of an RDSP reaches age 60 they must start withdrawing funds no later than the end of that year as an LDAP. The formula limits withdrawal amounts each year and is based on a life expectancy of 83 years. When you are age 70, for example, it is assumed that you have thirteen years to live and therefore the maximum withdrawal amount is based on your age at the beginning of the year (69) - one fourteenth of the plan balance at the beginning of the year, or in this case, 7.14%.

Figure 7.10 shows the LDAP withdrawal amounts starting at age 60 assuming there is $100,000 in the plan.

Figure 7.10 LDAP Withdrawal Amount

Age at January 1	Withdrawal	Age at January 1	Withdrawal	Age at January 1	Withdrawal
60	4,348	67	6,250	74	11,111
61	4,545	68	6,667	75	12,500
62	4,762	69	7,143	76	14,286
63	5,000	70	7,682	77	16,667
64	5,263	71	8,333	78	20,000
65	5,556	72	9,091	79	25,000
66	5,882	73	10,000	80	33,333

The withdrawal percent stays at 33.33% of the plan value after age 80. As a general rule, an RDSP provides an indexed pension starting at age 60 with the first payment being 4.17% of the plan value.

Figure 7.11 shows maximum withdrawals at different ages.

Figure 7.11 LDAP Withdrawals Starting at Age 60

Age at January 1	Opening Plan Balance	Required Withdrawal
59	$100,000	$4,167
65	$100,000	$5,556
70	$100,000	$7,692
75	$100,000	$12,500
80	$100,000	$33,333

Given the fact that some individuals with disabilities may have a shorter life expectancy than the population in general, it is difficult to understand why the pension is based on a life expectancy of 83 years. In many cases this will result in substantial balances being left in the plan on the death of the beneficiary. The maximum amount they are allowed to withdraw in a year is the greater of the LDAP formula or 10% of the market value of the account on January 1 of the year in question. In the early years, 10% of the account will be greater than the LDAP.

Shortened Life Expectancy

Where an individual can show that he/she has a shortened life expectancy by five years or less based on a medical practitioner's opinion, the LDAP limit will not apply and up to $10,000 per year can be withdrawn without penalty. Also, the requirement to repay bonds and grants in the previous ten years is eliminated. As well, the individual is not allowed to make contributions to the RDSP once they make this election and the government will not provide any further bond or grant contributions.

Taxation of Payments to Beneficiary

The taxation of amounts withdrawn from an RDSP takes into account personal contributions to the RDSP for which no tax deduction is available. The formula to determine the non-taxable portion equals the total contributions times the amount of the payment divided by the value of the RDSP at that time. The taxable portion of the payment therefore is equal to the total payment less the non-taxable part of the payment. It also considers previous non-taxable payments.

If, for example, there was a $20,000 withdrawal with no previous withdrawal and the total personal contribution to the plan equals $65,000, then when the fair market value of the RDSP plan is $400,000, the non-taxable amount would be calculated as follows.

$$\frac{\$20,000 \times \$65,000}{\$400,000} = \$3,250$$

The non-taxable portion would therefore be $3,250 and the taxable portion would be $16,750.

Early Withdrawals

RDSPs are meant to be for long-term use to provide pensions to individuals with a disability. Consequently, restrictions apply when funds are withdrawn from RDSP plans early in life. In simple terms, the rules are as follows.

- In any year when government grants and bond payments into the plan exceed private contributions (in a government-assisted plan), the DAP payment will be reduced to the greater of the LDAP formula and 10% of plan assets at the beginning of the year.

- When an amount is withdrawn from an RDSP, for each $1 withdrawn, $3 of grants and bonds paid into the plan in the previous ten years must be repaid (proportional payment rule).

RDSPs are meant to be pension plans and should be treated as such.

Events Requiring Grant and Bond Repayments

If any of the following events occur, RDSP rules require the repayment of bonds and grants received in the previous ten years.

Figure 7.12   Events Requiring the Repayment of Bonds and Grants

- RDSP is terminated
- Plan ceases to be an RDSP
- Beneficiary is no longer eligible for the disability tax credit (DTC)
- The election to keep a plan is not filed and the plan expires
- The beneficiary dies

The application of this rule and the formula to be used is complex and beyond the scope of this book.

Death of a Beneficiary

On the death of an RDSP beneficiary, an RDSP must be wound up. The plan must be closed by the end of the following calendar year of the death. In this situation, grants and bonds received within the last ten years must be repaid to the government.

The remaining funds will be paid to the beneficiary's estate and will be dealt with under the terms of the beneficiary's will if there is one. In the case of an individual with an intellectual disability who legally cannot have a will, the funds at death will be dealt with under provincial estate laws.

PART 4 – PLANNING FOR RDSPS

Financial Advisors

To manage their RDSP account, families should consider working with a financial advisor who has demonstrated experience in managing RDSP funds. Be explicit in asking about the qualifications and experience.

Planning for Early Withdrawals

RDSP plans allow lump sum withdrawals before age 60 as DAPs and periodic withdrawals as a pension starting any time; these withdrawals are mandatory at age 60. Since bonds and grants end at age 49, there can be no penalties from the periodic pension withdrawals after age 59. However, as mentioned previously in this chapter, lump sum withdrawals will require the repayment of three times the withdrawal amount to a maximum of the bonds and grants in the ten years preceding the withdrawal.

Some families may need to use RDSP funds for their child with a disability before age 60 to cover unexpected payments of large amounts. The question is whether or not they should withdraw funds if other planning options can fulfill the need for funds. Some beneficiaries will be able to make withdrawals without penalty before age 60. For example, a beneficiary who was age 19, for instance, can collect all the grants/bonds by the year they turn 39. Adding the ten-year vesting period will take them to age 49 and will allow them to withdraw funds the year they turn 50 without penalty.

An RDSP has three major advantages: tax-free compounding, social assistance exemption and bonds and grants. If a beneficiary loses some of the bonds and grants due to early payouts, an RDSP plan is still vastly superior to saving outside of a plan. And even if the beneficiary must return some of the grant and bond contributions on the premature withdrawal, the investment growth associated with the government contributions within the account can be thought of as an interest-free investment loan from the government.

Contribution Planning

Families with limited income may have trouble setting aside money to make contributions to an RDSP plan. In such cases, families may want to consider directing tax credit refunds such as the disability tax credit or the Canada Child Benefit towards RDSP contributions.

It is certainly a good idea to contribute to the plan as early as possible. The sooner contributions to an RDSP are made, the sooner the government will provide its matching contributions. Typically, the matching RDSP grants are received one to two months after a personal contribution is made. An important reason for early contributions is the benefit of long-term tax-free compounding. In addition, it may allow you to escape or minimize the claw back of bonds and grants should you need to make DAP withdrawals.

Only $30,000 in contributions are needed beginning the year the beneficiary turns age 19, or $1,500 a year for 20 years to get the maximum $90,000 of bonds and grants. This means that additional contributions of up to $170,000 can be made at any time. Early lump sum contributions would vastly improve RDSP pension income. This is a strategy that can easily be overlooked.

RDSPs are for the Long-term

Contributions to RDSPs can start at any time and last until a beneficiary is age 59. Normally, contributions start sometime in the early life of a person with a disability, such as at age 10. This means that the funds will be invested for about fifty years before any withdrawals would normally start. The bottom line is that RDSPs are long-term pension investments and are highly valuable for families.

Comparing an RDSP to a Henson Trust

Henson trusts and RDSPs are the most common vehicles for accumulating and preserving wealth for individuals with disabilities. The Henson trust is primarily used to protect and supplement social assistance while the RDSP is used to produce retirement income. Figure 7.13 compares the two plans.

Figure 7.13 An RDSP Compared with a Henson Trust

	RDSP	Henson trust
Distributions restricted to beneficiary	Yes	No
Distributions fully discretionary	No	Yes
Annual contribution limit	No	No
Lifetime contribution limit	Yes	No
Generally, assets and income can be structured to not affect provincial assistance	Yes	Yes
Ability to collect federal CDSG and CDSB amounts	Yes	No
Effective way to fund long-term savings	Yes	N/A
Assets can be sprinkled to others	No	Yes
Distributions on death may be subject to provincial intestacy laws	Yes	No

The RDSP is designed for long-term savings whereas the Henson trust is designed to optimize social assistance throughout the lifetime of an individual with a disability.

In some provinces, payments to the beneficiary of an RDSP do not affect social assistance, whereas Henson trust payments over certain limits (where they are allowed) will usually reduce social assistance (see Figure 3.2).

Estate Planning

If an RDSP beneficiary is legally competent then they can make a will and more flexibility in estate planning is possible. The RDSP beneficiary will have to decide in his or her will to whom the RDSP balance will go upon death. With an RDSP there is no option except to take the funds into the estate of the beneficiary—this is unlike an RRSP where a beneficiary can be named. If the person with a disability is not legally competent to have a will, the RDSP proceeds will be distributed under applicable provincial succession laws.

RDSP and Guardianship

As previously stated, the only recipient of RDSP funds is the beneficiary of the RDSP. In essence, that means a financial institution holding RDSP funds will have its hands tied in terms of distributions without the authority of the beneficiary. Essentially, the RDSP funds are vested in the beneficiary and belong to him or her and no one else.

In cases where the beneficiary has an intellectual disability and is unable to make binding legal agreements, the RDSP plan effectively comes under the control of the Public Trustee. Once the individual with a disability reaches the age of majority and a significant amount of funds are in the plan, the financial institution where the plan resides is likely to look to the Public Trustee to approve all decisions with respect to the plan including changes to its investment portfolio and early distribution as DAPs by age 60.

In order to take back some control, a family member of the individual with a disability needs to make an application to the Public Trustee to become personal legal guardian of property belonging to the individual. They must submit a management plan showing how the funds will be spent and file a report with the Public Trustee every few years showing the receipts and payments of funds to prove their compliance with the management plan.

Summing Up

RDSPs should definitely be part of long-term financial planning for an individual with a disability, even though the technical issues are complicated. RDSPs offer a significant tax-free government contribution and tax-free compounding. RDSP income does not usually affect social assistance benefits and income is taxed in the hands of the person with a disability who is usually in a lower tax bracket. Without question, RDSPs are better than other tax-deferred income plans.

There are significant problems when the RDSP beneficiary has an intellectual disability. Since handing over control to the Public Trustee may not be desirable, many families will want to apply for personal guardianship in order to control financial planning in a personal way. Families should do some calculations to determine how much financial assistance is available to their loved one and whether it fully meets their needs.

Figure 7.14 shows the five ways that funds can be added to an RDSP as well as which funds will be taxable on withdrawal. The beneficiary will receive pension income from the plan starting at age 60. Any funds remaining in the plan will pass to the beneficiary's estate to be dealt with in his or her will or as determined by provincial law if the person with a disability does not have a will.

Figure 7.14   RDSP Flow of Funds

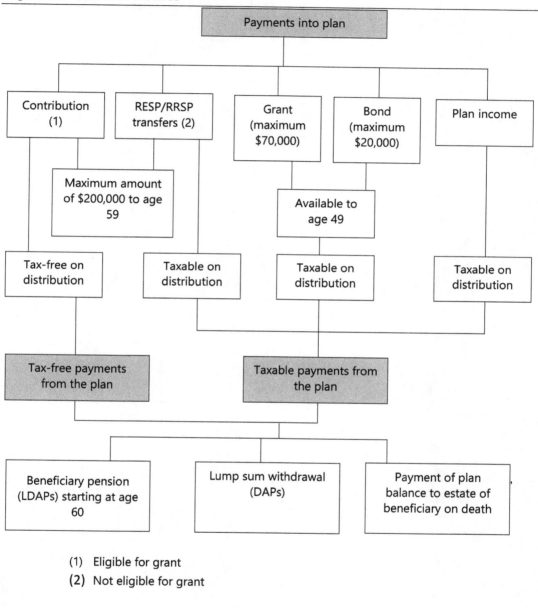

(1) Eligible for grant
(2) Not eligible for grant

CHAPTER 8

Estate Planning – A Different Path

Disability makes estate planning challenging because your loved one may not be able to own property or be able to pass it on to other members of your family as you would wish. This may be due to their lack of legal competence or because owning property would limit their right to government assistance. Their inheritances almost always need to be handled differently than for other family members. Conflict and legal complexity can be an issue from the beginning. Recent changes to the tax rules for trusts has made estate planning for a family member with a disability more difficult.

Before starting down the estate planning path, families should ponder some important questions regarding their loved one with a disability: How much money do they need to live out their life? Who will manage the funds? What type of accommodation is suitable? How should ownership of their property be structured? Who is going to take care of this when you are gone? Of course, you also need to consider if the plan you develop is fair to others in the family. Will siblings and others in your family participate in the structure you have designed?

Estate planning doesn't start with the writing of a will. It begins much earlier in life as a family goes through the rigours of comprehensive financial planning starting with retirement planning and then estate planning—it's a continuum. The bridge between your situation today and the time when your will takes effect on your death will be governed by you or your financial power of attorney if you cannot handle life's financial decisions. That too may need different structuring than normal.

In some cases, an individual with a disability could outlive parents by several years. Does the structure you have designed facilitate that, and are the documents flexible enough to allow for changes to a new caregiver as you give up that responsibility? Has guardianship been put in place to handle tax and legal issues for your loved one and are successor guardians recommended in your will?

Hopefully this chapter will encourage you to think about your will and its important estate planning considerations. With the background information provided here you can have a conversation with your advisors and start the process.

PART 1 – ESTATE PLANNING FOR DISABILITY – AN OVERVIEW

Why Estate Planning for Disability is Different

In estate planning for a loved one with a disability, it is important to accumulate enough capital to provide income over a long period of time. In many cases, the funds cannot be owned by the individual due to his or her inability to legally own property or competently deal with it.

A proper estate planning structure to meet the above objective must also deal with the following.

- Social assistance rules and restrictions
- Complexity of tax laws
- Provincial laws that restrict the ownership of assets or the accumulation of income
- Trusts - statutory or common law provisions
- Family wishes for fairness and equity

It takes a combined effort of professionals in financial planning, taxation and legal issues to properly structure estate planning for a loved one with a disability. This chapter should be read in conjunction with chapter 3 on provincial income assistance, chapter 5 on trusts and chapter 6 on taxes.

Estate Planning Overview

Estate planning (testamentary planning) and the use of trusts are very much intertwined. Estate planning for disability relies on the use of trusts if one of your estate beneficiaries has an intellectual disability preventing him or her from owning property. To simplify the complexity of this, the two areas have been separated in this book. Trusts are discussed in chapter 5 and estate planning in this chapter.

Upon death, you will have an estate that is governed by the terms of your will. You may want to provide that trusts will be established for certain beneficiaries of your estate—for a child with a disability, for example. The challenge is to separate the planning for a loved one with a disability from other beneficiaries because the plan is usually quite different.

There is also significant planning complexity today because of new rules for trusts arising on death. Recent tax changes, for example, saw the introduction of the qualified disability trust (QDT) which is highly beneficial for disability, but has its limitations. A QDT is a testamentary trust established in your will for a child who has a disability and qualifies for the disability tax credit.

Beyond the actual transfer of property in your will to an individual or to a trust, there may also be a transfer of certain financial plans such as RRSPs and RESPs to a beneficiary with a disability. Figure 8.1 shows the two types of transfers.

Figure 8.1   Transfers from an Estate

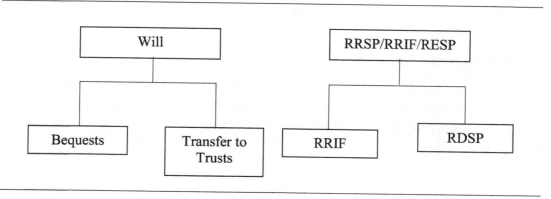

Financial planning sometimes misses the mark with respect to well-planned objectives. For example, Henson trusts are on everyone's estate planning to-do list but their possible uses, beyond maximizing social assistance, are usually overlooked. People continue to open RDSPs without knowing the amount of funds needed for the future or whether the RDSP account someday will fall under the control of the Public Trustee.

It is surprising that many people do not do the math to determine the amount of capital required to fund the financial needs of a loved one. Families need to think carefully about questions such as where the funds will come from, how the various income components fit together and whether or not there is a way to minimize income tax.

Two Kinds of Beneficiaries

If disability is not an issue, estate planning simply means distributing your assets to family and others according to your wishes. Sometimes it can get a little more complicated for tax reasons, but for the most part, beneficiaries will receive their inheritance and then do with it what they wish.

Estate planning for a loved one with a disability, particularly when the disability is an intellectual one, is more complex. You need assurance that the funds you leave will cover your loved one's financial needs, possibly for many years, and that administration of the funds will have proper checks and balances. Money should not be misdirected nor should your expectations for its use be overly complex, confusing or inexact. In that regard, this book discusses a letter of wishes in part 1 of chapter 5.

Life Plan

To properly plan for the financial needs of a loved one with a disability, you must first develop a life plan. Do you want your loved one to live a lifestyle beyond what social assistance will allow? If you can afford it and they are capable, do you want your loved one to live in their own home or with others where families might pool their resources? Is your loved one's disability at a level where they must eventually live in supportive accommodation? In this case, very little extra income support may be required. You should consider all of these issues and then work through your planning to make it happen.

Trusts or Outright Bequests

If your loved one has a physical disability, then your planning may not be much different than it would be for a child without a disability. However, if your loved one's disability is intellectual, then a different approach is needed. In these cases, as previously stated, one or more kinds of trusts may be needed for the following reasons.

- Your loved one may not be legally competent to own property
- Your loved one, even if legally competent, may not be suitable for ownership of significant property
- Social assistance may be denied
- Your loved one may need protection from individuals who might inappropriately diminish their assets
- Transfer of certain funds may have to pass to a trust to achieve tax and social assistance objectives
- Home ownership may be desirable

Several different trusts to accomplish your objectives were discussed in chapter 5. The objectives of many of these trusts can often be combined in a single trust.

Choosing Trustees, Executors and Others

People often choose the closest family member as a trustee of a trust or executor of an estate. This can lead to unfortunate results if the person selected is not suitable or does not have the emotional or financial competence to do the job. The situation can sometimes be mitigated by having more than one trustee or executor, in the case of an estate, or by appointing a corporate executor. Additionally, the person in whom you have the most confidence might be required to be in the group approving decisions which also has the ability to veto poor decisions.

Caregiver Succession

There will come a time when parents are no longer able to act as the primary caregivers (financial or personal) for their loved one with a disability. Paying the bills, finding housing, administering trusts and making other personal decisions may become too much for some as they grow older.

If you have put your legal documents in order and there have been frequent family conversations, it will be a less burdensome job for a new caregiver. You should start the conversations with successor caregivers as soon as you can. Certainly, it's important that they want to do the job, which means that mentoring should start years earlier. You should decide if they will be paid a fee or if, instead, they will share in the assets of the loved one with a disability. In all likelihood, the financial caregiver will also be your attorney under your financial power of attorney.

Capacity and Its Implications

The lack of intellectual capacity of a loved one with a disability completely changes estate planning. Limited capacity will prevent this individual from making a will or power of attorney, owning property or making certain elections under the Income Tax Act. These are all significant restrictions.

Because of these limitations, property is usually held in trust for, rather than owned by, your loved one. If ownership of property were to be transferred to a person with an intellectual disability, it would more than likely be administered by the Public Trustee, which this should be avoided except as a last resort.

When a person is not legally competent, tax rules will prevent him or her from doing the following.

- Opening an RDSP after the age of majority
- Making an annual qualified disability trust (QDT) election
- Making the preferred beneficiary election to shift the trust tax liability to a beneficiary

Each of these issues is discussed in more detail in chapter 6.

Guardianship and Estate Planning

Frequently, families have not applied for guardianship of an adult child with an intellectual disability—perhaps because of cost and legal complexity. Court approval for guardianship is needed and it can difficult to obtain because the courts frown on taking away the personal freedom of anyone.

There may be advantages in allowing family members to make decisions for a person with an intellectual disability rather than a Public Trustee because they can personalize decision-making and truly understand the needs of their loved one.

Personal guardianship also allows a guardian to make elections for an individual with a disability under the Income Tax Act or to have access to tax plans such as an RDSP or qualified disability trusts. Without the written consent of the person with a disability or by the person's legal representative, it is not possible to open an RDSP for an adult with a disability (subject to a temporary exemption), elect that a trust be a qualified disability trust or make certain elections under the Income Tax Act. Nor is it possible for RDSP funds to be directed by the plan holder, such as early withdrawals, without legal authority vested in the RDSP beneficiary.

Personal guardianship can be applied for by a parent during the lifetime of a child and then by another family member after the death of parents. In both cases, it is only a recommendation and the courts still have the final say. A recommendation coming from a family member can positively influence the court's decision.

Some provinces have instituted streamlined processes for the appointment of a trusted person to manage the personal finances of an adult who is incapable of making decisions. It would be helpful for all provinces to move forward on this. It would also simplify issues under the Income Tax Act.

Figure 8.2 shows the relationship between guardianship (public and personal) and the use of a personal trust to manage the finances of a loved one with a disability.

Figure 8.2 Guardianship Compared to Trusteeship

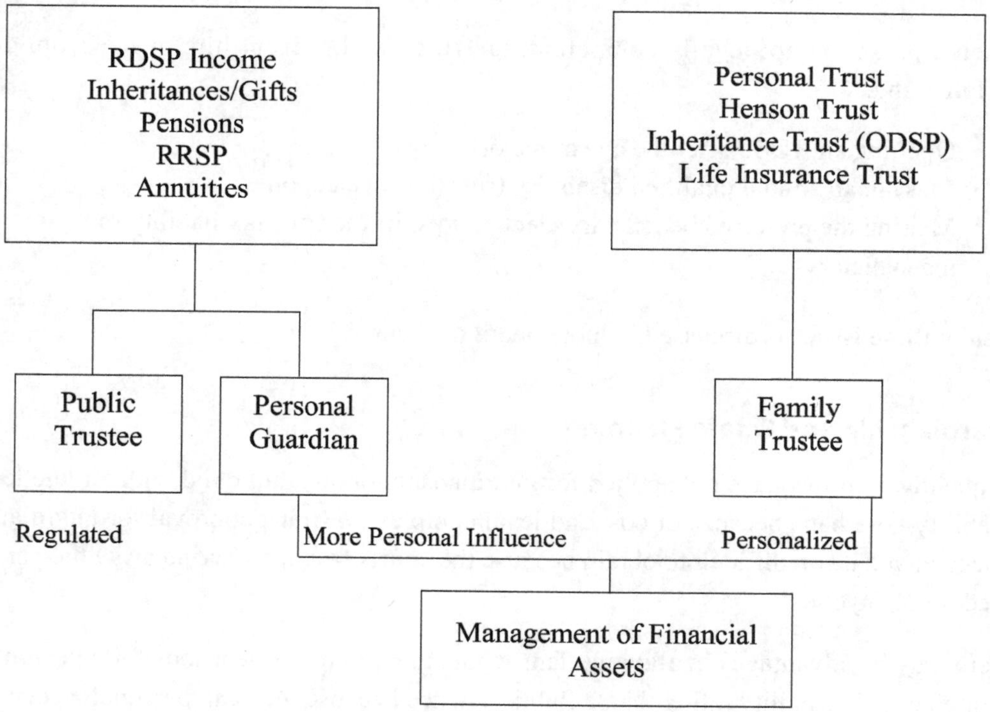

Families have less influence over decision-making if the Public Trustee is in charge. However, with a properly structured management plan, significant family input can happen through personal guardianship. The most financial flexibility is available through a family trust.

Treating Beneficiaries Differently

Sometimes under the terms of wills and trusts, there may be an unequal distribution of assets between beneficiaries. This may seem unfair, but it is the preference of the creator of the will or the trust.

The dilemma of how to distribute assets is becoming more common with the large amount of wealth being distributed by families. Parents should obtain legal advice if they think that any of their beneficiaries might object to a distribution. Even if it appears that a distribution cannot be successfully challenged, it is still a good idea to have a discussion with beneficiaries to inform them of what you intend to do and why.

When there is more than one discretionary beneficiary of an estate or trust, language of the document may allow executors or trustees the freedom to favour one beneficiary over others if that flexibility was intended. If the executor or the trustee can demonstrate the deceased's or settlor's actual intentions, then beneficiaries who feel the outcome is unfair will have less opportunity for a legal challenge. Keep your legal documents clear and unambiguous so your executors don't end up in court.

Provincial Social Assistance Constraints

As discussed, the Henson trust is a common element in estate planning in order to keep income and ownership of assets of a person with a disability within the social assistance exemption amounts. However, some provinces allow other exempt assets which broaden the financial options in estate planning. In Ontario, for example, a person under social assistance can own up to $100,000 in cash value of life insurance and the amount in an inheritance trust. If you combine the value of these assets with the general $40,000 asset exemption, a person with a disability could have $140,000 in exempt assets plus whatever is in a Henson trust or a RDSP. Proper planning will be needed to maximize these exemptions.

PART 2 – WILLS, PROBATE AND RELATED ISSUES

Practical Estate Planning

Some of the questions parents might ask themselves when making decisions about their estate are as follows.

- Who will receive my assets?

- When will they receive them?
- If trusts are involved, who gets the remaining assets after the needs of lifetime beneficiaries are met?
- Who will make the decisions based on directions in my will, trusts and any memorandum I might provide?
- Who will manage the money in my estate or trust and protect it from losses or poor administration?

These questions will take time to answer. As you move forward, you will likely want to re-visit the decisions of your wills, trusts and other legal agreements.

Figures 8.3 and 8.7 provide a practical will planning checklist for estate planning.

Figure 8.3   Estate Planning – Fifteen Practical Ideas

- Start the transfer of wealth now while you can still get some glory—a gift or trust for your grandkids' education or a significant gift to your favourite charity may be worth considering.
- Talk to your family about your will—start with one-on-one conversations and then move to a full family meeting.
- Complete your will while you are still able so no one can question your competence as they may do if you start to show signs of forgetfulness or uncertainty.
- Do what you can to save taxes but make sure taxes are always in second place behind your personal wishes.
- Look carefully at the influence that others have on you when making your decisions; this could later be perceived as undue influence on you by those who feel they were edged out in some way.
- Make sure your executors have the skills to act responsibly, perhaps with some checks and balances to resolve the tough issues when you aren't there to referee.
- Honour all of your legal obligations, including statutory ones, such as your obligations to adult dependents who you are still supporting.
- Trusts have major advantages both for tax planning and estate administration purposes—use them.
- Have lots of liquidity to meet your personal needs in retirement so you don't have to live below the poverty line. You may live longer than you think.
- Make the provisions of your will as detailed as possible to prevent arguments among your beneficiaries as to what you really intended.
- If you are able, compartmentalize bequests of specific assets to specific beneficiaries—this will make the job of your executors much easier.
- Make sure beneficiary designations outside your will (RRSP's, etc.) are consistent with the terms of your will.
- Know how income taxes will be applied to your estate assets so a misplaced tax liability does not destroy a bequest for a beneficiary.
- Make sure any bequest for individuals with disabilities has sufficient capital to meet their needs.

Estate Distributions

Figure 8.4 shows the many ways that property is distributed by an estate to its beneficiaries. Distributing property to or for a beneficiary with a disability by using trusts can be far more complicated than the distribution of assets outright to other beneficiaries. In the end, property not used by a beneficiary with a disability will likely pass to other family members or to charity.

Figure 8.4   Flow of Assets Under a Will

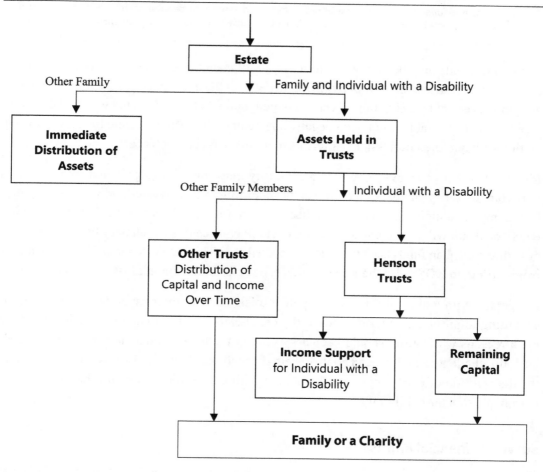

Capacity to Make a Will

The legal competence of an individual to sign a valid will is not based on statute law (as it is for power of attorney under the Substitute Decisions Act in Ontario). Rather, legal competence is based on long held principles of common law which have evolved over time. They are summarized in Figure 8.5.

Figure 8.5   Competency to Sign a Will

The person signing a will must be able to understand the following in order for the will to be valid.

- Understand the nature of the testamentary act—know that they are giving instruction on who their beneficiaries will be and what property they will receive.

- Understand who their legal relatives are and know how they might be affected by their inheritance.

- Understand their property—know what their estate consists of and its value in a broad general sense (bank accounts, real estate, investments, etc.)

- Must not suffer from a cognitive disorder that could result in a bequest to someone who would not ordinarily be a beneficiary had the individual had the capacity to make good judgements.

Some individuals may be competent to make a will even though they may have a cognitive disability that restricts them from living a conventional lifestyle. Having a cognitive limitation does, however, set up a situation in which challenges could be made to the will based on your loved one with a disability not being legally competent. It's worth investing time and working on this with qualified professional advisors to assess legal competence.

It's possible that your loved one with a disability may come into significant wealth so it is important that they can pass on their wealth according to their wishes and without disputes. For example, an individual with an intellectual disability who becomes the beneficiary of an RDSP on death will not be able to direct the RDSP balance to a beneficiary of their choice or even direct the plan funds back to the RDSP contributor. This may discourage family members from setting up RDSPs for their loved ones, especially if matrimonial issues are complex.

If a person with a disability is not competent to sign a will, their estate will be distributed according to provincial laws and not to the beneficiaries of their choice. This is one of the main reasons why family should keep assets out of the hands of dependents who are intellectually challenged and instead control them through family trusts. Family trusts still allow the distribution of trust income to the person with a disability to ensure that they have a reasonable standard of living.

Survivor Financial Rights

There is a large and varied amount of legislation across Canada that establishes financial rights relating to the property of a deceased person. These rights usually fall under one of these three categories.

- Dependent Relief Provisions
- Matrimonial Property Rules
- Pension Survivor Benefits

The impact of these rules should be a consideration in all estate planning.

Dependent Relief Provisions

The meaning of a "dependent" for dependent relief provision purposes in wills can vary from province to province. Perhaps surprisingly, in some provinces a family member doesn't even need to be a dependent to have property rights—just being a member of the family gives them these rights. Dependents for financial relief applications ordinarily include spouses, minor children, adult children, parents, siblings and common-law partners.

While it is sometimes assumed that an individual can include or exclude anyone he or she wishes from a will, this is not the case. Provinces and territories of Canada have dependent relief provisions that provide differing levels of fairness. The obligation to provide dependent relief can vary from an absolute right to a right based on dependency of a family member.

Survivor Pension Benefits

Private pension plan provisions usually include pension benefits for a plan member's child (or children) who has long-term disabilities and is dependent on the member for the necessities of life. The plan tends to require that the level of disability be severe and long-term.

Pension plan members should review their pension benefits under their pension plan to determine the conditions for eligibility of their dependent child with a disability for survivorship income.

Survivorship benefits are also available under the Canada Pension Plan providing certain criteria are met, including the years of contributions. If the surviving spouse has a child age 18 or over who had a disability since age 18, then the CPP survivor pension may be available.

Corporate Executors

Your will may be more complex than most because one of the beneficiaries is a loved one with a disability. Depending on the financial and tax skills of your personal executors, you may want to add a corporate executor. Issues to consider when using a corporate trustee are similar as discussed in Part 1 of Chapter 5 under the heading Corporate Trustees.

A Will Checklist

In addition to the technical issues you will need to deal with, there are some common sense, big picture things to keep in mind when creating a will. Figure 8.6 outlines a basic estate planning checklist that should be considered in any estate planning situation.

Figure 8.6 Estate Planning – A Will Checklist

- Make sure there are enough *liquid assets* or *insurance* in your estate to pay all taxes, fees, etc. on death and leave surviving dependents with adequate assets and income.
- *Review* wills regularly and *revise* when necessary.
- Decide how much you wish to leave to your children and at what stages it will be distributed.
- Consider ways to *minimize income taxes* on death.
- Make sure you deal with a family member who could claim for a share of your estate because of financial dependency or because of provincial law.
- Consider the use of *trusts to control and allocate assets and income* on a planned basis.
- Choose *executors* who understand your personal wishes and will carry them out as you wish.
- Make sure *proper beneficiary designations* are made in insurance policies, RRSPs, pensions and similar plans.
- Determine how your estate planning is impacted by the following.
  - Joint ownership of property
  - Family law
  - Marriage contract
  - Business contracts and agreements
  - Informal trusts
  - Beneficiary designations in insurance, pension and RRSPs
  - Joint ownership of property

These guidelines can be helpful in the drafting of any will, even if disability is not an issue.

PART 3 – TRUSTS IN ESTATE PLANNING

Trusts – Issues, Tax Benefits and Other Considerations

Trusts can be difficult to wrap your head around, but they are a valuable financial tool. Understanding that they are not legal entities is the first hurdle. Figure 8.7 provides an overview of trusts.

Figure 8.7   Trusts: An Overview

Documentation Issues

Pay attention to the legal formality of a trust. Do-it-yourself trusts are fraught with uncertainty.

The CRA is watching closely

The CRA will test the documentation of trusts and challenge their validity

Trustees tend to be ineffective at documenting their decisions

Tax Benefits

Property usually rolls out of trusts tax free for capital distributions and on wind up (except spousal trusts)

The tax on qualified disability trusts allows graduated rates

Trusts arising on death (QDTs) can hold a principal residence for certain beneficiaries with a disability

Trust assets distributed are not taxed as capital gains at the time of distribution, in most cases

Trusts avoid probate fees

Other Considerations

Use of trusts means that you will give up beneficial ownership to property but control legal ownership through the trustees

Terms of the trust can provide broad discretion to trustees to carry out your wishes

Trusts maintain secrecy of the document that is not available in a will which is a public document

Trusts aren't just for the wealthy anymore

The complexity of trusts comes from both the legalities surrounding them, but also from the myriad of tax rules that limit or expand their uses. You will need both legal and tax advice if you use trusts in your estate planning for your loved one.

Six Trusts For Estate Planning

Various types of trusts and their attributes were reviewed in chapter 5, parts 2 to 7. There are six kinds of trusts used to accomplish different objectives, as shown in Figure 5.5 on trusts. The trusts that are commonly used to support someone with a disability are as follows.

- Henson trust
- Principal residence trust
- Inheritance trust
- Lifetime benefit trust
- Life insurance trust
- Qualified disability trust

The tax benefits of these trusts (discussed in detail in chapter 5) can sometimes be combined in a single trust, making it unnecessary to have a separate trust for each need.

Qualified Disability Trusts

Until recently, an individual could have several testamentary trusts arising from their will which allowed several opportunities for graduated tax rates. This is no longer possible because only one qualified disability trust (QDT) is permitted for each person with a disability and other testamentary trusts do not qualify for graduated tax rates. To be eligible for a QDT, one or more of the trust beneficiaries must qualify for the disability tax credit (DTC).

The new rule that restricts family estate planning to a single QDT is unhelpful and unfair. For instance, the first family member to die who has included a QDT in his or her will for a loved one with a disability may not offer the best use of the one allowable QDT. A further problem to a QDT is that the loved one with a disability must be signatory to an annual election to be a QDT. But if that loved one is intellectually challenged and a guardianship does not exist, the benefits of a QDT will be lost. However, if guardianship exists, the guardian should be able to make the annual QDT election.

The Henson Trust

While some parents are willing to give modest amounts to their children during their lifetimes, many are reluctant to make significant transfers of wealth while they are alive. For parents who want to start the process of wealth transfer now but don't want to let go of significant funds while still living, there is a solution. An inter vivos Henson trust will give parents reasonable control and some ability to re-direct assets if things change. Another attraction of this trust is that families can reduce the value of their estates to avoid additional taxes upon death and to allow future growth in the value of transferred assets to benefit children. All of this also comes with significant flexibility when structured properly.

Since an inter vivos Henson trust structure is set up earlier in the life of a person with a disability than it is for others, it has a longer period of time to provide benefits to this person and his or her family. In addition to holding a portfolio of assets to provide income, an inter vivos trust might also own a home for the person with a disability (although the property will not qualify as a principal residence after 2016 under recent tax changes).

The key to this flexible structuring is the use of inter vivos trusts. Where disability is involved, the trust is most often a Henson trust, although other discretionary family trusts are also an option. The structure would look much the same for a testamentary trust through a will. Figure 8.8 shows a possible arrangement for either a testamentary or an inter vivos Henson trust.

Figure 8.8   Trust Funding Structure

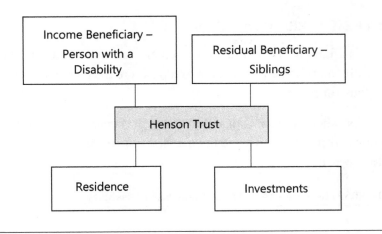

One of the significant advantages of including a Henson trust in your will rather than establishing it during your lifetime is that graduated tax rates will be allowed in a testamentary trust.

Who are the Final Trust Beneficiaries?

When assets are placed in a trust to support the income needs of a person with a disability, what happens to these assets when they are no longer needed and the trust is wound up? The trust terms in the will provide for this. The two obvious choices for remaining trust funds are as follows (see Figure 8.4).

- Assets are distributed to family members
- Assets are distributed to charity

The choice between the two types of distributions is entirely a personal one. Some families may want to give to charity in appreciation for the many benefits they received from the community. Others may want to pass residual assets of a trust to surviving family members.

PART 4 – PLAN TRANSFERS

Death of a RRSP or RRIF Plan Holder

RRSPs/RRIFs are used to accumulate retirement income. On death, the balances in such accounts usually must come into income except where the plan balances are transferred to a plan for a spouse or partner.

In certain cases, when a person with a disability is the beneficiary of an RRSP/RRIF or RESP, similar options are available to avoid tax and defer the income over the life of the individual owning the new plan.

Figure 8.9 RRSP / RRIF Transferred to an Adult with a Disability

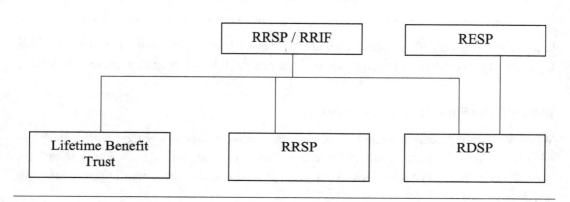

The RRSP/RRIF beneficiary must be a child or grandchild of the plan holder who is a dependent person, as discussed in chapter 7, part 2. In the case of a transfer to an RDSP, the RDSP holder must approve the transfer.

The problem with transfers to an RRSP held by the person with a disability is that RRSP pension income received could reduce social assistance. A transfer to an RDSP avoids this problem both for the funds held in an RDSP and the income received from an RDSP. Generally speaking, most people do not use lifetime benefit trusts, although perhaps they should. The consensus is that it's better to put any proceeds into an RDSP.

RRSP/RRIF and RESP Rollover to RDSP

An individual may decide to make a child or grandchild a beneficiary of an RRSP or an RRIF. The transfer to an RDSP can take place on a tax-free basis and the RDSP is an exempt asset for social assistance. The RDSP holder would have to authorize the contribution and the contribution must fit within the contribution limit of the RDSP. The contribution is not eligible for RDSP grants.

If an RDSP and a RESP share a common beneficiary, it is possible in certain situations to transfer RESP funds to an RDSP. The transfer is allowed based on either of two conditions.

- The beneficiary has an intellectual disability that prevents the individual from pursuing post-secondary education.
- The RESP plan has been in existence for more than thirty-five years.

The amount transferred will also be subject to the rules for RDSPs.

Lifetime Benefit Trust

The lifetime benefit trust is a vehicle that allows a tax-free transfer of proceeds of an RRSP/RRIF to a beneficiary with a disability. The recipient must be a child or grandchild of a deceased person and dependent for support on the deceased person because of a mental infirmity. Dependency means having taxable income of less than $19,475. Part 5 of chapter 5 discusses this in more detail.

Inheritance Trust

Sometimes family members will leave an inheritance to a family member with a disability without realizing that this could disqualify the individual from social assistance. In some provinces the individual is allowed to transfer a sum of this inheritance to an inheritance trust and the trust assets will be exempt under social assistance rules so that assistance can continue. Details about this and other uses of trusts are discussed in chapter 5.

Summing Up

Estate planning is highly personal and emotionally driven but also constrained by the need for fairness to all. This chapter gives the reader some guidelines on the possibilities and limitations of estate planning and how they can be resolved. In some cases, your wishes will be frustrated by legal roadblocks. Clear direction in legal documents is important because your executors will be charged with the responsibility of carrying out final wishes as they understand them.

In the end you must look to the advice from advisors who are familiar with the many issues of disability. Most importantly, find a lawyer who will help you draft your will and other related legal documents that will communicate your wishes as best you can.

CHAPTER 9

Charitable Giving –
A Winning Proposition

Making donations provides financial support for national and community organizations of your choice. At the same time, you will reduce your taxes with tax credits you will receive from making a charitable donation. And finally, your loved one with a disability may indirectly benefit from your generosity since your contributions help improve the services that they get from charities that provide them. Tax benefit from charitable giving comes from a generous non-refundable donation tax credit of just under 50% and sometimes from a tax exemption on the capital gain on a donated property.

At some point you will have fulfilled your financial need to support a loved one with a disability and there may still be funds available for making a donation—perhaps a significant amount. Since you have probably structured your financial planning to delay taxes to the last possible moment, there could be more taxes than normal at the time. Giving now or later through your estate presents significant tax saving opportunities. Donating to charity is a good way to say thank you for the benefits that may have been received by your family.

PART 1 – THE CASE FOR GIVING BACK

A Winning Proposition

There are two wins from charitable giving. First, donations give community organizations the resources to provide much needed services and to expand them as needs change. Secondly, there are several tax benefits that come with making a charitable donation such as non-refundable tax credits and exemption from tax on capital gains. Families and their loved ones have much to gain from charitable giving, not to mention the good feeling that comes from helping others.

Charitable giving can be done now or as part of your estate planning through your will. Contributing to capital campaigns gives you a tax credit now even though your charity of choice may only utilize the funds over several years.

How Will Your Gift be Used?

There is little doubt that a charity close to you has many ways to use the funds that you give. In general, funds will either be used to run their programs or to meet capital needs such as buying or maintaining equipment, buildings, or infrastructure costs. Some donors prefer that their donations not be used for operations but be used for long-term capital projects. In either case, a donation receipt will usually be issued to you for the total amount of the donation.

Tax Credits for Donations

Tax credits through making charitable donations are significant. Anyone planning to give a large donation to a registered charity should therefore seek out tax advice so tax credits can be fully utilized. As previously mentioned, charitable giving can happen while you are living or through your will on your death. The rules for giving through an estate are more complicated if you want your donation tax credits to match taxes payable at the time.

For each donation to a registered charity, a non-refundable tax credit is received. Taxpayers with higher incomes and paying a provincial surtax get an even higher credit. Since this tax credit can only be used to offset taxes payable, individuals will want to give their charitable donation in a year when their taxes are higher.

Our Canadian tax rules allow a five-year carryover of non-refundable donation tax credits, so this provides some added flexibility for those making large donations that might exceed their taxes payable in one year. Donations claimed cannot exceed 75% of income, so that is another restriction to keep in mind. In the year of death, your estate can claim up to 100% of income arising on death and can carry over unused credit to certain other years. In some cases, individuals make very large donations in their wills but due to poor planning the tax credits are not fully allowable. Donations of publicly traded securities and capital property (real estate) have some advantageous rules that will be discussed later.

Community Foundations

In many communities, foundations have been established to help donors tailor their giving to community needs. These foundations generally offer a number of plans to help families make a donation that can have a lasting impact in their communities. Community foundations also allow family members to have a say on an ongoing basis through capital donations and donor-advised funds. Some examples of community foundation plans are as follows.

Field of Interest Funds
- Enable donors to identify an area of interest to support (children, arts, entertainment, etc.)

Donor Advised Funds
- Allow donors to have ongoing participation in the selection of charities that will benefit from your gift

Designated Funds
- Allow donors the opportunity to specify the charitable organization they wish to support in perpetuity

Charitable Endowment Funds
- Allow for the establishment of a permanent endowment to provide a source of income to an organization so it can carry out its work

Flow-Through Funds
- Allow non-endowed gifts that are distributed on a short-term basis

One important advantage of community foundations is that, through them, you can direct part of a lump sum amount to a charity of your choice and change the charity of choice as you wish. You can even make an anonymous gift to charities through community foundations. Community foundations offer many of the benefits that were once only available to the very wealthy through private foundations.

What's the Value to You of a Donation?

The amount you receive as a tax credit for charitable donations will depend on your tax bracket and your province of residence. The rules are complicated, but Figure 9.1 below shows an approximation of the percentage of a charitable donation allowed as a tax credit based on income bracket.

Figure 9.1 Donation Tax Benefit Percent	
Income level $0-$200	25%
Income level $200 - $200,000	45%
Income level over $200,000	50%

Even though the tax credit for donations under $200 is smaller, the tax benefit of donations overall for most taxpayers is about half the amount given. I use the tax credit percentage of 45% for my examples in this and other chapters. Compare this to other non-refundable tax credits that are worth only about 20%, as discussed in chapter 6.

Current and Testamentary Gifts

Changes to the rules for donation-related tax credits over the years have created more opportunities and flexibility for tax payers to reduce or eliminate taxes. This chapter reviews gifts that can be made during your lifetime (current gift) and those that can be made at the time of death (testamentary gifts). Figure 9.2 depicts the kinds of gifts most likely to be given.

Figure 9.2   Current and Testamentary Gifts

Current Gifts	Testamentary Gifts
Cash	Life Insurance proceeds upon death
Capital property	Trust capital balances
Publicly listed securities	Residual Interest in property
Life Insurance cash value	RRSPs and RRIFs

In addition to making a gift now or upon death, individuals can donate different kinds of assets such as cash, real estate, art or publicly listed securities. Each type of asset offers different tax benefits.

Charitable Bequests

If your will provides for charitable bequests there is more flexibility in using these as tax credits. To begin, the 75% of net income limitation is increased to 100%. However, there are often significant gifts provided by a will which may mean that your bequests to charity exceed the net income limitation. Fortunately, there is some added flexibility. Gifts made through a will are deemed to be made when the gift is actually made to the charity, which is usually in the estate of the deceased and not on the individual's final tax return. However, the donation can be claimed on the estate tax return or on the last two years of the individual's personal tax returns. The gift can be made up to 60 months after the date of death.

Despite this flexibility, it may be difficult to use all of the charitable donation tax refunds upon death because of inadequate estate income, so careful planning is needed.

PART 2 – CURRENT GIFT GIVING

Donating Cash

There is nothing complicated about giving cash. When you send in your $100 donation, you get $45 back as a tax credit. Put another way, when you want to make a $100 donation, it only costs you $55 because the government will give a $45 tax refund. That's what makes charitable giving such a good deal—the government almost matches your contribution. In the sections that follow, the book discusses how you can make your donation go even further.

Donating Capital Property

When donated to a charity, capital property receives a number of tax benefits, depending on the type of property. Capital property is property that would show as a capital gain on your tax return if you sold it. This is different from other property where the capital is fully taxed. Property that you buy and sell quickly at a profit (speculation) is not capital property, and the capital property gift rules do not apply.

Another tax advantage of a gift of capital property to a registered charity is that you can elect a value of the property for the donation amount and the proceeds. Essentially, the elected amount must be between the fair market value of the property and its cost. A low elected amount would lower your capital gain but would also lower the amount of the donation. You should do some calculations to determine the optimum elected amount.

Donating Publicly Listed Securities and Other Assets

Donating certain securities to a charity will provide you with even greater benefits than donating most other kinds of property. When you donate publicly traded funds, mutual funds and segregated funds, you receive a charitable donation receipt for the full fair market value, but none of the capital gain is included in your income. Such gifts at the time of death must be made by a graduated rate estate to receive this benefit. Form T1170 must be filed with the personal or estate tax return. It is usually much better for the donor to donate the securities themselves than it is to sell them and then donate the after tax proceeds.

Donating Life Insurance - Cash Value

Sometimes an insurance policy has no use to you in your estate planning. If you wish, you can give the policy to charity. You will receive a charitable donation receipt for its cash surrender value plus any accumulated dividends or interest less any loans against the policy. However, if the value of the policy exceeds the cost, you will have to declare the income on your tax return.

After you donate the policy you will receive a donation receipt for any premiums you pay to keep the policy in force for the charity.

PART 3 - DONATING WHAT'S LEFT OVER

GOLD MEDAL STORY - Breaking New Ground On Children's Rehabilitation

The following story appeared in the Globe and Mail on August 31, 2013.

About ten years ago, business-woman Robynne Anderson became involved with a local charity near her home in Winnipeg called the Rehabilitation Centre for Children. The Centre provides a variety of services for children with disabilities and special needs, but like many organizations offering similar care, resources were spread across the city.

For years, the Rehabilitation Centre and other agencies tried to find a place where many of these services could be provided in one location, sparing families the ordeal of travelling to more than a dozen places.

Ms. Anderson shared that vision. So when she sold her business, an agricultural publication, a few years ago, she donated $10,000 to help make it happen. That gift helped kick-start a campaign that has finally culminated in the construction of a building that will soon house 14 separate agencies, including one for children's rehab.

The Manitoba government is contributing $17-million to the project, known as Specialized Services for Children and Youth, and the centre is raising another $5 million through donations. The building is expected to be completed in 2015 and will be able to accommodate 30,000 visits annually.

Ms. Anderson, who now runs another agriculture-related business called Emerging Ag, has recently given a second gift of $10,000. "When you consider the challenges that the kids face every day and that their parents face every day, the least we can do as agencies trying to assist them is overcome our challenges in terms of the structure of how we work," she said. The centre "will be a great, great gift."

Life Insurance Proceeds

If you have an insurance policy on your life at the time of your death, you might consider leaving the proceeds to a charity. If you do, your estate will receive a tax credit equal to the policy amount.

Often taxes are payable on the capital gain on property realized at the time of death. A tax credit from donated insurance is often structured to help pay the taxes on other assets.

What's Left in a Henson Trust?

A Henson trust is commonly set up to preserve social assistance. Since it's impossible to assess how much money will be needed for that purpose, there may well be a surplus when the trust is no longer required to support your loved one's cost of living. What does the trust do with the remaining funds? The two most common choices for dealing with left over funds are to give the amount to either family members or to a charity.

If the charitable route is chosen, planning should be done in advance to determine which charities will receive funds and for what amount. Also, you will need to pay attention to the donation amount so the tax credit can be used by the trust.

Residual Interest in Property

A bequest of residual interest in a home is an opportunity sometimes overlooked. The bequest has the condition that your loved one with a disability can occupy the property during his or her lifetime. For tax purposes, the donation amount would be calculated as the present value of the future gift. In such an arrangement, provisions would have to be made as to how the annual operating costs of the home would be paid.

RRSPs and RRIFs

There are numerous ways to deal with RRSP/RRIF balances at the time of your death. They have been reviewed in more detail in other chapters. For instance, you may want to leave these proceeds

- to an RDSP for a child or grandchild; or
- to a lifetime benefit trust for a child or grandchild.

A third option is to leave the RRSP/RRIF proceeds to a charity. You will be taxed on the RRSP/RRIF balance in your estate, probably at a high tax rate, so the gift tax credit will reduce or eliminate this tax.

Summing Up

This chapter has provided an overview of gift giving to a registered charity. If you wish to proceed with this kind of planning and your gift will be significant, you should seek tax advice well in advance.

Many people with disabilities have no family and friends to help them out. If you can help sponsor the acquisition of assisted housing, financially support a local service provider or give money to a charity, your gifts will improve the lives of some individuals for years to come.

CHAPTER 10

Seniors – Plan Ahead to Stay Ahead

As we age, we will face challenging health issues at some point. These issues sometimes happen slowly, and sometimes come without warning. Unfortunately, you never know when your health might decline, so advanced financial planning is important. This chapter concentrates on financial risks to seniors.

Sometimes family members go too far in imposing their views on the financial decisions of parents and older family members. There is an increasing amount of litigation that proves this. To what degree should family members try to influence elderly parents in making important life choices?

Seniors should start planning their financial future well in advance of old age and declining health. This will take away the uncertainty about their legal competence. The day will come for each of us when we have declining abilities and can no longer make good decisions. Until then, seniors should make their own choices as much as possible. As this chapter will show, legal advice in drafting wills, powers of attorney and other documents is extremely important.

PART 1 – AGING CAN INFLUENCE FINANCIAL OUTCOMES

Financial Planning For Seniors

This chapter deals with the issues of protecting the property of seniors from too much family influence. The following issues are beyond the scope of this chapter.

- Budgeting for retirement
- Preparing wills, powers of attorney and other documents
- Understanding proper organization of personal finances

- Drawing up a personal budget
- Insurance needs
- Changing lifestyle in a healthy and happy way

Financial Care For Your Aging Parent, written by Lise Andreana and published by Self-Counsel Press, is a highly recommended book that can help seniors in many of these areas.

The Wisdom that Comes with Age

Linda Hazlett, a wise friend, shared with me her thoughts on growing old.

> *"Age makes us all vulnerable even though we have reasonable mental capacity. The only solution is having a clear cut plan laid out in advance in anticipation of encroaching vulnerability. Even if we know exactly what is going on ... we may lose the desire to look after ourselves.*
>
> *Everyone should reflect their own will in their will ... some think they can control everyone this way when they are gone ... some hold favouritism of one form or another ... and some, like me, think it is a chance to repair and heal old issues of sibling rivalry and perceived favouritism ... but ... it is a last impression we leave to the living and we have the right to do it according to our own likes.*
>
> *Be happy ... enjoy life ... and look to ourselves first ... the people we can't count on are sometimes the people we love and we should still love them but ... not be blind to their human frailties."*

Risk Changes in Retirement

When you fast forward to retirement years, your investment motives changes. In your working years, your investments are directed towards growing your capital by taking on some level of risk. When you retire, your investments are there to provide you with income for the rest of your life. In retirement, there is little, if any, ability to recover your capital if it is depleted by risky investment decisions. Inflation also depletes capital over time. The two approaches to investing during your working years compared to your retirement years are shown in Figure 10.1.

Figure 10.1 Investing Changes in Retirement

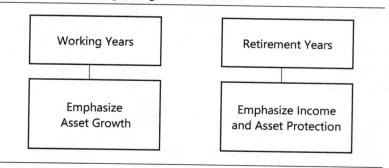

You might expect a return of 8% to 10% on your portfolio or RRSP investments as you accumulate capital in your working years. In retirement this will probably drop to around 5% to 6%, and maybe less. That's just the reality of low risk investing. It seems simple, but the shift in the way you manage your new normal can be hard to adjust to—especially if advisors are pushing you in the other direction. If this is the case, you should ask your advisor to change the dial and give you a new investment policy statement—one that emphasizes secure income and asset protection.

The Scarcity of Funds

It's not a foregone conclusion that parents will have a significant amount of money in their retirement. Some do, but many do not. Family members should not assume that parents have the flexibility to share their savings.

Costs in retirement shift away from paying for a mortgage and the costs of children's education. Here are some of the new costs that are likely to increase when you retire.

- Health care
- Retirement home costs
- Attendant care

Attendant care and long-term care costs tend to be the biggest expenses. Your savings can be depleted by the cost of retirement home accommodation and uninsured medical costs. Planning should be done in advance for this new paradigm.

Time to Recover Is Short

After you retire there is little time to recover from significant financial losses. Therefore, your saving habits need to change and the emphasis should move from growth of capital to preservation of capital. That means that your portfolio allocation must also change. You should be holding more cash and fixed income securities and fewer stocks and other equities.

Pensions and annuities will also maximize security but provide income. Your planning can be improved by allocating your retirement assets into these three pots.

- Assets to guarantee retirement income
- Assets to supplement income and support capital needs
- Assets for spending or giving away to family or charity

Put another way, retirement assets fall into three different pots.

- Guaranteed Income Pot (income certainty)
- Capital Preservation Pot (capital preservation with modest income)
- Investment/Legacy Pot (growth assets with some risk)

The guaranteed income pot should be made up of assets that you know will generate income for the rest of your life. The only assets that should be in this pot are pensions (private and government), annuities and possibly short-term money market funds. Hopefully they can also provide some inflation protection, but if not, your capital is still secure.

The capital preservation pot consists of assets with secure capital but still modest income. This pot might contain such investments as segregated funds, laddered GICs or high quality corporate or government bonds.

The last pot of savings is the investment/legacy pot that you use to invest in the equity market to a higher degree. Hopefully it will show some growth and may even support the need for extra income. There is always some chance of loss so the portfolio should be conservative. Investments in this pot should be blue chip investment grade to keep risk low.

Family Financial Advice

When parents get older, there may be a tendency to give up control of their finances to their children. This is an area where parents should act carefully. They should get a money manager on board with some strict investment guidelines such as preserving capital rather than trying to grow it. It is difficult to overrule well-intentioned family members who may not be as skilled as they think.

Borrowing Money from the Bank of Mom and Dad

The difficulty with transferring money to children is that they might not understand what is expected of them in terms of paying it back. You too may have left this unclear. Documentation of family money transfers is important.

Parents should decide on terms they can live with that are also fair to others in the family and are not a major financial imposition on themselves. It's sometimes not the money that matters, but the uncertainty that it creates. Parents should prepare documents with terms that everyone can live with and should never lend more than they can lose without impairing their own financial well-being.

Family money transfers should be well-documented to avoid confusion and problems in the future. Was it a loan or a gift? When do mom or dad want to be repaid? What happens to the loan on death—does it come out of the borrower's share of assets or is it forgiven? Does it affect the distribution of assets among family members on death? All of this needs to be made clear in written documents supported by legal advice.

The Family Cottage

Family loans are difficult, but they pale in comparison to the complexity of who in the family gets the family cottage and how this works out financially for everyone. Who will bear the costs of maintaining the cottage—taxes, insurance and repairs? Such costs can put a real strain on retirement income of parents, yet it's surprising when adult children don't share these costs even though they continue to use the cottage.

Parents hope that all of their kids will be fair-minded and willing to work out a plan as to how to share the family cottage and who contributes to the expenses. Nevertheless, you should be prepared to have family discussions to work out a plan. More than likely, you will need professional tax and legal advice to complete the legal documentation needed.

A cottage set aside for one of the children may cause a huge imbalance in estate assets because it is such a material part of an estate. If the cottage is left to one or more children through a will, there may need to be a condition that the child receiving the cottage will make a cash payment to other children to balance out the benefits received by all. And then of course, parents may have to pay tax on the cottage appreciation on death, depending whether or not they can elect it to be their principal residence.

PART 2 – CAPACITY AND UNDUE INFLUENCE

It's a Complex World For Seniors

As you get older your ability to make clear decisions may start to diminish. Even so, seniors do what they can to safeguard their finances from their own mistakes and sometimes from the influence of others.

Figure 10.2 shows some of the threats to seniors with respect to their decision-making.

Figure 10.2 Seniors and Decision-Making

- Clear thinking diminishes as they age
- Inability to use modern communication tools
- Increased complexity of laws
- Increased isolation from family
- Privacy rules that inhibit communication

The complexity of today's world can leave seniors behind and out of touch. Family members can help alleviate this stress by assisting them in navigating through today's technical window.

Seniors – Age Reduces Capacity

It is a difficult world today for seniors. New threats exist that were not part of the simple life of the past. Some may feel that these threats are overblown and do not apply to them, but they shouldn't be so sure—the courts say otherwise.

Figure 10.3 depicts depleting capacity over time.

Figure 10.3 Age Reduces Personal Capacity

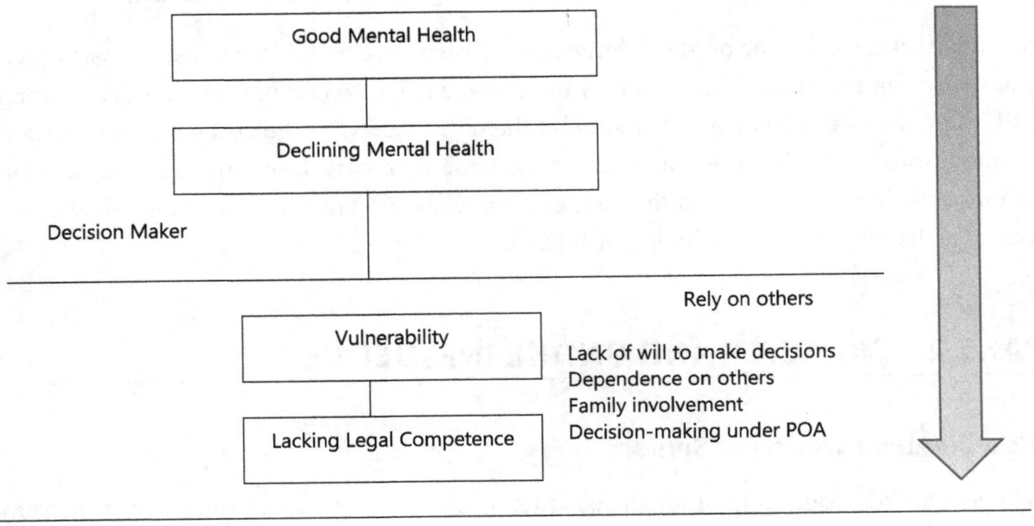

Good Mental Health

Declining Mental Health

Decision Maker

Vulnerability

Lacking Legal Competence

Rely on others

Lack of will to make decisions
Dependence on others
Family involvement
Decision-making under POA

Capacity Tests Can Be Different

In general, our laws say that an individual is capable of making legal decisions until there is evidence to the contrary. There isn't a single definition of capacity. There are different rules defining capacity in different situations. Here are some example areas where knowing the applicable capacity definition is important.

- Contracts
- Selling property
- Making or revoking a will
- Granting power of attorney and revoking it
- Managing property
- Personal care decisions
- Making a gift
- Creating a trust

The legal capacity to make and document decisions is complicated. There is no ordering of tests for capacity as one might think; instead, capacity depends on the particular transaction. In general, a person must understand what they are doing and the outcomes and future consequences of their actions.

Finally, the ability to show capacity has three different influencers.

- **The Decision** - your understanding of what it is you are agreeing to
- **The Time** - your ability to make decisions at the time
- **The Situation** - whether you are comfortable making a decision where you are situated at the time

A person with an intellectual disability may not be able to function on their own but they may still be able to comprehend what a transaction is about and its implications; therefore, this person may have legal capacity. Proper testing by a qualified person is important in order to avoid doubt about the legality of documents some years later. There are various tests of capacity depending on the transaction you are contemplating, as shown in Figure 10.4.

Figure 10.4 Capacity Test Criteria

Contract

Understand the contract

Understand the contract effect

Make a Gift

Understand the nature of the gift

Understand the effect of the gift

Intention to make a gift

Make or Revoke a Will

Understand the nature and effect of making a will

Understand the extent of the property involved

Understand the possible claims of persons that would normally expect to benefit from the will

Create a Trust

Understand the nature of the trust

Understand the trust's effects under the circumstances

Undertake Real Estate Transactions

Understand the nature of the contract

Understand the contract's specific effects

Testamentary capacity is likely required for a gift

Seniors can show early decline in their thought processes. For example, individuals showing early signs of dementia may have days when they are confused and out of touch. Because legal competency is time and place specific, a person with dementia may be able to make legally binding decisions on their good days in the right surroundings. At other times when their thinking is not as clear, this may completely prevent them from making legally binding decisions.

Legal capacity should not be confused with impairments due to cognitive lapses. Also, an individual with adaptive challenges as opposed to intellectual challenges may still be able to make legally binding decisions.

Vulnerability

Although an individual may have legal capacity, they may still be vulnerable in making well thought out decisions as they age simply because they want to avoid conflict. The symptoms of such vulnerability are listed in Figure 10.5.

Figure 10.5 Symptoms of Vulnerability

• Making Poor Decisions	✓
• Financial irresponsibility	✓
• Not wanting to face issues	✓
• Easily taken advantage of	✓
• Financial planning is not structured	✓
• Life plan is difficult to work out	✓
• Communicating poorly	✓
• Fighting back or refusing to act	✓
• Making decisions that are inconsistent with past decisions	✓

Vulnerability is an area giving rise to family disputes and even litigation. Seniors should document as many decisions as possible early in life before vulnerability becomes an issue.

Signs of Undue Influence

Undue influence is defined as dominating the will of someone through manipulation, coercion or the subtle use of power. The main signs of undue influence developed through the courts are as follows.

- Increasing isolation
- Substantial gifts and property transfers
- Inability to provide an explanation for large transfers
- Turnover in advisors
- Material change in terms of a will or power of attorney
- Family wanting to attend advisor meetings
- Parents being overly anxious
- New relationships or material changes in previous relationships

Family members should be vigilant and protect parents and other loved ones from financial manipulation.

Financial Literacy and Risk

Technology has changed the way we communicate and access information, making life increasingly difficult for the elderly. Unfortunately, dishonesty against seniors is becoming more prevalent. Seniors may be at risk of abuse simply because they see themselves as having greater financial competence than they actually do.

Four risk factors relating to undue influence are as follows.

- Substantial savings or assets
- Limited contact with family
- High sense of trust
- Declining health

Seniors should act prudently, get independent advice and put a financial records system in place with good checks and balances. Financial institutions and even law enforcement are increasingly aware of signs of elder abuse and some have even established special resources to deal with this.

PART 3 – DOCUMENTATION AND THE BLURRING OF PROPERTY OWNERSHIP

Did You Mean to Give Up Ownership?

Seniors can experience pressure from family members or even from advisors to register their assets into joint ownership with a family member. The most common reason given is to save on probate fees. However, in the grand scheme of things, probate fees are relatively small, so the decision is rarely well-founded given the modest cost of probate relative to total assets.

Four adverse effects you should consider before changing property ownership from sole to joint ownership are as follows.

- Unless there is documentation to the contrary, you may be giving up ownership of half of your property.
- For tax purposes, when you transfer ownership of property to someone other than your spouse, you will have a deemed sale at fair market value. That means that you must report any capital gain as income. Furthermore, losses on such transfers are not likely deductible in family transactions.
- The new co-owner of the property may squander the asset, use it as security for a debt, or in some other way diminish the value of the property to the transferor.
- The new co-owner could expose the property to claims from his or her spouse in the event of marriage breakdown.

Finally, on death, your interest in the jointly held property would normally pass to the survivor, absent evidence to the contrary. This may mean that a provision in your will with respect to the property cannot be enforced.

In summary, the concerns about joint ownership could result in the following unintended consequences:

- assets being exposed to new creditors;
- failure to avoid probate;
- adverse tax implications;
- frustration of the terms of the will;
- disputes resulting from poor documentation as to intention; and/or
- court challenges.

These are significant downsides that overshadow the small cost savings through joint ownership registration.

Financial Power Of Attorney

A power of attorney (POA) is a more powerful document than most realize. Too often, individuals sign it without realizing they are turning over control of their assets with very few safeguards. Figure 10.6 outlines important facts you should know about your financial POA.

Figure 10.6 Power of Attorney Checklist

- the POA can be revoked
- you have knowledge of the assets covered by the POA
- you know your obligations to your dependents
- the attorney must give an accounting
- property could decline in value with poor management
- your attorney could misuse funds

Issues relating to having more than one power of attorney

- You may want to have a power of attorney for different asset classes or if assets are located in different jurisdictions
- Bank power of attorney can be separate
- Be careful not to cancel existing powers of attorney when creating new ones
- Multiple POAs are difficult to structure
- Bank must accept your POA—work with them if they refuse

Trusts Can Replace Wills

Sometimes the privacy of your will may concern you because it will be a public document after you die. One way to avoid public disclosure of your will when you die is to transfer your assets to a trust while you are living. The terms of the trust rather than the terms of your will dictate the distribution of its assets. There should be symmetry between the terms of the two documents in regards to your total estate distribution.

PART 4 – PROFESSIONAL ADVISORS

Advisors Should Be Holistic

If you meet with a financial advisor, it's important that you understand each other. Sometimes this is difficult if good communication falls by the wayside. Advisors need to be qualified in their area of expertise and should stay within their area of specialty. Financial advisors should not offer legal advice and lawyers should not offer investment advice and so on.

Independent Advice

Sometimes there is an inclination for family members to insert themselves directly into parents' decision-making. For example, family members may wish to attend their parents' meeting with a lawyer. Professional advisors should be vigilant about this. Lawyers, accountants and investment advisors should listen to their clients and less to children or other family members trying to influence decisions.

Professionals are aware that it is part of their duty to watch for undue influence. Such influence may be occurring if a professional notices certain things.

- the family directs the conversation;
- plans have already been decided before the first meeting;
- the client easily agrees without showing any indication of putting forth their own thought; or
- the client has dismissed their longtime advisor.

Choosing a Suitable Money Manager

It is difficult for many of us to find a money manager who understands our needs and is able to meet them. When seeking out an advisor, seniors should look for someone who

- appreciates a portfolio design that has a shorter time horizon;
- understands the need to maintain income and not risk a loss of capital;
- sells financial products relevant to their needs;

- is willing to redirect sales of financial products to others if they don't offer these products; and
- has a level of advisor expertise that matches the level of client complexity.

Fiduciary Obligations of Advisors

Advisors have a fiduciary responsibility to their client. This means that their client's interests must rank ahead of their advisor's interests. Consequently, advisors should avoid directing their client to financial products and services they sell which may not be in their client's best interest.

Summing Up

It is difficult for seniors to navigate today's legal system and make fair decisions for everyone in the family. Aging can diminish the legal capacity of seniors so that they are no longer allowed to change or initiate legal documents such as wills and powers of attorney. Even though family input is important, it should not unduly influence mom and dad. Valid documentation of family decisions is important along with legal advice. Financial security for seniors is about several things—capacity, independent decision-making, documentation and competent and independent advice.

CHAPTER 11

Financial Planning and Investing – Some Guiding Principles

Considering the long-term finances of a person with a disability raises a number of important questions. How much do you want to participate in their lives? How much do they want you to participate? Is what you are proposing fair to others in the family? Financial plans are complex and this book can't give you a course on that, but it can make you aware of the issues involved and some possible solutions. You will need to develop a well-structured financial plan which goes beyond numbers on a spreadsheet.

Planning for the income needs for a loved one with a disability for years beyond your lifetime is akin to planning your own income needs in retirement. For people with disabilities, income is less plentiful and tends to come from sources other than employment, personal investments and pension plans.

Over time, a family must develop an understanding of what lies ahead. Not only does this involve a plan for the accumulation of long-term savings for the future, but families also need to structure complementary income sources from those savings. Financial planning for an individual with a disability is difficult because it encompasses complex rules relating to social assistance, taxation, trusts and laws that relate to dependency, competency, guardianship and other legal issues.

PART 1 – FINANCIAL PLANNING

What's in a Financial Plan?

A financial plan should be a working document that articulates financial decisions based on an assessment of a family's financial circumstances, priorities and stated objectives. This plan is the road map that helps families and their loved one with a disability reach their financial destination. It ensures financial security when you are no longer around.

Financial plans should define family financial objectives with regard to the family member with a disability. These objectives include

- meeting lifestyle needs and expectations;
- protecting and growing capital;
- managing taxes effectively;
- guarding against the unexpected; and
- having income every year.

Based on this list, it's obvious that a financial plan goes well beyond cash flow and net worth projections. A good plan is necessary to have strong personal ingredients tailored to the specific needs of a person with a disability.

A good plan should meet the needs of the individual in a very personal way. Goals and priorities must be defined for the current situation and identify recommendations for change. Financial plans themselves have both strengths and weaknesses and therefore trade-offs may need to be found between financial goals and the ability to meet them with available resources. The plan must also meet the comfort level of family members in terms of financial sharing or it should be discarded and re-worked until everyone is satisfied.

A Personal Financial Check-up

Figure 1.10 in chapter 1 provides the ten key ingredients for building your financial plan. In addition, our website, www.thefamilyguide.ca, provides a detailed questionnaire (Disability – Financial and Life Plan Questionnaire) to get you started with your financial check-up.

Budgeting for the Future

It's important to know the ins and outs of personal finances as they relate to a person in the family with a disability as well as to the entire family. Before getting into the details, however, families should give more thought to the long-term. The following questions need to be answered before starting an assessment of financial needs.

- What are the income sources?

- What is the expected annual cost of living for the person with a disability after all forms of known financial assistance are determined?
- How long will these expenses continue and will they change throughout the stages of life? (See Disability - Financial and Life Plan Questionnaire on our website at www.thefamilyguide.ca).
- How much capital should be accumulated to take care of expenses after current providers will no longer be paying for day-to-day support?
- Have the right investments been purchased to assure that funds will be there to guarantee future income needs from accumulated capital?

Many families are setting aside significant savings to pay for future expenses but have no idea how much money is really needed. They should get professional advice on this. One-off advice on RDSPs, Henson trusts or social assistance income is helpful but doesn't provide an answer on how each fits into the total picture.

The budgeting process should first set out possible income and the cost of living. For example, possible income would usually include social assistance, tax credits and pension benefits (OAS, CPP and GIS) arising later in life. Income might also include amounts to be received as survivor pensions and amounts from trusts that you may set up (Henson, Inheritance and Lifetime Benefit trusts). Cost of living expenses include basic cost of living, housing and possible attendant care.

Once you have done this, you should incorporate it into a financial projection including a cost of living adjustment. Our website, www.thefamilyguide.ca, provides a basic proforma to get you started.

Typically, family support comes to an end when parents near retirement. Plans need to be made to replace direct family support with income from accumulated savings.

Unfortunately, many people invest in an RDSP or set up a Henson trust without considering the amount of funds that will actually be needed. For example, individuals with a physical disability may be financially secure. They may own a home, be employed and can pass on an inheritance to their families. For others with significant intellectual disabilities none of this may be possible and more financial support from family will be required. All of this should be considered and verified with written budget projections.

Timing is important when it comes to matching expenses with income. Expenses are perhaps easier to predict than incomes, except possibly for significant costs with respect to health and personal care that may appear unexpectedly.

The projection of incomes listed below is much less certain with respect to amounts, timing and even expectation. It will be important to understand possible income that may occur before you prepare a lifetime budget for your loved one.

Pensions

- Old age security
- Canada pension
- Canada pension survivor pension
- Private pension survivor pension
- Guaranteed income supplement
- RDSP – LDAPS

Trusts

- Henson trust
- Inheritance trust
- Lifetime benefit trust
- Life insurance trust

Other

- Family and government
- Tax credits
- Inheritances
- Community support
- Gifts
- RDSP – DAPS
- Social assistance income and benefits

Reaching Out for Financial Advice

Most of us know when we should reach out for financial advice but sometimes there are barriers to doing this. Financial services are confusing and there are silos everywhere (legal, financial, taxation) that don't all connect. One of the purposes of this book is to help readers understand the relationships amongst various sources of financial assistance.

Disability usually requires a team of advisors because there are many overlapping areas to cover such as maintaining social assistance, minimizing taxes, and dealing with issues that arise when assets move from the person with a disability to other family members.

Lifetime Financial Needs

The costs of relating the support of a loved one with a disability are as follows.

- Housing – with family, independently or assisted living
- Personal expenses
- Attendant Care
- Medical Expenses
- Therapies and Training
- Travel

Funding the lifelong finances of a person with a disability is a big undertaking. It requires a plan not only to manage day-to-day finances but also to keep on top of the long-term issues. Then, of course, the structures must endure into the future.

Financial Concerns Unique to People with Disabilities

Planning for a person with disabilities is different than long-term financial planning for others in the family. The financial future of an individual with a disability cannot be left to chance. Here is a list of questions to consider.

- Is there enough money to last the lifetime of the individual with a disability?
- If funds are insufficient, should insurance be purchased? If so, how much?
- How do we maximize the benefits of an RDSP instead of investing the funds?
- Is cash flow arranged so that social assistance is maximized?
- Are we taking advantage of all tax credits and other incentives?
- Are pension benefits available?
- Are there appropriate discretionary structures in place to meet unexpected changes in the financial requirements of the individual?
- Are the supporting documents such as wills and trusts up to date and compatible with the financial plan?
- Have we dealt fairly with siblings and other members of the family?
- Have we had a family conversation to get buy-in from everyone?

It will take most families some time to process these financial issues and seek out advice from advisors experienced with disability.

Phasing in Family Support

Individuals with disabilities who are not capable of earning significant amounts of income or perhaps no income at all obviously need financial help to survive. Government does provide basic support which is below the poverty level. Obviously, family must be involved to raise living standards to a more acceptable level. This is done in three ways.

Family Income Support
- Direct money support for day-to-day living

Family Capital Support
- Money support in future years through investments and savings plans put in place by family, including contributions to registered plans such as RDSPs
- Bequests and life insurance proceeds which can be invested and paid out as income over time to support the cost of living of your loved one, usually through a Henson trust

Registered Plan Transfers
- On death, the Income Tax Act allows generous tax-free transfers from your RRSPs, pension plans and RESP plans to other plans for a person with a disability

Capital Needs – A Snapshot

It is important to know how much capital will be required to fund the expenses of a loved one with a disability over many years. Figure 11.1 is designed to give you a snapshot of approximate needed savings.

To illustrate, let's assume you will need $10,000 a year (in today's dollars) in 10 years for 20 years. The chart assumes inflation going up by 2.5% a year and a 3% return after tax. Figure 11.1 shows that you will need to have $241,920 of capital in ten years.

Assuming that there are other siblings in the family that will also benefit from your estate in a fair and equitable way, you might choose to purchase life insurance to fund the needed capital of about $250,000 ten years from now. If the life expectancy of your loved one is longer, then you would increase the insurance coverage accordingly. Part 3 of this chapter comments on the use of life insurance to fund disability.

Figure 11.1 Estimating the Capital Needs of Life Funding

YEARS TO FUNDING START	INFLATION ADJUSTED PAYMENT	CAPITAL SUM REQUIRED TO MAKE PAYMENTS FOR YEARS INDICATED				
		10	15	20	25	30
NOW	1,000	9,700	14,300	18,900	23,300	27,600
10	1,280	12,416	18,304	24,192	29,824	35,328
20	1,638	15,889	23,423	30,958	38,165	45,209
30	2,097	20,341	29,987	39,633	48,860	57,877
40	2,685	26,045	38,396	50,747	62,561	74,106
NOW	3,000	29,100	42,900	56,700	69,900	82,800
10	3,840	37,248	54,912	72,576	89,472	105,984
20	4,914	47,666	70,270	92,875	114,496	135,626
30	6,291	61,023	89,961	118,900	146,580	173,632
40	8,055	78,134	115,187	152,240	187,682	222,318
NOW	5,000	48,500	71,500	94,500	116,500	138,000
10	6,400	62,080	91,520	120,960	149,120	176,640
20	8,190	79,443	117,117	154,791	190,827	226,044
30	10,485	101,705	149,936	198,167	244,301	289,386
40	13,425	130,223	191,978	253,733	312,803	370,530
NOW	10,000	97,000	143,000	189,000	233,000	276,000
10	12,800	124,160	183,040	241,920	298,240	353,280
20	16,380	158,886	234,234	309,582	381,654	452,088
30	20,970	203,409	299,871	396,333	488,601	578,772
40	26,850	260,445	383,955	507,465	625,605	741,060

There could, of course, be a need for more funds for significant periodic costs such as equipment or other property. The required amounts will be less if the rate of return is higher than the conservative 3% used in the calculations, but the estimates are intentionally conservative.

The degree to which you financially support your loved one with a disability will depend on three things:

- the degree to which you wish to or are able to enhance the lifestyle of the individual;
- the period of time that funds are required based on life expectancy of the individual; and
- the degree to which the individual will be financially supported by government and other outside sources.

If the individual requires extensive personal care, the need for funds from family may be minimal since the individual may live in assisted living largely paid for by government. If, on the other hand, the disability allows the individual to have a more conventional lifestyle, then there may be a need for enhanced funding. Others with disabilities who are partly independent can often function largely on their own with the help of community services.

Structuring Financial Support and Asset Ownership

Structuring the finances of an individual with a disability is a tricky job. Finances are often not coordinated even after Henson trusts, social assistance and an RDSP have all been put in place. The missing ingredient is a financial plan that takes into consideration the financial tools being used and how they all fit together.

Individuals with an intellectual disability are unlikely to be able to own property, make a will or control their finances. Therefore, ownership of the assets usually must vest in a trust or in someone else. If possible, ownership should also be structured so that the assets eventually pass to other family members as tax efficiently as possible when no longer needed.

Figure 11.2 shows where a family member with a disability fits into the support picture. Perhaps they qualify for social assistance, perhaps they don't. Perhaps they can own property or maybe not. Figure 11.2 has three major parts: 1) day to day financial support, 2) long term financial support and 3) property ownership. In the big picture, these are the three areas that individuals with disabilities and their families need to focus on.

Figure 11.2 Financial Support and Property Ownership

	LEGALLY COMPETENT			NOT LEGALLY COMPETENT		
	Self-Supporting	Not Self-Supporting		Self-Supporting	Not Self-Supporting	
	No ODSP	Receives ODSP	No ODSP	No ODSP	Receives ODSP	No ODSP
Day-to-day Financial Support						
Can receive minimal family support	Yes	Yes	Yes	Yes	Yes	Yes
Can receive significant family support	Yes	No	Yes	Yes	No	Yes
Long-term Financial Support						
Can be an RDSP beneficiary	Yes	Yes	Yes	Yes	Yes	Yes
Can utilize absolute discretionary trust	Yes	Yes	Yes	Yes	Yes	Yes
Can utilize (ODSP) inheritance trust	N/A	Yes	N/A	N/A	Yes	N/A
Can utilize other trusts	Yes	No	Yes	Yes	No	Yes
Can have a life annuity	Yes	No	Yes	Yes	No	Yes
Can receive significant bequests	Yes	No	Yes	No	No	No
Property Ownership						
Can own a home	Yes	Yes	Yes	No	No	No
Can own a vehicle	Yes	Yes	Yes	No	No	No
Can own other property	Yes	No	Yes	No	No	No
Can make a will	Yes	Yes	Yes	No	No	No

The answers above are general and could change depending on particular circumstances. We have assumed Ontario rules for social assistance under the Ontario Disability Support Program (ODSP), which, of course, may be different in other provinces. The 'no' answers usually arise because of lack of legal capacity or because social assistance has limitations that cannot be met.

Consider Inflation

You may or may not know how much it costs per year to pay the expenses for your loved one. He or she may be living at home so there is no significant out-of-pocket cost for accommodation right now, but in future there will be. Of course, costs increase over time due to inflation, so this must be factored into your financial plan.

Set out in Figure 11.3 is a projection of annual costs in the future assuming an inflation rate of 2.5%. In order to simplify the math, calculations are based on your loved one being 20 years old today.

Figure 11.3 Inflation Adjusted Cost of Living

When	At Age	Future Cost		
Today	20	$10,000	$20,000	$30,000
In 10 years	30	12,800	25,600	38,400
In 20 years	40	16,400	32,000	49,200
In 30 years	50	21,000	42,000	63,000
In 40 years	60	26,900	53,800	80,700

Figure 11.3 shows a projection of 40 years into the future, which is quite possible depending on the age gap and life expectancy of the caregiver and the individual with a disability.

The Time Value of Money

The time value of money refers to the fact that money gains more value the longer it's invested. As a general rule, a person should invest money as soon as possible to maximize resources for the future.

Suppose Pat is 20 years old and starts investing $5,000 now at 6% for 30 years. Assume that Pat does not invest anything from ages 51 to 60. At the age of 60, with the interest, Pat will have a whopping $750,000! Mike, on the other hand, puts his investment plan on hold for ten years and starts investing at age 30. He also invests for 30 years until he is age 60. Using the same 6% rate of return, Mike will only have $419,000 at age 60. Although they both invested for 30 years, Pat has $231,000 more than Mike at age 60 because Pat started investing ten years earlier than Mike. It is clear through this example that the time value of money is important.

Maximizing Financial Resources

Maximizing financial resources beyond your own personal contributions is the holy grail of financial planning for disability. There are three effective ways to do this, as shown in Figure 11.4.

Figure 11.4 Maximizing Financial Resources

Maximize Social Assistance

Maximize exempt income

Maximize disability expenses

Maximize exempt assets

Maximize Tax Incentives

Utilize all available tax credits

Utilize RDSP

Use tax effective structures and transfers

Utilize Community Resources

Qualify for community assistance programs

Document retention for multiple applications as age changes

In the process of maximizing financial resources, care needs to be taken so that taxes and wealth continuity is kept in mind. This usually dictates the use of trusts and registered plans that assist with the transfer of funds efficiently.

Capital Resources

Expenses can be paid out of pocket or from savings. Savings, in turn, can be from money and investments that you own or that are owned for the benefit of your loved one with a disability. Capital resources are summarized in Figure 11.5.

Figure 11.5 Capital Resources

Family savings and investments

RDSPs

Personal pensions (RRSP, etc.)

Bequests and Henson trusts

Registered plan transfers

Lifetime Benefit trusts

Pension plan survivor rights

Life insurance proceeds

RDSPs, Henson trusts and insurance trusts are incredibly appropriate structures but need to be tailored to your family's situation. They are like pots that you fill up in your early years and empty in later years of life when you no longer want to draw on current family income to support expenses.

The Income Gap

One of the difficulties of financial planning is to have income match expenses throughout the life of your loved one with a disability. The chart in Figure 11.6 compares the ages of the child and parent. It assumes that the age difference between the parents and the child with a disability is 25 years, the life expectancy of parents is 85 years and the life expectancy of the child is slightly shorter—75 years in this example.

Figure 11.6 Age Gap

Life Stages	Child Age	Parent Age
Birth of loved one with a disability		25
Social assistance begins (if any)	18	43
Child lives outside of the family home	30	55
Parents retire	40	65
Parents die	60	85
RDSP income begins	60	85
OAS/CPP/GIS begin	65	

If we assume that parents want to end personal support when they retire, then the only income available to the loved one with a disability at that point is social assistance. This means that parents should have some accumulated savings (in a Henson trust) to support their loved one for twenty years until RDSP income starts to come in.

OAS, CPP and GIS can all reduce social assistance income on a dollar-for-dollar basis. Consequently, social assistance income and benefits could be replaced by these other income sources. Loss of social assistance benefits can be devastating to some individuals.

The message from this is that parents must set aside funds throughout their lives in order to have a pool of funds which will produce income later in life for their loved one with a disability.

Maximizing RDSP Income

While chapter 7 discusses some of the technical rules relating to RDSPs, this chapter offers a few guidelines for how to maximize RDSP income when your loved one with a disability reaches age 60, or even before that, if possible. In addition, you will want to avoid any repayment of bonds and grants which means there should be a ten-year gap between the time when the last contribution is made and the time when the RDSP pension begins in order to avoid repayments. Here are some basic guidelines for maximizing RDSP income.

- Open an RDSP plan as soon as possible.

- Contribute an amount each year that will maximize grant income—usually contributions of $1,000 per year until your loved one reaches age 18, and then $1,500 per year at age 19 and thereafter.
- Try to end contributions by the time your loved one reaches age 39.

Based on these guidelines, Figure 11.7 shows the balances in the RDSP excluding investment income for an individual at age 39.

Figure 11.7 RDSP Balances

Age	Years	Contribution Per Year	Total Contribution	Grant	Bond	Total
1-18	18	$ 1,000	$ 18,000			$ 18,000
19-39	20	$ 1,500	$ 30,000	$ 70,000	$ 20,000	$ 120,000
			$ 38,000	$ 70,000	$ 20,000	$138,000

You can see from Figure 11.7 that having contributed only $38,000 to an RDSP leaves a balance of $138,000. This does not include investment income which will increase the plan to about $270,000 at age 39 using an interest rate of 5%. This balance would balloon to almost $800,000 at age 60 when the plan would start to pay out. In this example, there is still $162,000 of contribution room left which can be utilized at any time and will increase the RDSP plan balance. RDSP plans provide an excellent source of pension capital over time even if contributions are more comparatively modest as shown in this example.

Tax and Legal Constraints of Trusts

Complex tax rules and legal constraints are part of the reality of investing through trusts. For individuals with disabilities, the use of trusts is likely to arise when your loved one has an intellectual disability and could otherwise be a recipient of income that would reduce social assistance. The solution to this is one or more special trusts, as shown in Figure 5.5 in chapter 5.

Figure 11.8 outlines the tax and legal constraints of trusts that need to be dealt with.

Figure 11.8 Tax and Legal Constraints of a Trust

- 21 year deemed disposition of assets under the Income Tax Act
- Rule Against Accumulations
- Rule Against Perpetuities

Part 8 of chapter 5 discusses the 21 year deemed disposition under the Income Tax Act. Part 1 of chapter 5 discusses the rules against accumulation and perpetuities.

Bedrock Rules for Investing

If you read the business section of your newspaper, it seems that there is a new theory for investing almost every day. It can be confusing for the average person trying to make good investment decisions. Often, too much attention is devoted to maximizing income returns and growing capital and too little to capital preservation. This failure to focus on preserving capital can sometimes cause the novice investor to make poor choices. Most people do not adjust the risk level in their portfolios when they need asset security and start to dip into their capital to support their cost of living.

When your invested funds are a primary source of income, reducing risk is always more important than maximizing reward. If you lose a significant portion of your long-term savings, it will take a long time to get back to where you once were. As you get older there is less time to recover from loss, so the risk factor becomes highly important.

Try to obey these basic tips of successful investing.

- Show an interest in your portfolio even if someone else manages your money
- Acquire as much knowledge as you can
- Be persistent in sticking to the basic rules
- Be patient and think long-term
- Use your personal acumen
- If you use an advisor, choose one you can learn from

If you follow these basic guidelines, you will have a good shot at successful investing.

Accumulation Years and Preservation Years

There are two distinct periods in financial planning: 1) the years in which funds are accumulating wealth (accumulation years) and 2) the years in which you are spending the accumulated wealth on your cost of living (preservation years). In other words, they are your working years and your retirement years. The rules for investing and protecting capital change dramatically between these two periods.

Figure 11.9 Accumulation and Preservation Years

Accumulation Years	Preservation Years
Moderate to Aggressive Risk	Conservative - Capital Preservation and Income
Growth objective for investments	Income objective for investments
Can absorb losses	Can't absorb losses
No income needs	Income needs
Inflation not an issue	Inflation must be considered
Capital growth objective	Income certainty objective

Investing funds for an individual with a disability usually involves planning for someone with less ability to earn income, make financial decisions or own property. From a financial point of view, you will have some of the same goals for your loved one for their lifetime as you have for yourself in retirement:

- provide a secure income;
- protect against losses and
- deal with inflation.

So your approach to investing should always change as you get older—risk needs to be adjusted by the shorter time frame available to recover.

Long-Term Investing

To practice wise investing, you should take time to educate yourself in the basic principles of handling a portfolio, especially when investing for the long term.

Generally speaking, too much emphasis is placed on maximizing growth and not enough on preserving capital. But if you are a long-term investor putting aside money for yourself or a loved one with a disability, you need to think about changes to a strategy to avoid losses. The core issues of long-term investing and accumulating savings discussed in this chapter are as follows.

- **Start early** - the longer you save the more you will accumulate.
- **Moderate risk** - Aim for a reasonable rate of return (most likely 5% to 7%). If you aim higher you increase the risk of significant loss of your capital.
- **Avoid high fees** - High fees that do not improve performance squander returns.
- **Diversify your investments** - Include the best investments in your portfolio you can find but diversify them across industry sectors, countries or even groups of countries.
- **Match risk with the available time to invest** - As discussed, the shorter period of time you have to invest, the more important it is to lower your risk since you have less time to recover from significant loss.

Family Support - The Savings Pots

We work much of our lives for the enjoyment it brings and, from a financial perspective, to save for our retirement. Families of a loved one with a disability not only have their own retirement savings pot but also need a savings pot to support their loved one. The two pots are somewhat independent of each other, but you can move funds between them as times change.

There may also be a third pot for surplus funds that can be used to make family gifts now or bequests later on.

11.10   The Savings Pots

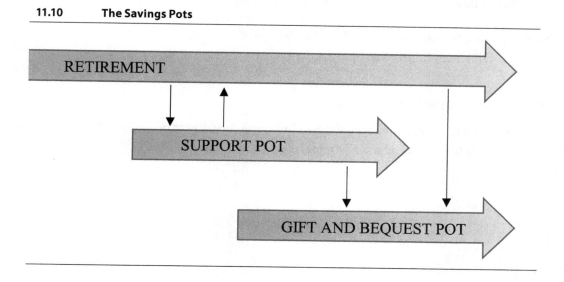

Self-Investing - Can You Do It on Your Own?

It can be difficult to know if you should self-invest or use an advisor. Advisors come with a wide range of skill sets. Not everyone is cut out to self-invest: it requires analytical skills and the willingness to spend time doing research and gaining knowledge.

If you decide to self-invest you will need to find an online broker—a firm that will make the trades for you according to your instructions. You may be attracted to the services of an online broker because of their

- account reporting information;
- research and tools and/or
- innovation and report design.

It's important to compare services before selecting one. The research and services that an online account brings should help with your investment decisions.

Why Do Investors Fail?

One of the reasons more people employ money managers rather than managing funds on their own is because individuals have a difficult time keeping personal biases out of their decision-making. Investors fail at managing their own money for the following reasons:

- they put too much emphasis on recent events;
- they seek information that supports pre-existing opinions;
- they are resistant to information that contradicts personal beliefs and
- they follow the herd and listen too much to others.

People who are less influenced by these factors tend to be contrarians, but that's not easy for everyone. Do you fit this mold?

Advisors and Personal Finances

When it comes to money management and investing for a loved one with a disability, there are many tools to support financial strategies, as shown in Figure 11.11.

Figure 11.11 Disability and the Levers of Your Personal Finances

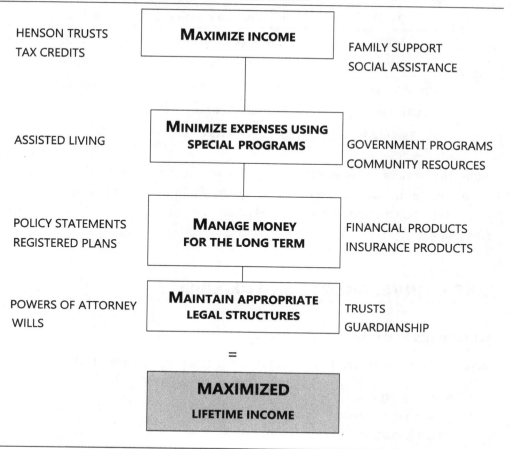

You can see from Figure 11.11 that there are four basic criteria important to maximize income and reduce costs for an individual with a disability.

Financial Institutions Provide Expertise and Special Financial Products

Financial institutions and their advisors may be able to play a big role in your financial planning for disability. They offer special products and services that you will find useful and important for good financial planning. Some may come with an added cost because they are designed to provide extra services such as insurance not always needed by the general population to the same extent.

Figure 11.12 shows some of the important products and services a financial institution may offer.

Figure 11.12 Products offered by Financial Institutions

Banks	Insurance Companies	Credit Unions
RDSPs	Segregated Funds	RDSPs
RESPs	Annuities	RESPs
Income Management	Corporate Trustees	Investment Planning
Estate Planning	Estate Planning	
Tax Advice	Tax Advice	

Finding the services and products you require will take some searching. Financial institutions help their clients through their own staff or through financial planning representatives qualified to sell their products. Look for a qualified person who also specializes in the financial issues of disability.

PART 3 – INVESTMENTS AND DISABILITY

Investments and Financial Products

There is an array of special financial products to meet certain needs and purposes such as

- protecting capital,
- guaranteeing income,
- deferring income,
- reducing income taxes, and
- providing a hedge against inflation.

The degree to which financial products are used for the above reasons and their success in doing that varies. Some investment products have added costs because they provide unique benefits. You will need to assess if the extra cost of these investments is worthwhile. However, the benefits of segregated funds and sometimes annuities can be helpful where disability is involved.

Figure 11.13 Characteristics of Market Investments and Financial Products

	Tax Effective	Growth	Income	Capital Protection	Income Certainty	Lifetime Income
Market Investments						
Growth/Income						
Cash				✓		
Stocks	✓	✓				
Segregated Funds			✓	✓		
Bonds			✓		✓	
Guaranteed Investment Certificates			✓	✓	✓	
Real Estate	✓	✓	✓			
Financial Products						
Guaranteed Income						
Annuities			✓		✓	✓
Prescribed Annuities	✓		✓		✓	✓
Insured Annuities	✓		✓	✓	✓	✓
Income Protection or Deferment						
T Series Mutual Funds	✓		✓			
Total Return Index ETFs	✓	✓				
Capital Protection						
Indexed Linked GICs			✓	✓		
Principal Protected Notes				✓		
Strip Bonds		✓		✓		

Tax-Free Savings Accounts

Failing to properly use tax-free savings is losing one of the most important tax incentives available. Many people view a tax-free savings account (TFSA) as an emergency fund for unexpected expenses—this is a mistake. Most investments are readily cashable, so it's not necessary to only put cash in a TFSA. If you are looking for security, laddered GIC's, savings accounts or laddered bonds are better tools for this purpose than a TFSA. Because your income from TFSAs is not taxed, that's where you should put your investments with the highest potential rate of return—your equity portfolio.

Figure 11.14 compares a TFSA non-taxable account with an investment account of $5,000 annually at a rate of return of 6% and a tax rate of 30%.

Figure 11.14 TFSAs Compared to a Portfolio Account

When	TFSA (6%)	Investment (4.2%)	Extra
Today			
In 10 years	69,900	63,100	6,800
In 15 years	123,300	105,900	17,400
In 20 years	195,000	158,000	37,000

It is clear from Figure 11.14 that a TFSA generates significantly more after-tax income than non-TFSA investing, especially so over longer periods of time.

Life Insurance

Life insurance is often misunderstood—people may assume they don't need it, it's too expensive, they are better off investing their money elsewhere and so on. But this overlooks the protection element of insurance which is sometimes needed at a particular stage of life. If you pick the wrong type of policy for your situation then you might encounter some of these problems.

On the other hand, if you pick the right policy for your situation, it can help protect you from the unexpected. You will need a skilled and knowledgeable insurance advisor who is able to match you to the best insurance product for your situation, age, and income level.

In broad terms, life insurance provides two valuable, but distinct benefits.

- It provides you with a pool of capital in the event of an unexpected tragedy. This is the pure insurance aspect.
- It is a savings vehicle and an excellent alternative to investing in the market for several reasons, such as the following.
  - It has reduced risk
  - Proceeds are not taxable to certain limits
  - Policy growth accumulates tax free
  - Returns are better than fixed income investments
  - It provides a disciplined approach to investing
  - It offers reasonable returns without increased volatility

There are a few core benefits to using life insurance as an investment and estate planning vehicle as compared with non-registered investment accounts. They are as follows.

- You commit yourself to regular savings through your monthly premiums
- There is less risk than investing in the market
- You have a guaranteed payment when you die without concern about the amount
- You can borrow against the policy to pay premiums or for other personal reasons

- It normally offers reasonable returns, and exceptional returns if you die prematurely
- You can deposit large sums to universal life policies
- You can bypass probate
- You can put the proceeds of insurance in a qualified disability trust (RDSP) with a low tax rate

Life insurance can play a valuable role in your savings and security plans if the product fits your situation.

Term, Whole Life or Universal Life?

Life insurance policies can be classified under three categories as follows.

- Term insurance - insurance coverage only with no cash value but a limited term
- Whole life insurance - insurance with a cash value earning income that is not segregated in the policy
- Universal life insurance - insurance with a cash value (savings) component that is segregated in the policy

Term insurance is pure insurance with no special add ons and has its place in certain circumstances. Both whole life and universal life insurance have a savings component. Generally speaking, younger people buy term insurance because it is cheaper than whole life or universal insurance when their main goal is to guard against loss of long-term income because of the death of the breadwinner. People over the age of 60 with investment portfolios tend to purchase whole life or universal insurance for financial diversification and as a tax-free investment to provide capital to pay taxes or other debts due on death.

Insurance and Disability

The financial needs of a loved one with a disability are, for the most part, financed by parents and social assistance throughout the parents' lifetimes. Upon death, parents need to have a pool of capital to continue this funding. This is usually an amount of funds transferred to a Henson trust which, if planned properly, is also a qualified disability trust taxed at graduated rates. If the child has an intellectual disability this will not be possible unless an annual QDT election is made.

When an insurance policy is paid out it can either be done as a lump sum amount or as an annuity to the beneficiary. If the policy and its ownership are structured properly, the proceeds can be paid into an insurance trust which is usually also a Henson trust. The terms of the trust will then dictate how funds will be distributed to benefit a child with a disability. The policy proceeds might also be structured so that an annuity is paid directly to a child with a disability. Unfortunately, this could reduce or eliminate social assistance.

Annuities

An annuity is an amount payable over your lifetime or a defined period of time, with or without a guarantee, and is purchased by a lump sum payment. Annuities work because they provide a person with a fixed amount of annual income guaranteed for a lifetime. Annuities can be indexed and a guaranteed period can be chosen if that is important. Certain kinds of annuities receive more favourable tax treatment than others.

Annuities are sometimes criticized as being expensive because they can result in a loss of capital on an early death. There is some truth to this, but this drawback may be minor compared to the certainty of guaranteed capital and income for your lifetime. Some of the benefits of annuities are outlined in Figure 11.15.

Under the Income Tax Act, payments received from an annuity are a combination of a repayment of the original cost of the annuity (not taxable) and annuity income (taxable). Under the prescribed annuity rules in the Income Tax Act, the return of principal is allocated equally to all years making annuities very tax effective. An annuity must be purchased if a Lifetime Benefit trust is used as discussed in part 5 of chapter 5.

Figure 11.15 Benefits of Annuities

- Tax effective ✓
- Guaranteed income ✓
- No investment management required ✓
- Income can be guaranteed for different periods of time ✓
- Can be set up in a will ✓
- Trade off of market risk for longevity risk ✓

Segregated Funds - A Good Product for Disability

Unlike other investments, segregated funds guarantee to protect between 75% and 100% of the amount invested in them. This is true even if the underlying investments decline in value providing you hold your funds for a certain period of time—usually 10 years. Even though you pay a higher fee for this, it is often worthwhile if you need to protect your capital—to assure income for a loved one with a disability, for example. Segregated fund investors will not be able to retain the insurance benefit if they cash out their investments before their maturity date, but will always get back the current value of their segregated fund investment.

A significant advantage of investing in a segregated fund is that it is an investment product that can also be an exempt asset with respect to social assistance under some provincial jurisdictions. Segregated funds offer other special advantages because they are not only an investment product, but they offer insurance protection as well.

Segregated funds hold the following other advantages for an individual investing for a loved one with a disability.

- Principal guarantee
- Guaranteed death benefit
- No probate fees if the contract has named beneficiaries
- Creditor protection
- An exempt asset under some social assistance programs

On the other hand, there are a few disadvantages to segregated fund investing.

- Funds will be locked in to retain the principal guarantee
- Higher fees to cover insurance features
- Possible penalties for early withdrawal

Because security of capital is so important to investing where disability is a factor, individuals should consider the insurance benefits and security offered by segregated funds despite the higher cost of these funds.

Life Funding Road Map

It's difficult to get a clear picture of the many possible sources of financial support for individuals and their families. In general, support comes from government assistance, tax benefits, community services and family. Figure 11.16 provides an overview of the possible sources. It's ironic that Figure 11.16 is the first one I did when I started this book and now it is the last one in the book. It was my compass in writing the book; now it can be yours.

My website, www.thefamilyguide.ca, provides an excellent tool called Disability – Financial and Life Plan Questionnaire. It covers the core elements of disability and personal finance, as discussed in chapter 1, into the ten separate components. The questionnaire should help families and their advisors work through each of these areas in a more systematic way.

Figure 11.16 A Life Funding Road Map

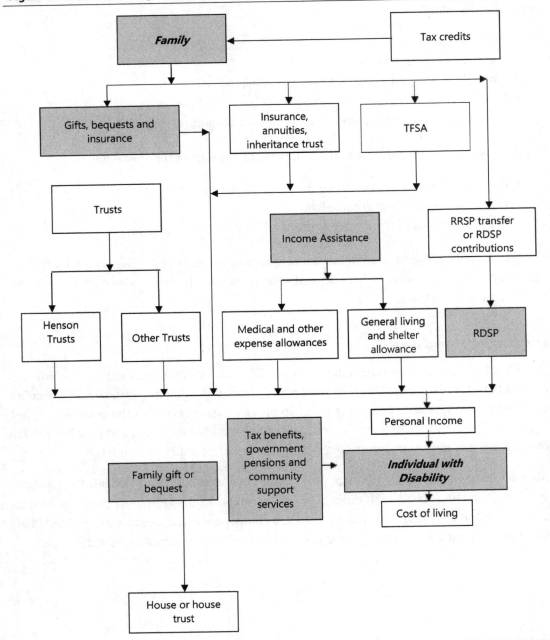

Letter of Wishes

It is so important to provide clear instructions to your attorneys under a power of attorney, your executors in your wills and your trustees in trusts about the scope of their authority with respect to a person with a disability. Each of these documents on their own will likely lack specificity to do such things as making gifts or loans to prevent self-dealing or an encroachment on distributions to others. The following are some suggestions:

- Provide some guidelines on the frequency and amounts of discretionary payments
- Make sure that professional advisors are aware of your intentions
- Discuss this at family meetings
- Prepare a non-binding letter of wishes discussing your intentions in a general way

Powers of attorney, wills and trusts start with template precedents and are then customized for the particular needs of the individual for whom they are prepared. Help your advisors to understand your wishes and create a document that reflects your particular requirements.

Engage and Move Forward

Planning your family finances when disability is involved is highly personal and incredibly difficult. Surround yourself with experienced professionals and listen carefully to what they have to say. If you do that, you should do well in managing your personal finances that will pass on to a loved one with a disability. Financial planning requires knowledge beyond straight forward money management and investing. It's not only about the money – it's about the structures you use to maximize your financial resources for a loved one to match their financial needs as they occur.

The Family Guide covers a huge territory about disability and personal finances – confusing to be sure. Engage your family, engage your community, engage yourself and move forward. I wish you well.

Bibliography

Andreana, Lise. *Financial Care for Your Aging Parent.* Vancouver: Self-Counsel Press, 2014.

Bala, Nicholas, Michael Kim Zapf, R James Williams, Robin Vogl, Joseph P Hornick. *Canadian Child Welfare Law.* Toronto: Thompson Educational Publishing Inc., 2004.

Biscott, Lynn. *The Boomers Retire: A Guide for Financial Advisors and Their Clients.* Toronto: Carswell, 2010.

Chilton, David. *The Wealthy Barber.* Toronto: Stoddart, 2002.

Chilton, David. *The Wealthy Barber Returns.* Kitchener: Financial Awareness Corp., 2011.

Diamond, Daryl. *Your Retirement Income Blueprint: A Six-Step Plan to Design and Build a Secure Retirement.* Etobicoke: Wiley, 2011.

Emmerson, Jeff and Robert Yehling. *Beyond ADHD: Overcoming the Label and Thriving.* Lanham, MD: Rowman & Littlefield Pub., 2017.

Foster, Sandra. *You Can't Take It With You: Common-Sense Estate Planning for Canadians.* Etobicoke: Wiley, 2006.

Freedman, Janet and Marie Howes. *Hit by an Iceberg.* Victoria: Trafford Publishing, 2003.

Gray, Douglas and John Budd. *The Canadian Guide to Will and Estate Planning.* Whitby: McGraw-Hill Education, 2011.

Law Commission of Ontario, *A Framework for the Law as it Affects Persons with Disabilities,* Toronto: September, 2012, https://www.lco-cdo.org/wp-content/uploads/2012/12/disabilities-framework.pdf.

McCaw, Donna. *It's Your Time.* Toronto: BPS Books, 2011.

Milevsky, Moshe and Alexandra Macqueen. *Pensionize Your Nest Egg: How to Use Product Allocation to Create a Guaranteed Income for Life.* Etobicoke: Wiley, 2010.

Poyser, John E.S., Larry H. Frostiak and Grace Chow. *Taxation of Trusts and Estates.* Toronto: Carswell, 2011.

Shields, Simon. *Ontario Disability Support Program (ODSP) Law.* Greece: 2016, http://isthatlegal.ca/index.php?name=start.odsp.

Treeby, Graeme S. *Removing the Mystery: An Estate Planning Guide for Families of People With Disabilities.* Toronto: Ontario Federation for Cerebral Palsy, 2008.

Treeby, Graeme. *Trustee Reference Manual.* Toronto: Ontario Federation for Cerebral Palsy, 2008.

Van Cauwenberghe, Christine. *Wealth Planning Strategies for Canadians 2017.* Toronto: Carswell, 2016.

Whaley, Kimberly, Albert H. Oosterhoff, Ameena Sultan, Benjamin D. Arkin, Heather B. Hogan and Birute Lyons. *Whaley Estate Litigation on Fiduciary Accounting.* Toronto: Whaley Estate Litigation, 2014.

Whaley, Kimberly and Heather Hogan. *Elder Financial Abuse.* Whaley Estate Litigation, 2015.

Appendices

Appendix A – Summary of Figures

Appendix B – Helpful References

Appendix C – Publications

A – Summary of Figures

FIGURES

1.1   ODSP Definition of Disability
1.2   ITA Definition of Disability
1.3   Physical or Cognitive Disability
1.4   Common Attributes of the Vulnerable
1.5   The Disability and Lifestyle Continuum
1.6   The Levels of Challenge
1.7   Family Life Cycle and Personal Finances
1.8   Four Financial Contributors
1.9   Life Plan Considerations
1.10 Disability – The Ten Most Important Components of Financial Planning
1.11 Core Financial Issues and Concerns

2.1   Community Service Organizations
2.2   Charity Funding
2.3   Housing Options for Individuals with Disabilities
2.4   Provincial Home Care

3.1   Provincial Disability Support Acts and Regulations
3.2   ODSP Exempt Assets
3.3   Provincial Social Assistance – Exempt Assets and Their Limits
3.4   ODSP Monthly Benefits
3.5   ODSP Prescribed Benefits
3.6   Ontario Disability Support Program and Incomes
3.7   ODSP Monthly Support Calculation
3.8   ODSP Exempt Income
3.9   Qualification for ODSP Support
3.10 Ontario Disability Support Program – Act, Regulations and Policy Statements
3.11 Ontario Disability Support Program – Important Definitions

4.1   Family Support for Individuals with a Disability
4.2   Living Arrangements and Family Support
4.3   Property Ownership/Contract Ability and Disability

5.1   The Purpose of Trusts Relating to Disability
5.2   Trust Property and Distributions
5.3   Features for Inclusion in a Family Trust
5.4   Tax Rate Comparison
5.5   Trusts for Persons with Disabilities
5.6   Lifetime Benefit Trusts

6.1   Income Tax Act References
6.2   Actual Taxes Payable (Ontario resident)
6.3   The Sources of Non-Refundable Tax Credits
6.4   Provincial Tax Credit Rates
6.5   Disability-Related Tax Benefits
6.6   Qualifications for the Disability Tax Credit
6.7   Disability Tax Credit
6.8   RESP for Individuals with Disabilities
6.9   Attendant Care Costs (Medical Expenses)
6.10   Comparison of Non-Registered and Registered Fund investments
6.11   Non-Refundable Tax Credit Amounts
6.12   Tax Benefits – Individuals Qualified for DTC and the Vulnerable
6.13   Tax Credits Available for Family Members Age 18 and Older

7.1   RDSP Loss of Eligibility
7.2   RDSP Savings Advantage
7.3   RDSP Life Cycle
7.4   Important RDSP Budget Amendments
7.5   Bond Entitlements
7.6   Grant Entitlement
7.7   Maximum Retroactive Contribution Entitlement
7.8   CDSB/CDSG Received
7.9   Transfer of RESP Income to a RDSP
7.10   LDAP Withdrawal Amount
7.11   LDAP Withdrawals Starting at Age 60
7.12   Events Requiring the Repayment of Bonds and Grants
7.13   A RDSP Compared with a Henson Trust
7.14   RDSP Flow of Funds

8.1   Transfers from an Estate
8.2   Guardianship Compared to Trusteeship

8.3   Estate Planning – Fifteen Practical Ideas

8.4   Flow of Assets Under a Will

8.5   Competency to Sign a Will

8.6   Estate Planning – A Will Checklist

8.7   Trusts: An Overview

8.8   Trust Funding Structure

8.9   RRSP / RRIF Transferred to an Adult Individual with a Disability

9.1   Donation Tax Benefit Percent

9.2   Current and Testamentary Gifts

10.1   Investing Changes in Retirement

10.2   Seniors and Decision-Making

10.3   Age Reduces Personal Capacity

10.4   Capacity Test Criteria

10.5   Symptoms of Vulnerability

10.6   Power of Attorney Checklist

11.1   Estimating the Capital Needs of Life Funding

11.2   Financial Support and Property Ownership

11.3   Inflation Adjusted Cost of Living

11.4   Maximizing Financial Resources

11.5   Capital Resources

11.6   Age Gap

11.7   RDSP Balances

11.8   Tax and Legal Constraints of a Trust

11.9   Accumulation and Preservation Years

11.10   The Savings Pots

11.11   Disability and the Levers of Your Personal Finances

11.12   Products Offered by Financial Institutions

11.13   Characteristics of Market Investments and Financial Products

11.14   TFSAs Compared to a Portfolio Account

11.15   Benefits of Annuities

11.16   A Life Funding Road Map

B – Helpful References

RELEVANT LEGISLATION/REGULATIONS (ONTARIO)

Accessibility for Ontarians with Disabilities Act, 2005

   Age of Majority and Accountability Act

   Child and Family Services Act

   Children's Law Reform Act

   Consent to Treatment Act

   Dependent's Relief Act

   Estate Act

   Estates Administration Tax Act

Excellent Care for All Act, 2010

   Freedom of Information and Protection of Privacy Act

   Health Care Consent Act

Home Care and Community Services Act, 1994

Home for the Aged and Rest Homes Act

   Insurance Act

Long-Term Care Homes Act, 2007

   Mental Health Act

   Ontario Disability Support Program Act, Regulations and Policy Statements

Ontario Drug Benefit Act, 1990

   Personal Health Information and Protection Act

   Powers of Attorney Act

Retirement Homes Act, 2010

Services and Supports to Promote the Social Inclusion of Persons with Developmental Disabilities Act

   Substitute Decisions Act

   Succession Law Reform Act

   Trustee Act

HELPFUL STUDIES AND SUBMISSIONS

Law Commission of Ontario, *A Framework for the Law as it Affects Persons with Disabilities*

Law Commission of Ontario, *Capacity and Legal Representation for the Federal RDSP*

Law Commission of Ontario, *Legal Capacity, Decision Making and Guardianship*

Select Committee on Developmental Service, *Inclusions and Opportunity: A New Path in Ontario*

STEP Canada, *Submission on the Proposals to Improve the Integrity of the Federal Tax System by Limiting Access to Graduated Rates for Trusts and Certain Estates*

PROVINCIAL LAWS IMPACTING INDIVIDUALS WITH DISABILITIES

Alberta – Assured Income for the Severely Handicapped Act
British Columbia – Employment and Assistance for Persons with Disabilities Act
Manitoba – The Family Maintenance Act
New Brunswick – Family Income Security Act
Newfoundland – Income and Employment Regulations
Nova Scotia – Employment Support and Income Assistance Regulations
Ontario – Ontario Disability Support Program Act
Prince Edward Island – Social Assistance Regulations
Quebec – Quebec Pension Plan
Saskatchewan – The Saskatchewan Assistance Regulations

WEBSITES

Federal Government

Canada Revenue Agency
www.cra-arc.gc.ca

Human Resources and Skills Development Canada
www.hrsdc.gc.ca

Benefits Finder
www.benefitsfinder.gc.ca

Employment and Social Development Canada
www.esdc.gc.ca

Provincial Government

Alberta Finance and Enterprise
www.finance.gov.ab.ca

British Columbia Ministry of Finance
www.gov.bc.ca/fin

Manitoba Finance
www.gov.mb.ca/finance

New Brunswick Department of Finance
www.gnb.ca/0024

Newfoundland and Labrador Finance
www.fin.gov.nl.ca/fin

Nova Scotia Finance
www.gov.ns.ca/finance

Ontario Ministry of Finance
www.gov.on.ca

Prince Edward Island Department of Finance and Municipal Affairs
www.gov.pe.ca/finance

Revenue Quebec
www.revenuquebec.ca

Ministere des Finances du Quebec
www.finances.gouv.qc.ca

Saskatchewan Finance
www.finance.gov.sk.ca

Other

Simon Shields, Lawyer
www.isthatlegal.ca

C - *Publications*

The Canada Revenue Agency is updating their previous bulletins and other publications and compiling a new publication called Income Tax Folios. So far, the following folios that may be of interest to individuals with disabilities have been issued.

INCOME TAX FOLIOS

The folios are organized into seven different series with a number of folio topics under each series. Series 1 relates to disability in some way or another.

Folio 1   **Health and Medical**
S1-F1-C1   Medical Expense Tax Credit
S1-F1-C2   Disability Tax Credit
S1-F1-C3   Disability Supports Deduction

Folio 2   **Students**
S1-F2-C1   Education and Textbook Tax Credits
S1-F2-C2   Tuition Tax Credit

Folio 3   **Family Unit Issues**
S1-F3-C1   Child Care Expense Deduction
S1-F3-C2   Principal Residence

Folio 4   **Tax Credits**
S1-F4-C1   Basic Personal and Dependent Tax Credits

Forms

TD1 Personal Tax Credit Return
T2201   Disability Tax Credit Certificate
RC4460   Registered Disability Savings Plan

Publications

5000-G	General Income Tax and Benefit Guide
RC4064	Disability Related Information – 2016
RC4065	Medical Expenses
IC99-1R1	Registered Disability Savings Plan
T4013	T3 Trust Guide
T4040	RRSPs and Other Registered Plans for Retirement – 2016

Personal Wealth Strategies issues several *Disability Alerts* each year. Listed below is a sample of articles that relate to issues faced by people with disabilities. These *Alerts* can also be found on the www.thefamilyguide.ca website.

ALERTS

2017 Ontario Budget - ODSP
All Our Children Deserve a Home
Changes to the Principal Residence Rules
Disability – A Long Term Funding Structure for Families
Disability – Life Needs Should Drive Financial Planning
Disability – The new Tax Rules for Trusts
Disability Tax Credit – Adaptive Functioning
Disability – Pension Transfers to Adult Children
Disability Tax Credit Review and Analysis
Financial Support, Asset Ownership and Legal Capacity
Lifetime Financial Planning for Individuals with Disability
Qualified Disability Trusts
RDSPs and Intellectual Disability
Registered Disability Savings Plans
Seniors, Vulnerability and Legal Consequences
Seniors and New Home Modification Tax Benefits
Tax Credits for Individuals with Disabilities
Tax Credits, Medical Expenses and Family Support
The Henson Trust – The Mysteries Explored and Explained
Trusts, Taxes and Disability
Seniors, Vulnerability and Legal Consequences
Seniors and Home Modification Tax Benefits

Our financial planning website, www.personalwealthstrategies.net, contains even more *Alerts* such as Financial Planning Alerts, Estate Planning Alerts, Tax Alerts, and Seniors Alerts.

Glossary

ABBREVIATIONS

ACB	Adjusted Cost Base
AGM	Age of Majority
CDSB	Canada Disability Savings Bond (RDSP)
CDSG	Canada Disability Savings Grant (RDSP)
CFP	Certified Financial Planner
CPP	Canada Pension Plan
CRA	Canada Revenue Agency
CSB	Canada Savings Bond
CV	Commuted Value
DAPs	Disability Assistance Payment (RDSP)
DTC	Disability Tax Credit
ETF	Exchange Traded Fund
GIC	Guaranteed Investment Certificate
GIS	Guaranteed Income Supplement
GRE	Graduated Rate Estate
GST	Goods and Service Tax
HBP	Home Buyers Plan
HST	Harmonized Sales Tax
IA	Income Assistance (Provincial)
ITA	Income Tax Act
IWD	Individual with Disabilities
LDAPs	Lifetime Disability Assistance Payment (RDSP)
LIF	Life Income Fund
LIRA	Locked-in Retirement Account
LRIF	Locked-in Retirement Income Fund
LTD	Long-Term Disability
MER	Management Expense Ratio

NAV	Net Asset Value
NRTC	Non-Refundable Tax Credit
ODSP	Ontario Disability Support Program
PBE	Preferred Beneficiary Election
PGT	Public Guardian and Trustee
POA	Power of Attorney
PSW	Personal Support Worker
QDT	Qualified Disability Trust
RDSP	Registered Disability Savings Plan
RESP	Registered Education Savings Plan
ROE	Record of Employment
RRIF	Registered Retirement Income Fund
RRSP	Registered Retirement Savings Plan
REIT	Real Estate Investment Trust
SDA	Substitute Decisions Act (Ontario)
SIN	Social Insurance Number
TFSA	Tax Free Savings Account
TSX	Toronto Stock Exchange
YMPE	Year's Maximum Pensionable Earnings

Most of the above abbreviations and terms are in general use, but some have been adapted for this book.

There are many legal terms and acronyms used in publications and laws. Set out below is an explanation of such terms for the purposes of this book. These explanations may not be precise, but they are included to give readers a general understanding of some of the concepts discussed in this book.

Absolute Discretionary Trust: A trust whose terms provide that none of the beneficiaries have any power or ability to demand any of the income or capital of the trust at any time. This is generally known as a Henson trust.

Adaptive Disability: A disability that limits one's ability to take on personal responsibility or function within the community within accepted social norms.

Accumulation Years: These are the years when individuals accumulate savings for their retirement or for the years when a loved one will need income to meet or improve their standard of living.

Adjusted Cost Base: The cost of property for tax purposes which is generally the original purchase price plus purchase costs and costs of improvements.

Advanced Health Care Directive: A document outlining your wishes with respect to the refusal or consent to medical treatment and who should decide for you if you are unable.

Affidavit: A sworn statement in writing made before an authorized person.

Agent for Executor: A person or company hired by the executor to provide advice or professional services.

Alter Ego Trust: A trust (meeting CRA requirements) to hold personal assets if you are age 65 or older.

Annuity: A contract that provides a series of payments at regular intervals in return for a lump sum deposit.

Attorney: The person named in your power of attorney to carry out its instructions.

Attribution Rules: Rules in the Income Tax Act that govern the attribution of income (including capital gains) for tax purposes.

Beneficiary: A person who receives a benefit under a will or a trust.

Bequest: A gift of property in a will.

Budgetary Requirements: The amount of assistance provided under ODSP for basic needs and shelter allowance.

Capital: Accumulated savings usually for use later in life.

Capital Beneficiary: A beneficiary who is entitled to the capital of a trust.

Capital Gain: The gain earned on the sale of an asset.

Cash Surrender Value: The money paid on cancellation of life insurance.

Chargeable Income: This is the amount remaining under ODSP rules after deducting all exemptions from actual income.

Charity: A charity that is registered under the Income Tax Act.

Charitable Gift Annuity: A life annuity issued by a registered charity.

Codicil: An alteration to terms of a will after it is created.

Cognitive Disability: A disability that affects either intellectual or adaptive functioning.

Committee: The name for a legal guardian in certain provinces.

Continuing Power of Attorney: A power of attorney that remains in effect even if you become mentally incapable.

Convertible Term Insurance: An insurance policy that allows the policy holder to change term insurance to a whole life policy without evidence of insurability.

Creditor: Person to whom money is owing.

Curator: Legal guardian in Quebec.

Deemed Disposition: Income Tax Act deems that assets are sold even if no actual sale takes place.

Deferred Gift: A donation commitment now for payment in the future.

Developmental: Relating to physical or mental development.

Disability Assistance Payment (DAP): Single payments from an RDSP before age 60.

Estate Trustee: An individual appointed by the settlor of the trust to make all decisions to carry out the terms of the trust.

Exchange Trades Funds (ETF): Low cost funds that track stock market sectors that are in some ways similar to mutual funds without any management.

Executor/Executrix: The person or persons named in a will to administer and carry out its terms. The executor/executrix may or may not be the same person who administers specific trusts established under the will.

Fair Market Value: The price in the open market that a person would pay for property.

Family Trust: This book uses this term to describe a trust to serve the general needs of family members including a person with a disability. The trust could be set up during lifetime or upon death. A Henson trust is a family trust but used for very special reasons.

Fiduciary: An individual under a legal obligation to act for the benefit of another party.

Fiduciary Duty: The obligation required of a person to act for another person implying a reasonable standard of care, independence and judgement.

Financial Products: Plans offered by financial institutions which offer some type of benefit beyond the normal attributes of investments such as certainty of income or protection of capital. They can be thought of as an insurance product of sorts and involve extra fees.

General Power of Attorney: A document which gives someone authority to make decisions relating to your assets.

Gift In Kind: A gift of property rather than cash.

Gift Over: A gift of property to a second recipient when a certain event happens which might, for example, include the death of the beneficiary—often used in trusts.

Graduated Rate Estate (GRE): A trust arising on the death of an individual that is eligible for graduated rates of tax for a period of three years after death.

Grant of Probate: A certificate issued by the court confirming the authority set out in a will to administer an estate.

Guardian: A person appointed by the court and legally responsible for another person (in relation to property or personal care) who is unable to take care of themselves.

Health Care Practitioner: A person licensed under provincial legislation to provide health or personal care.

Henson Trust: A special use family discretionary trust designed to maximize social assistance. It is sometimes called an absolute discretionary trust.

Holograph Will: A hand written will having no witnesses.

Income Assistance: Various sources of provincial assistance that supplement income.

Income Beneficiary: The person entitled to the income of a trust which may not include capital gains.

Inheritance Trust: A trust recognized under some provincial assistance programs to hold funds to meet disability related costs, usually with a maximum amount of capital.

Intellectual Disability: A disability relating to brain function resulting in an inability to understand basic information, sometimes referred to as IQ.

Inter vivos Trust: A trust established during the lifetime of the settlor.

Intestate: Dying without a will.

Intestate Distribution: The distribution of assets according to rules of applicable provincial law when a person dies without a will.

Irrevocable: A document which cannot be changed or cancelled.

Issue: All descendents of a common ancestor.

Jointly Owned Property: Property registered in more than one name such that the survivor of the first to die will acquire full ownership of the property.

Legal Decision Maker: An individual legally authorized to manage the financial affairs of another person such as an attorney under a power of attorney.

Lifetime Benefit Trust (LBT): A trust allowed under the Income Tax Act for the sole benefit of a mentally infirm individual to receive RRSP and RRIF proceeds on death of a parent or grandparent.

Lifetime Disability Assistance Payment: Periodic payments from an RDSP starting at age 60.

Life Insurance Policy: A contractual agreement with a life insurance company to pay the beneficiaries a death benefit in exchange for premium payments.

Life Interest: A benefit to enjoy or have the use of property for the beneficiary's lifetime only.

Life Interest Trust: Trust: Trusts under the Income Tax Act to provide for special tax treatment on the transfer of property to the trust on a tax-free basis for certain family beneficiaries—trusts are alter ego trusts, joint partner trusts and spousal trusts.

Life Tenant: A person who has an interest in trust property for that beneficiary's life.

Liquidator: An executor in Quebec.

Living Will: A document that outlines your wishes regarding medical treatment and health care and may convey wishes to prolong life.

Mandate: A power of attorney document in Quebec.

Mental Incapacity: The inability to understand information that is relevant to making decisions or to appreciate the reasonable foreseeable consequences of making a decision.

Minor: A person who has not reached the age of majority.

Mutual Fund: An actively managed pool of investments for which you pay a fee.

Notarized Copy: A copy of an original document certified as being a true copy.

Not-For-Profit Organization: an organization that does community service but is not necessarily a registered charity.

Oath: A solemn affirmation of the truth of what a person has said.

Palliative Care: Health or personal care that relieves pain but does not attempt to cure it.

Partner: In this book, partner refers to a spouse or common law partner.

Passport Program: A cash allowance program in Ontario fostering community outreach for individuals with disabilities in addition to ODSP benefits.

Power of Attorney for Property: A document that gives someone else legal responsibility for your assets.

Power of Attorney for Personal Care: A document which gives your representative authority to make personal care decisions if you become mentally incapacitated.

Prescribed Annuity: An annuity that meets requirements of the Income Tax Act that allows income deferment over the life of the annuitant.

Primary Caregiver: The person who takes responsibility for the support and care of an individual who may or may not be related or live with the person who has a disability.

Probate: The process by which a court reviews your will after death and declares it valid. Probate gives your executor legal authority to settle your estate.

Proceeds of Disposition: The proceeds from the sale of an asset.

Public Guardian and Trustee (Public Trustee): A government body that makes decisions on behalf of individuals who cannot make decisions for themselves. The office is referred to by different names in different provinces such as committee, tutor, trustee, curator, or representative.

Qualified Disability Trust (QDT): A testamentary trust for individuals with a disability that qualifies for graduated tax rates providing the beneficiary qualifies for the disability tax credit.

Real Property: Land and buildings.

Registered Disability Savings Plan (RDSP): A plan for individuals with disabilities authorized by the Income Tax Act to provide retirement savings and supported by government contributions.

Remainder Beneficiary: The person entitled to the balance left in a trust or estate after all specific distributions to beneficiaries have been paid.

Renewable Term Insurance: Term insurance gives the policy owner the right to renew the coverage without evidence of insurability.

Residuary Beneficiary: The beneficiary to whom the residue of the estate or trust belongs when the trust is terminated.

Rollover: A transfer of property on a tax-free basis under the Income Tax Act.

Segregated (Seg) Fund: Funds offered by insurance companies which offer security of the capital in the fund.

Settlement: The transfer of property to a trust.

Settlor: The person establishing a trust and its terms.

Special Needs Trust: A trust set up in order to pay disability-related expenses under certain provincial disability support rules.

Spousal Trust: A trust under which the spouse is entitled to all of the trust income during his/her lifetime and nobody except the spouse has a right to any of the trust capital while the spouse is living.

Strip Bonds: A bond without any coupon that is purchased at a discount and sold at par on maturity.

Substitute Decision Maker: The person or persons who are legally designated to make decisions for someone else, usually under a power of attorney or similar documents.

Tax Deferred Plans: A plan authorized under the Income Tax Act that allows taxpayers to delay the taxation of income until some future event such as going to school or retirement.

Testamentary Trust: A trust created under a will.

Trust: A legal arrangement whereby someone holds legal ownership to property but does not actually own it and carries out the instructions with respect to the property according to the wishes of the settlor as outlined in the terms of the trust.

Trustee: The person appointed to administer a trust.

Whole Life Insurance: Life insurance that builds a cash value while in existence.

Will: A written document expressing the terms under which property of the deceased will be distributed after death of the deceased to heirs and beneficiaries.

Let's Keep the Conversation Going

This book was written as a comprehensive guide outlining the financial levers of disability and tying them together so they make sense for the average person. First and foremost, this book was put together for families unfamiliar with complex rules. My hope it that it will also be useful for banks, insurance companies, charitable organizations, universities and colleges, and parent groups who help spread knowledge about disability and personal finances. This book is available in e-book format through amazon.com

SOCIAL MEDIA

www.thefamilyguide.ca

thefamilyguide@outlook.com

205-30 Dupont Street East
Waterloo, ON N2J 2G9
(519) 884-7087

/thefamilyguide

/thefamily_guide

/thefamilyguide

We hope to be able to keep in touch through our website, Facebook, Twitter and LinkedIn. You can order a copy of the book by contacting us at our email address: thefamilyguide@outlook.com.

NEWSLETTERS

Don't hesitate to sign up for our mailing lists to receive our Disability Alerts which are sent out regularly. They are available on either of our websites, www.thefamilyguide.ca for disability and www.personalwealthstrategies.net for general financial planning.

BOOK DISCOUNT PRIVILEGES

We want this book to get out to as many users as possible. Discounts for bulk orders are available to charities, not-for-profits, educational institutions and parent groups. **See our website for details.**

SPEAKING

If you are looking for a speaker who is knowledgeable about disability and personal finances, please contact us. Ed Arbuckle offers a down-to-earth approach to addressing your financial concerns which he combines with professional knowledge and personal insight.